AFRICAN-AMERICAN HISTORY HEROES IN HARDSHIP

LISBETH GANT STEVENSON

Cambridgeport Press · Cambridge, Massachusetts

ABOUT THE AUTHOR

Lisbeth Gant Stevenson is an author and award-winning journalist. She has also written and produced for public television and for network television news programs. A former lecturer at the Claremont Colleges in California, she is a frequent speaker at schools and universities in this country and abroad.

Stevenson's own family is a heroic blend of African, Indian, and white ancestry. Her great-grandfather was a rancher in Mississippi who, despite discrimination, helped his illiterate neighbors—both black and white—learn to write. Her maternal grandparents attended college in the early 1900s, a rare accomplishment in Mississippi, and her paternal grandfather was one of the early successful insurance executives in Chicago.

Lisbeth Gant Stevenson has had a long-standing interest in African-American achievement, and she hopes that, after studying this book, every reader will say, "If those heroes could do it, I can too."

For her work on *African -American History: Heroes in Hardship*, Lisbeth Gant Stevenson has been awarded the Los Angeles Mayor's Proclamation of Merit, Toyota Motors USA Black History Month Award, and the National Association of Market Developers "PRAME" Award.

Please direct all inquiries about this publication to:
Publisher
Cambridgeport Press
15 Chalk Street
Cambridge, MA 02139

Design by Wendy Bedenbaugh.

Photo Credits
29, 83, 109, 135, 169, 205, 258, 281. The Bettmann Archive. **250** U.S.S. Arizona Memorial, National Park Service. All other photos and illustrations, courtesy of the Library of Congress.

Printed in the U.S.A.
ISBN: 0-944348-01-7
BCDEFGHIJ-998765432

CONTENTS

A LETTER FROM LISBETH GANT STEVENSON

This book is a look at selected men and women in African-American history who were, quite literally, heroes in hardship. As you read, you may think of other people who should have been included. Great. Please let us know who they are. Because of space limitations, it has been impossible to include in this edition everyone who has made significant contributions. But, when you think about it, this fact, in and of itself, is a great tribute to the many accomplished African-Americans throughout history.

In this book you may notice references to either "African-Americans" or "black Americans". I decided to use these terms interchangeably. Whatever your preferred manner of description, I hope you will read into these lines the respect with which I used the terms. Throughout the history of the United States, we, as African-Americans, have described ourselves in many ways. Whatever the name, the accomplishments remain the same.

To a person, the men and women in this book certainly accomplished a great deal. And they did so under the most dire circumstances. But they never let that stop them. Instead, they simply made up their minds to overcome every obstacle, one by one, until they accomplished their goal, be it social, scientific, political, educational, or financial.

Because of them, we are what we are today. We are who we are today. Because of them, not one of us needs to give up hope. Ever. If they could do it, so can we.

I, for one, was able to write this book because, throughout the course of my life, there were people who took the time to assure me that I could achieve anything I wanted. I sincerely hope that when you finish reading these pages, if you don't feel that way already, you will too. And if you do feel that way, that you will share your conviction with someone else who needs to hear it.

With my deepest appreciation, I would like to thank the many people who, directly and indirectly, helped make this book happen. Of course, like the heroes and heroines in these pages, it is impossible to list everyone right here. But you know who you are.

I would, however, like to give the following people special thanks:
To my beloved family which has always believed in me; to John H. Johnson of Johnson Publishing and Ed Lewis of ESSENCE who gave me my first writing breaks, and to my many other educational and business associates who have provided understanding and support; to the good people at the libraries and other institutions I consulted, who provided much needed help; and to "SGI-USA" and Soka Gakkai International President Daisaku Ikeda for their incredible example of what an individual can do if he or she really tries.

BLACK AFRICAN CIVILIZATIONS

Why should anyone study black history? The answer is simple. Because no matter what your race, your very own great, great, great ancestors came from Africa!

That's right. Did you think the world began with Fred Flintstone? Well, scientists will tell you that life began in none other than Africa.

But there's another reason to study black history. Many of the contributions that black people have made to the world have been misinterpreted or misunderstood over the years. We know now that, no matter what the era or the adversity, there have always been black people who have been active participants in history. It's a good idea to look at the roles they've played, so that you will not think black people have spent the last several centuries just sitting on the sidelines.

The place where the story begins is Africa.

SECTION ONE

THE RISE OF EGYPT—AFRICA'S FIRST CIVILIZATION

VOCABULARY civilization B.C. A.D. pharaoh dynasty census hieroglyphics

MAIN IDEA Egypt, in northeastern Africa, was one of the world's first great civilizations.

OBJECTIVES As you read, look for answers to the following questions:
1. Why did a great civilization rise in Egypt?
2. Why can ancient Egypt be called a land of "firsts"?

civilization:
an advanced level of culture, characterized by organized government and religion, a system of writing, and a class structure.

Ancient Egypt, in the northeastern corner of Africa, was the home of a glorious **civilization** that lasted 3,000 years. When

The first great African civilization arose in Egypt. This Egyptian wall painting recorded the arrival of nobles from the kingdom of Kush to attend a pharaoh's funeral in 1290 B.C.

Egypt flourished around 2,000 **B.C.**, ancient Rome was still just a village of simple farmers and shepherds scattered over a few hills. Rome only began to emerge as a large civilization around the time of the decline of ancient Egypt.

Ancient Egypt existed many centuries before the rise of modern Europe as well. A thousand years after Egypt reached its height, tribes of pelt-wearing natives known as Franks, Goths, and Vandals began forming loose alliances in what is now known as Europe. It wasn't until much later (the 11th century **A.D.**) that the warlike Franks banded together to form the beginnings of what is now France.

B.C.:
the years before the birth of Christ.

A.D.:
the years since the birth of Christ.

Why Did Ancient Egypt Develop So Early?

Ancient Egypt developed before other civilizations for one main reason—it had a great location. It was situated right

1

in the middle of the tremendously fertile Nile River valley. Every year, after the rains, the Nile would overflow its banks, sending a healthy, fresh layer of black topsoil to cover the land for miles around. Thus, the people of the Nile region found that because of their fortunate location they no longer had to roam in nomadic groups in search of food. They could stay in one place and grow their own food.

By being able to stay in one place and raise their own food, the groups in the Nile region did not have to spend all their time scratching out a bare existence. Over the next few hundreds of years, they formed communities. They invented things. They experimented, without fear of starvation. Development naturally quickened. The result? Some important "firsts" for human beings.

Ancient Egypt—A Land of "Firsts"

As each farm community flourished, the ancient Egyptians naturally had to develop systems of organization. These various communities eventually became linked, leading to the first national government. The first capital of Egypt was called Memphis. (And you thought it was only in Tennessee!)

The Egyptian ruler, or emperor, became known as the **pharaoh**. The pharaohs were so powerful that they were looked upon as gods. Thousands of officials and priests helped the pharaohs run their lavish courts.

pharaoh:
a ruler of ancient Egypt.

dynasty:
a series of rulers from the same family.

Strong **dynasties**, or families of rulers, brought stability to Egypt. There were 28 dynasties in all during the 1,500 years when ancient Egypt was at top strength. These dynasties were divided into the Old, Middle, and New Kingdoms. The periods in between marked the times when Egypt was dominated by invaders.

When pharaohs died, they were buried in gigantic tombs with huge stone slab monuments called *stelae*. Court secretaries, or clerks—called scribes—carved on these *stelae*. They wrote the accounts of various important battles and other milestones in each pharaoh's life. To move the huge heavy stones needed for the creation of these monuments, the ancient Egyptians invented the first wheel. The wheel soon proved helpful in other means of transport as well.

Egyptian engineers and architects used their skill in

building the great pyramids that served as the pharaohs' tombs. In addition, they were the first to use stone columns in homes, palaces, and temples.

One disadvantage of having a pharaoh was that the Egyptian people had to be taxed to provide for the lavish court. In order to collect taxes, Egyptian officials took the first known **census**. The early census-takers counted up to four million Egyptian people at one time. (This was probably more than the population of all the rest of the African continent put together.)

census:
an official count of the population.

To communicate more clearly and to keep records over the years, the ancient Egyptians created one of the first systems of writing. It was called **hieroglyphics** and consisted of intricate combinations of pictures.

In 500 B.C. a famous Greek scholar and traveler, Herodotus, traveled to Egypt. In writing about his journey, he expressed amazement at the Egyptians' sophisticated and accurate calendars and systems of record-keeping and mathematics. He called the Egyptians "the best historians of any nation of which I have had experience." He said he was awestruck at the precise written account of no less than "three hundred and thirty monarchs."

hieroglyphics:
ancient Egyptian writing that used pictures to symbolize words and sounds.

So, Egypt truly was a land of "firsts." The first national government. The first wheel. The first stone columns. The first census. One of the first writing systems. Think about it. All of these important "firsts" came from Africa. Where would we be today without them?

The Life of the Average Egyptian

Now, if what you know about Egypt is limited to seeing Elizabeth Taylor in the movie "Cleopatra," you have some rethinking to do!

The great majority of ancient Egyptians had dark hair and dark skin. Most of the people came originally from the central-west Sahara region of Africa. Others included lighter-skinned peoples from the Middle East.

We know that Egypt's rulers, the pharaohs—with their large courts, many wives and retainers—fared well in pomp and splendor. But what about the average Egyptian?

Well, it seems they were saddled with a system of bureaucracy, not unlike the one we struggle with today!

The 9-to-5'ers in ancient Egypt were part of a huge civil service, with clerks and tax-gatherers everywhere.

The following account, written in about 3,200 B.C. by a court clerk to a friend, sympathizes with the farmers' plight:

> I am told you have abandoned writing and taken to sport.... But do you not remember the condition of the farmer who is faced with paying his harvest-tax when the snake had carried off half the corn and the hippopotamus has eaten the rest? Then the mice abound, the locusts come, the cattle devour, the sparrows bring disaster, and what remains on the thrashing floor is taken by thieves. And now the clerk lands on the river bank to collect the tax. With him are guards ... and they say, 'Hand over the corn,' though there is none. And the farmer is beaten, bound, and dunked in the well.

Indeed, in many instances, the farmers also were forced to help build the huge pyramids during the periods when their lands were covered with flood waters and they could not plow their fields.

First Decline of Ancient Egypt

By about 2,200 B.C., many Egyptians had become fed up with supporting their pharaohs. Tired of heavy taxation, they rose in revolt. The rulers already had their hands full fighting off raiders who had started to venture from their dry, desert homes in Libya and Syria to invade Egypt.

For years, chaos reigned. It would take another generation for the pharaohs to regain control of the vast empire.

The "Middle Kingdom"

After fighting off the attackers, the pharaohs renewed their own empire-building. (This period—2040–1786 B.C.—became known as Egypt's Middle Kingdom period.) This time, they concentrated on attacking their African neighbors to the south. Why? Because they had gold. And the Egyptian rulers needed gold to re-establish their lavish lifestyle.

In an effort to get more and more gold, the pharaohs became exploiters themselves. Soon, however, their armies were stretched thin. Some troops were busy rooting out gold from their neighbors to the south. Others were putting down uprisings at home. Still others were fighting off renewed attacks from Middle Eastern invaders. With all these various campaigns, the Egyptians were in trouble.

Where would they find new resources to fuel their sagging empire? Once again, they would look south.

SECTION ONE REVIEW

1. **VOCABULARY** Write a sentence for each of the following words: civilization, pharaoh, dynasty, census, hieroglyphics.

2. **GEOGRAPHY** How does Egypt's location explain its success?

3. **HISTORY** What were three of the "firsts" invented by the Egyptians?

4. **ECONOMICS** What were the sources of the pharaohs' income?

5. **CRITICAL THINKING** Of the "firsts" invented by the Egyptians, which do you think was the most important? Explain.

THE KINGDOM OF KUSH

SECTION TWO

VOCABULARY Nubia ebony Kush Meroë

MAIN IDEA The 2,000-year-old kingdom of Kush arose to the south of Egypt. It ruled Egypt for a century and later emerged as a major African trading center.

OBJECTIVES As you read, look for answers to the following questions:
1. Why did Egypt annex Kush?
2. How did Kush come to rule Egypt?
3. What were the highlights of Kush society?
4. What happened to Kush?

5

Nubia:
the land south of ancient Egypt, along the great bend of the middle Nile River.

ebony:
a very hard wood.

South of Egypt, along the great bend of the middle Nile River, was a region known to the Egyptians as **Nubia** (meaning "land of the blacks"). The Egyptians traded with the ancient Nubians for ivory and **ebony**, a very hard wood. The Nubians, in turn, got these goods from Africans who lived farther south.

By about 1,580 B.C., Egyptian troops conquered Nubia, making it a colony. For about 1,800 years, the Egyptians took ivory, ebony, gold, and other precious goods from Nubia. In fact, this southern area became so "Egyptianized" that the Nubian priests began to build Egyptian temples. Egypt, during these many hundreds of years, was looking south.

Kush Kingdom Emerges

Kush:
a kingdom established by the Nubians in about 2,600 B.C. in the part of Africa now occupied by Egypt, Sudan, and Ethiopia.

By 750 B.C., the Nubian state of **Kush** emerged as a fully developed kingdom under King Kashta. Its capital, Napata, was once an Egyptian "frontier" station.

By this time, Egypt was in decline. Several pharaohs ruled it, none of whom had control over the entire empire. The Kushites, tired of centuries of colonization, decided to turn the tables on Egypt.

Kush Conquers Egypt

King Kashta's son, Piankhi, in one of history's most dramatic turnarounds, invaded and conquered Egypt in about 72 B.C. A huge stone *stela* still exists describing Piankhi's siege of Memphis, the Egyptian capital.

Piankhi's arrival into Egypt from Kush, according to the giant stone document, coincided with the annual overflow of the Nile. When Piankhi and his troops reached the city, the floodwaters had already risen as far as the town walls. Piankhi then displayed his skill as a strategist by devising a shrewd plan of attack. The description on the *stela* picks up the story:

> Every man told his opinion among the army of his majesty [Piankhi], according to every rule of war. Every man said: 'Let us besiege it—; lo, its troops are numerous.' Others said: 'Let a causeway be

made against it; let us elevate the ground to its walls. We will divide it . . . on every side of it in order to find a way for our feet.'

Then his majesty was enraged against it like a panther. . . . He sent forth his fleet and his army to assault the harbor of Memphis; they brought to him every ferryboat, every cargo boat, every transport, and the ships, as many as there were, which had moored among its houses. There was not a citizen who wept, among all the soldiers of his majesty.

Then Memphis was taken as by a flood of water, a multitude of people were slain therein, and brought as living captives to the place where his majesty was.

Piankhi's brother, Shabaka, completed the work of establishing a dynasty of Kushite rulers of Egypt. Under Shabaka, the 25th or "Ethiopian Dynasty" of Egypt was formally founded. This was the only dynasty of Egypt to originate from an African neighbor. It lasted nearly 100 years.

"Then Memphis was taken as by a flood of water. . . ."
—Description of Kushite conquest of Egypt

Highlighting a Hero—King Taharka

By about 688 B.C., Taharka (Shabaka's nephew) came to the throne. Surviving sculptures indicate his obvious black features. He ruled in peace for at least another 13 years, restoring temples and erecting buildings and monuments in the cities of Memphis and Thebes. Taharka, a man of great ability, also made astute plans for what he knew was the return of the longtime enemy of Egypt—Assyria. Taharka was right. By 670 B.C., the regrouped Assyrian armies attacked Egypt.

Taharka and his troops fought valiantly, but for two years were dominated by the Assyrians. Finally, some twenty lesser kings of the region, disgusted with Assyrian rule, swore a new allegiance to Taharka. Together, they pushed the invaders back. This tug-of-war for power continued with Taharka ruling one part of Egypt and the Assyrians in control of another. The great Taharka continued to rule for another 25 years.

Egypt's Decline

In 663 B.C., Taharka died. His younger cousin, Tanutamon, succeeded him. Tanutamon defeated the Assyrians and was proclaimed Pharaoh of All Egypt. But Tanutamon was not a shrewd military leader. Just two years later the Assyrians, in an all-out battle, sacked and plundered Thebes. They were successful chiefly because they used iron weapons that were superior to the stone and bronze Egyptian weapons. Tanutamon, perhaps wisely, decided not to expend any more energy holding Egypt and retreated south to Kush.

Thereafter, the Kushite rulers directed all their attention to the development of their own land. As you will see, those new efforts would prove fruitful indeed.

Kush Society Develops

**Meroë:
the capital of Kush.**

Over the next 300 years, the Kushites gradually shifted more and more of their highly developed society out of the capital city of Napata south along the Nile to **Meroë** (MEHR-oh-ah). There they had more grazing land for cattle, plenty of trees, and rich mineral stores. Meroë was also located on a major trade route between Egypt and the African interior.

By 200 B.C. Meroë became a greater capital city than even Napata had been. It was located just north of present-day Khartoum, the capital of Sudan.

The Kushites developed their own form of writing, built brick buildings and fine temples, and made beautiful pottery. An energetic and proud people, the Kushites organized an ambitious international trade. Gold, ivory, ebony, leopard skins, and ostrich feathers flowed north through Meroë. Traders also carried goods east to parts of the Red Sea and then to India and China. Other routes under the control of the Kushites extended into central Africa.

Highlighting a Hero—King Nastasen

The Kushites had King Nastasen to thank for much of their development. His twenty-year reign, beginning in about 400 B.C., was a high point of Kushite power. Nastasen was dead-set against imitating Egypt, and so he promoted the development of a Kushite culture and economy.

Under Nastasen, Meroë lost no time in becoming one of the ancient world's biggest developers of the new "high tech"—iron. Indeed, the ancient world eventually knew Meroë as one of the biggest iron-working centers ever created. From iron, the Kushites made fine weapons and farming tools. Even today, huge mounds of slag (a by-product of iron smelting) can still be found amid the ruins of ancient Meroë.

Kush's Downfall

Over time, Kush attracted the interest of outsiders. A Roman army attacked Kush in 23 B.C., but failed to conquer it. Later, desert people began to attack Kush. Meroë was finally destroyed in A.D. 350 by the rival state of Aksum, located in the northern highlands of present-day Ethiopia.

Aksum, which defeated Kush, was an impressive kingdom. Aksum's people built a strong agricultural economy and a thriving trade. It also introduced a new religion to the continent—Christianity. Christianity came to Aksum in about A.D. 350, when two Syrian youths were shipwrecked on its coast. Brought to King Azana, the conqueror of Meroë, they converted him to Christianity. Over the centuries the religion survived in Ethiopia, where it remains strong today.

In spite of Kush's downfall, its civilization had dominated the middle Nile region for nearly 2,000 years. In the process, it created its own Egyptian-Nubian culture, a culture which left a positive influence among the people of the region for generations.

SECTION TWO REVIEW 〰〰〰〰〰〰〰〰〰〰〰〰〰〰〰

1. VOCABULARY Write a sentence for each of the following terms: Nubia, ebony, Kush, Meroë.

2. GEOGRAPHY Where was Kush located in relation to Egypt?

3. ECONOMICS Who did the people of Kush trade with? What products did they trade?

4. **TECHNOLOGY** What part did iron play in the history of Kush?

5. **CRITICAL THINKING** Before you read these pages, did you know there was a 2,000-year African kingdom along the Nile? Does that knowledge change your views about Africa? If so, how?

SECTION THREE

EAST AFRICAN TRADING CENTERS

VOCABULARY nomadic extended family Islam Swahili

MAIN IDEA The east coast of Africa became an important trading center. As a result of the trade with other regions, a new people arose and gained prominence.

OBJECTIVES As you read, look for answers to the following questions:
1. How did East Africa become an important center of trade?
2. Why did Arabs come to East Africa?

Farther south from Aksum, along Africa's east coast, hustling harbor towns grew up, the product of a growing trade with the Middle East and Asia. Around the beginning of the Christian era (1st century, A.D.), Arab sailors began writing accounts of their voyages to the exotic "lands of the blacks." One of the most famous accounts was the tale of "The Thousand and One Nights," which recounted Arab trade with East Africa. As this account explains:

"We sped on the foamy highways of the sea, trading from port to port...."
—Arab trader

We voyaged for many days and nights from port to port, and from island to island, selling and bartering our goods, and haggling with merchants and officials wherever we cast anchor. We sped on the foamy highways of the sea, trading from port to port and from island to island.

In exchange for African goods, traders and travelers introduced new foods to Africa. For instance, Malaysian travelers brought Africa the banana, the yam, and certain kinds of coconuts. This proved significant. These foods grew so well that many once-**nomadic** people were able to settle down and form communities because they no longer had to roam in search of new food supplies.

nomadic:
refering to people who have no fixed home and wander from place to place in search of food and water.

Legendary "Rhapta" and "The Land of Zanj"

By A.D. 60, ships routinely traded along the East African coast as far south as present-day Tanzania. One traveler, a Greek Egyptian named Periplus, published a small handbook in that year in which he left tantalizing hints of the East Africa of old. For example, he explained that the East African region was called "Azania" and mentioned cities with exotic names like "Rhapta." Periplus described the men as being of "very great stature" and having "separate chiefs for each place."

Later, in A.D. 915, the Arab traveler and historian Ali Masudi described an East African kingdom called "Zanj":

> The land of Zanj produces leopard skins. The people wear them as clothes or export them to Muslim countries. They are the largest leopard skins and the most beautiful for making saddles. They also export tortoise-shell for making combs for which ivory is likewise used.

Ali Masudi also described the king of the Zanj. He was called the Mflame and had a great reputation for honesty:

> He has 300,000 men. The Zanj use the ox as a beast of burden. It is from this country that come tusks weighing 50 pounds and more. They are sent to China and India. The Mfalme is chosen to govern them justly. If he is tyrannical or strays from the truth, they kill him and exclude his children from the throne; for they consider that in acting wrongfully he forfeits his position as the son of the Lord, the King of Heaven and Earth.

"If he is tyrannical or strays from the truth, they kill him and exclude his children from the throne...."
—Ali Masudi on the king of the Zanj

Arabs in East Africa

Arab traders began flocking to East Africa between the 11th and 13th centuries. These Arab trade "reps" married local

11

women and set up small trading settlements along the coast. They became intermediaries with other traders from African societies in the interior. They were also on hand to service the ships that sailed the Indian Ocean. Traders exchanged Arab axes, glass, and wheat for African ivory, tortoise shells, cinnamon, rhinoceros horns, and palm oil.

They also traded a great deal of Chinese porcelain. Remnants have been found from as early as the 7th century T'ang Chinese dynasty to the 13th century Sung Dynasty. And we have evidence that as early as the 10th century, the Chinese depended on East African ivory for making ceremonial objects as large as the ornately carved chairs on which they carried their kings and queens.

So, the Arabs thrived as middlemen in the growing African world trade.

Arabs and Africans

The Arabs who came to East Africa had two general similarities to African peoples. First, both placed great importance on the **extended family** as the major cultural and political unit. Second, both Arab and African rulers tended to leave local customs intact.

extended family:
a family that includes parents, children, and other close relatives, such as grandparents.

There were two major differences between Arabs and Africans, however. First, most Africans thought of land as being owned by the community as a whole, with everybody profiting. The Arabs, on the other hand, brought with them the notion of individual land ownership.

The second major difference was religion. The Arabs brought the religion of **Islam** with them, a religion that worships one God. Within a few hundred years Islam had spread across northern Africa, where it remains very strong today.

Islam:
the religion founded in Arabia by the prophet Mohammed during the 7th century A.D.

Swahili Society

The Arab trading cities were located on the **Swahili** (swah-HEE-lee) coast. The Swahili were a Bantu-speaking people who farmed the coastal lands, fished the ocean waters, and traded with foreign visitors. Over time, they mixed with the Arab merchants from Arabia and Persia who settled in the

Swahili:
people living along the coast of East Africa who interacted with Arab traders and merchants.

coastal cities. As trade spread, so did the Swahili language. Today, over 30 million Africans speak Swahili.

Probably because of Islam, the dress of the Swahili people changed from skins or grass clothing to imported cloth. If you were "in," you wore long skirts and robes of cotton or silk. Women began wearing scarves or loose hooded robes over their heads. Bare breasts were now out of fashion.

With trade no doubt as its impetus, the Swahili people began to write their language using Arabic characters. Later, a very broad store of history and poetry also developed. Although one central Swahili empire never emerged, this civilization spread for over 1,000 miles from present-day Somalia southward to Mozambique.

By the 14th century, the famed Moroccan scholar Ibn Battuta, who had already traveled to India and China, praised the Swahili city of Kilwa. He called it "one of the most beautiful and best-constructed towns in the world." Later, Portuguese sailors would describe the city as having "many fair houses of stone and mortar, very well-arranged streets with doors of wood, well-carved with excellent joinery."

"[Kilwa is] one of the most beautiful and best-constructed towns in the world."
—Ibn Battuta, 14th century Moroccan scholar

Indian Ocean Trade to the East—Sahara Trade to the West

As you have read, East African trade flourished across the Indian Ocean. In the 15th century, West African trade also began to spread across another ocean, this one of sand. It was the great desert known as the Sahara. Eventually, the West African trade would eclipse the East African trade in its magnitude and in its evil—because of outsiders' lust for gold and for slaves.

SECTION THREE REVIEW ‹‹‹‹‹‹‹‹‹‹‹‹‹‹‹‹‹‹‹‹‹‹‹‹‹‹‹

1. VOCABULARY Write a sentence for each of the following terms: nomadic, extended family, Islam, Swahili.

2. TECHNOLOGY What new foods did outsiders bring to East Africa?

3. **HISTORY** How were the Arabs similar to the African peoples with whom they came into contact? How were they different?

4. **GEOGRAPHY** Where did Swahili society develop?

5. **CRITICAL THINKING** How is trade an important part in human development?

SECTION FOUR

GHANA—THE FIRST WEST AFRICAN TRADING EMPIRE

VOCABULARY sub-Saharan Africa savanna Ghana silent trade

MAIN IDEA Ancient Ghana arose as the first great West African empire.

OBJECTIVES As you read, look for answers to the following questions:
1. What factors led to the rise of ancient Ghana?
2. How did Ghana's rule come to an end?

Travelers who journeyed across the continent to West Africa found that the "ships" they needed to cross their "ocean" were live ones—camels. But such rugged "voyages" were worth it. They knew that in this region lay great supplies of gold and other items.

Crossing the Sahara

For centuries, merchants from North Africa had crossed the Sahara to reach cities south of the desert. They wanted gold and slaves in return for salt and other goods. Unlike the East African trade, salt was a prized good. People in sub-Saharan Africa—the part of Africa south of the Sahara— lost a great deal of perspiration in their warm, tropical climate. To insure good health, they added salt to their diet.

In the 7th century A.D., Arab invaders conquered North Africa. To satisfy the growing demand of wealthy Arabs for luxuries, more and more camel trains began heading south

sub-Saharan Africa: that part of Africa lying south of the Sahara.

in search of West African gold and slaves. The people who lived in the broad **savannas** on the southern edge of the Sahara welcomed these traders. Among the savanna people were the Soninke (soh-NEEN-kay) of the Niger (NY-ghur) River area. Sometime after A.D. 500, the Soninke people rose to power as a result of their control of the trans-Saharan trade. They put together a large new empire known as **Ghana.**

savanna:
a flat, open grass land with scattered clumps of trees and shrubs.

Ancient Ghana—A Growing Empire

Thanks to its ideal location on the southern edge of the Sahara, ancient Ghana also came into prominence as a trading center. (Ancient Ghana lay much closer to the Sahara than does present-day Ghana—which is on the West African coast.) From the north the Arabs would send camel caravans, laden with goods the Africans south of the Sahara did not make themselves—silks and cottons, timepieces, and intricately carved knives. And on the journey south, they would pick up salt to trade with, which, as we have seen, the people south of the Sahara needed in order to survive in their hot climate.

Ghana:
the first great West African trading empire, located at the southern edge of the Sahara.

Once they had reached their destination, the Arab merchants would trade for gold. The state of Ghana taxed the gold—as well as the salt and all other goods offered for trade. Those taxes supported an army which kept peace within Ghana's borders.

From about 700 to 1000 Ghana was at the height of its power. The empire ruled lesser kingdoms on its borders, extracting taxes from them in the form of gold. (The term "ghana" referred to the king himself. Foreign visitors gave the kingdom the name Ghana, calling it the "land of gold.")

Highlighting a Hero—Tunka Menin

According to an Arab traveler in 1063, the reigning ghana, Tunka Menin, held great power. The traveler described his power along with the role of religion in the ghana's kingdom:

Tunka Menin wields great power and inspires respect as a ruler of a great empire. . . . The religion is

"Tunka Menin wields great power and inspires respect as a ruler of a great empire."
—Arab traveler, 1063

15

paganism, and the worship is of idols. . . . Around the royal town are domed dwellings, and woods where live their sorcerers, those in charge of their religious cults. There are also their idols and their kings' tombs.

When the king dies they construct a large dome of wood over the burial place. They put the king's ornaments and arms, his eating and drinking vessels, food and drink, and bring in those people who used to serve his food and drink. Then the dome's entrance is locked.

With every bit as much financial savvy as a Wall Street tycoon, the great ghana regulated the value of the gold he controlled. He is said to have kept the largest nuggets for himself and traded only the dust. He did this so the price of gold would not fall.

With the aid of his thousands of troops, the ghana made sure that almost all traders in the region had to go through him to have access to any gold. He would issue trading licenses and would extract regular tolls and taxes. For centuries, outside merchants were kept completely ignorant as to the whereabouts of the actual gold mines.

Ghana's Glory

**silent trade:
a method of trade in which goods were left at an agreed-upon place, without actual contact between individuals.**

Because the Ghanaians so mistrusted outsiders, they used a method of business known as **silent trade**. Merchants would place goods for trade on the ground near the gold-mining region and then leave. The local people, upon hearing the merchants' drums, would then come out. They would check over the goods and put out a certain amount of gold. Then they would leave. Trade was honorable and orderly, so no one took anything until both sides were satisfied with the arrangement.

Over time, trade made Ghana wealthy. An Italian merchant wrote from Ghana:

"The Egyptian merchants come to trade in the land of the blacks. . . ."
—Italian merchant

The Egyptian merchants come to trade in the land of the blacks with half a million head of cattle and camels—a figure which is not fantastic in this region. The place where I am is good for trade, as the merchants come hither from the land of the blacks bringing gold, which they exchange for copper and other goods. Thus everything sells well; until there is nothing left for sale.

Ancient Ghana's economy became so sophisticated that another trader claimed he saw a check from a single Moroccan merchant for 40,000 dinars—or well over $100,000!

And the great Ghana's army was so powerful that it had 200,000 men. To give you an idea of how awesome that was, let's make a comparison. In 1066, a century later, the Normans invaded England. To conquer England, the Norman army is said to have had only 20,000 men.

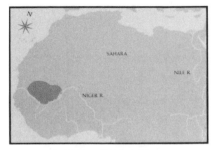

GHANA (700–1200 AD)

The Fall of Ghana

Like Egypt, ancient Ghana's wealth and fame eventually attracted ruthless invaders. Among them were North African warriors called Almoravids. Their continual attacks wreaked havoc on Ghana's agricultural system and eventually scared off most of the merchants who came to do business. Over time, traders and merchants alike began to move to the northeast, nearer the Niger River. The great ghana tried to move his capital, but it was too late. It proved impossible to re-establish the delicate balance of taxes and trade that had for so long been in place.

MALI (1200–1500)

In 1076 the Almoravids again swept across the Sahara, this time capturing Ghana's capital city. With its ravaged pastures and ruined wells gradually overtaken by the Sahara's sands, ancient Ghana lost its glory. But to its credit, it must be remembered that the empire of ancient Ghana had lasted nearly 500 years.

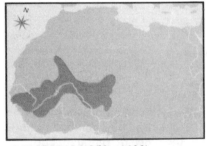

SONGHAI (1350–1600)

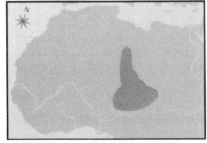

KANEM BORNU (800–1800)

SECTION FOUR REVIEW 〰〰〰〰〰〰〰〰〰〰

1. VOCABULARY Write a sentence for each of the following terms: sub-Saharan Africa, savanna, Ghana, silent trade.

2. HISTORY What development in the 7th century created new trading opportunities for Africans south of the Sahara?

17

3. **GEOGRAPHY** How did ancient Ghana's location affect its rise to power?

4. **ECONOMICS** What part did taxation play in Ghana's success?

5. **CRITICAL THINKING** Do you think it inevitable that a great empire will attract the envy of its neighbors, followed by an actual invasion?

SECTION FIVE

GREAT EMPIRES OF WEST AFRICA

VOCABULARY Mali griot pilgrimage Songhay

MAIN IDEA First Mali and then Songhay replaced Ghana as glorious West African empires.

OBJECTIVES As you read, look for answers to the following questions:
1. What caused the rise and fall of Mali?
2. What caused the rise and fall of Songhay?

Mali:
West African empire that at its height stretched from the Atlantic to the cities of Timbuktu and Gao.

After the fall of Ghana, ancient **Mali** developed into an even greater empire, thanks once again to the power of gold.

The Rise of Mali

The empire of Mali (MAH-lee) began as a small kingdom within the larger empire of Ghana. In the eleventh century its rulers became Muslims. Then, in 1203 the small kingdom came under the control of a king named Sumanguru. A ruthless, greedy ruler, Sumanguru angered the people by demanding large quantities of crops, gold, and other goods. He even stole daughters of local nobles, causing the people to hate him even more.

A few years before 1230, Sumanguru killed a local ruler and tried to take over his lands. In that battle, Sumanguru made the mistake of sparing his rival's son, Sundiata (son-JAH-tah), because he was crippled.

This proved to be Sumanguru's big mistake. Though

lame, in 1230 Sundiata gathered a force of loyal troops. In what would become one of the most famous battles in all of African history, he defeated and killed Sumanguru. This battle, fierce and decisive, is described by African **griots**, or oral historian, even today.

griot:
an African oral historian.

The victorious Sundiata became known as the "Lord Lion." After the battle, more of the surrounding states pledged allegiance to him, and the empire of Mali was born.

Sundiata reigned from 1230 to 1255. His new capital city was Niani. Mali, meanwhile, gained control of the caravan routes that crossed the Sahara.

What the great Sundiata started, two of his successors took to even greater heights. Sabakura was a freed slave who came to power in 1285. A fearsome fighter, he expanded Mali's territory from the Atlantic in the west to the Niger River in the east. (The empire was so large that in those days it took camel trains four months to cross it!)

Highlighting a Hero—Mansa Musa

But in all of Mali's long and prosperous history, it is one emperor who stands out in its most golden era. He was Mansa Musa. His reign, from 1312 to 1337, is known for the peace and security that prevailed throughout the huge empire. An Arab scholar of the day called him "the most powerful, the richest, the most fortunate, the most feared by his enemies, and the most able to do good to those around him."

"[T]he most powerful, the richest, the most fortunate, the most feared by his enemies, and the most able to do good to those around him."
—Arab scholar on Mansa Musa

Mansa Musa put great emphasis on education. He built great universities for religion and law in the cities of Timbuktu and Djenne. These centers of learning gained fame throughout the Muslim world. Indeed, books in Arabic became one of the hottest items on the trans-Saharan trade routes.

Mansa Musa is best-remembered for his famous **pilgrimage** to the Muslims' holy city of Mecca. Like many from the wealthy ruling classes, Mansa Musa practiced Islam. Still, the spread of Islam was superficial. The great majority of people still believed in their ancient magical and ancestral rites. Even Mansa Musa himself did not adhere to the Muslim rule of not having more than four wives.

pilgrimage:
a journey with a special religious purpose.

In 1324, taking with him thousands of slaves, Mansa Musa began the great trek across the Sahara to Mecca. The entire trip is said to have taken the better part of a year, including travel there and back. Like heads of state today, Mansa Musa visited the leaders of countries along the way. The following is from an account by an Egyptian official describing the mighty Mansa's arrival in Cairo:

> When I went out to greet him he treated me with the most careful politeness. But he would talk to me only through an interpreter, although he could speak perfect Arabic.
>
> The sultan of Egypt caused abundant quantities of foodstuffs to be bought for his suite and his followers, and gave a written order to look after and respect him. . . . This man spread upon Cairo the flood of his generosity: there was no person or holder of any office who did not receive a sum in gold from him. The people of Cairo earned incalculable sums from him, whether by buying and selling or by gifts.
>
> So much gold was current in Cairo that it ruined the value of money. That is how it has been for twelve years from that time, because of the great amounts of gold they brought to Egypt and spent.

"This man spread upon Cairo the flood of his generosity. . . ."
—Egyptian official on Mansa Musa

Indeed, historians have estimated that Mansa Musa's one trip caused the gold rate to drop 12 percent, such was the quantity of the rare metal that the enormously wealthy ruler brought with him!

The Rise of Songhay

As you saw, ancient Mali sprang from part of the Ghana empire. The next great West African empire, **Songhay** (SONG-hy), developed from the Mali empire.

Starting in the 7th century, the Songhay people had migrated northward along the Niger River until they came to a large fertile valley just south of the Sahara, near several important trade routes. By the 11th century, the Songhay

Songhay:
largest of the great West African empires, it reached its peak in the early 1500s.

20

had made the city of Gao (pronounced GOW) their capital and established a thriving state. For the next 300 years, Songhay prospered. Then, in 1325, Mansa Musa conquered Songhay. Mali's rule lasted about 50 years. Then, Songhay cast out the Malians and won back its independence.

In 1464, King Sunni Ali Ber came to power and began the expansion that would make Songhay a major empire. Sunni Ali, a brilliant strategist, was one of the first African kings to equip his army with horses. He also built a navy, made up of warriors in large canoes who patrolled up and down the Niger River. Sunni Ali was also a skilled politician, for 28 years maintaining an alliance between the two major factions in his empire. On the one side were the rural farmers and fishermen who continued to believe in the traditional Songhay gods; on the other were the townspeople who were mainly Muslim.

In 1492 Sunni Ali died (the same year Columbus sailed to the Americas). After that time, the Muslim townspeople came to dominate Songhay once and for all.

During Sunni Ali's reign the Songhay people captured Timbuktu and went on to conquer much of Mali's former empire. Songhay continued to grow, and at its height was as big as all of Western Europe.

Askia Muhammad Toure became ruler two years after Sunni Ali died. Askia Muhammad had gained renown as a general in Sunni Ali's army. He is said to have been as dynamic in government as he was in the armed forces. Soon, he formed a system of provinces, each under its own governor.

Under Askia Tuhammad, Songhay prospered. Its three main cities—Gao, Timbuktu, and Djenne—had populations of up to 40,000 people each. Philosophy, medicine, and law flourished in this stable atmosphere.

Invaders from Across the Sahara

In 1528, at the age of 80, Askia Muhammad allowed his son, Musa, to take over. This marked the end of one of the most intelligent and skillful periods of leadership in African history. Also, sadly, it marked the beginning of the end of the Songhay empire. In the years that followed, other states

21

Benin bronze

began to reassert their independence. Thus weakened, in 1591 Songhay faced an army of Moroccan soldiers and captured Europeans led by a Spanish mercenary. The following is a sad account written by a Timbuktu scholar after his city fell to the outsiders:

> I saw the ruin of learning and its utter collapse, and because learning is rich in beauty and fertile in its teaching, since it tells men of their fatherland, their ancestors, the names of their heroes and what lives these led, I decided to record all that I myself could gather on the Songhay princes, their adventures, their history, their achievements, and their wars.

The Songhay continued to fight valiantly to protect their land for many years. They developed a system of raiding their captors' camps guerrilla-style. As a result, the mercenaries never found the fabled vast stores of gold they searched for. After so much futile fighting, many of the mercenaries themselves are said to have decided to stay in Songhay, rather than go back home. They married local women and made their homes there. But by then it was too late to restore the Songhay empire to its previous heights of glory. So, the region fell back into groups of small neighboring states. No new power replaced it.

New Trade Routes, New Empires

As Songhay declined, the trade routes across the Sahara shifted to the east. Wanting to avoid the unrest in the Niger region, caravans traveled instead to the Hausa city-states and the empire of Bornu, in present-day Nigeria.

Meanwhile, by the early 1400s new trade routes were growing along the Atlantic coast. Portuguese explorers had sailed south along the coast, building forts where they traded for ivory, gold, cotton cloth, pepper—and slaves. Benin, near the mouth of the Niger River, profited greatly from this trade. With its capital city of broad avenues, Benin greatly impressed the Portuguese. Its sculptures of bronze and ivory remain today as one of the glories of world art.

SECTION FIVE REVIEW

1. VOCABULARY Write a sentence for each of the following terms: Mali, griot, pilgrimage, Songhay.

2. HISTORY Of what significance was Mansa Musa's journey to Mecca?

3. RELIGION What role did Islam play in the development of the West African empires?

4. ECONOMICS How did trading patterns change after the fall of Songhay?

5. CRITICAL THINKING Of the many achievements of the West African empires, which makes you most proud? Why?

KINGDOMS OF CENTRAL AND SOUTHERN AFRICA

SECTION SIX

VOCABULARY Bantu Zimbabwe

MAIN IDEA Great kingdoms also arose in central and southern Africa.

OBJECTIVES As you read, look for answers to the following questions:
1. What kingdom rose to power in central Africa?
2. What was the basis of Zimbabwe's wealth?

Mighty African kingdoms arose in central and southern Africa too. In the fertile lands along both banks of the Congo River, for instance, people had been farming since about A.D. 800. By 1400, small states governed by kings had emerged. One was the Kongo kingdom, centered near the mouth of the Congo River.

Kongo Kingdom

By 1500 the king of Kongo ruled over a huge area with an excellent structure of government. There were provincial governors. There were judges. And there were other administrators who regulated local disputes, as well as tax and trade matters.

It is important to remember that these governing structures were not run by ignorant "barbarians." They were developed by people who were every bit as gifted as their counterparts during the same time in Europe or Asia.

Beginning in the 1480s, Kongo traded heavily with the Portuguese. Some years later, a Portuguese captain described the Kongo capital:

"I made solemn entry into what is perhaps the greatest town of Central Africa."
—Portuguese captain on Kongo

I made solemn entry into what is perhaps the greatest town of Central Africa. Continuing our march we entered a long street of enclosures made with posts fixed into the ground and interlaced with grass to a height of ten or twelve spans. . . .

Arriving at the *musumba* [the king's residence] we found the great square filled with a throng of people. The warriors in the square comprised some five or six thousand men, all armed with bows and arrows and spears. . . .

The *mwata* [king] was seated. Many leopard skins served him as a carpet. Over these was an enormous lion skin, and on this a stool covered with a big green cloth. On this throne the *mwata* was seated, in greater elegance than any other African king I have seen. His head was ornamented with a kind of crown, pyramidal in shape and two spans high, made of brillliant scarlet feathers; round his forehead was a dazzling diadem of beads of various kinds and colors. Behind his head a band of green cloth, supported by two small ivory needles, fanned out from the back of his neck. . . .

Mwata Kazembe looks 50 years old, but we are told he is much older. He has a long beard, already turning grey. He is well built and tall and has a robustness and agility which promises a long life; his look is agreeable and majestic, and his style splendid in its fashion.

We certainly never expected to find so much ceremonial pomp and ostentation in the ruler of a region so remote from the seacoast and in a nation which appears so barbarous and savage.

First South African Settlers—The Bantu

Over the centuries, parts of central Africa became more and more populated due to the settled trading and farming ways of life. As a result, many African people picked up stakes and began moving south. After all, the giant continent seemed endless, and there was plenty of land for all. These travelers came from different ethnic groups. But because they had certain language and cultural similarities, we call them **Bantu**. One of the great Bantu kingdoms arose in southern Africa by the late 1400s. It was called **Zimbabwe** (zim-BAHB-way).

Bantu:
language and culture groups of people of central and southern Africa.

Zimbabwe:
empire of south-central Africa which reached its peak in the early 1400s.

Zimbabwe

Zimbabwe takes its name from the word for the residences of the kings and nobles of the region. These houses, made of stone, were called "Zimbabwes." The residence of the king was called the Great Zimbabwe.

Zimbabwe is best-remembered for its Great Wall, much as we associate China with the Great Wall of China. The Great Wall of Zimbabwe encircled the king's city. In some places more than 32 feet tall and 17 feet thick, the wall is a masterpiece of architecture. Many stones, for example, form intricate geometrical designs.

The Great Wall, like the pyramids so long before it, was so tightly constructed that no mortar was needed between the carefully placed stones. On one hill, reminiscent of the ancient Greek Acropolis, is a massive amphitheater with an elaborate system of walkways, steps, and hidden passages. For years, Europeans, upon seeing Zimbabwe's 60 acres of huge walls and buildings, refused to believe that black people could have built them.

Highlighting a Hero—Mutapa

A high point of the Zimbabwe empire came during the 30-year rule of Mutapa (moo-TAH-pah) in the mid-1400s. He is said to have combined conquest of weaker states with a widespread program for winning their trust. Mutapa's wealth came from his empire's gold mines. An extensive

25

trade was built up, as gold was exchanged with traders from as far away as the Indian Ocean. The Swahili city-states acted as middlemen in this trade. By the time of Mutapa's death in 1480, Zimbabwe's rule extended some 600 miles in any direction.

Paving the Way to Slavery

As we have seen, Africa was a continent of movement and change. This, unfortunately, would lead to disaster. Gradually, in the late 1400s, Europeans began to make their way south along the African coast. These Europeans had no intention of settling peacefully. Above all else, they were searching for slaves.

SECTION SIX REVIEW

1. VOCABULARY Write a sentence for each of the following terms: Bantu, Zimbabwe.

2. GEOGRAPHY What was the location of the Kongo kingdom?

3. GEOGRAPHY Why did many people from central Africa move south?

4. ECONOMICS What was the basis of Zimbabwe's wealth?

5. CRITICAL THINKING Reread the passage of the Portuguese captain describing the capital of Kongo. What had he expected to find in Africa? What surprised him? Why do you think he was so surprised?

CHAPTER ONE REVIEW

VOCABULARY

Write the numbered sentences on a separate sheet of paper. In each sentence fill in the blank with one of these terms: *Ghana, griot, Islam, nomadic, Swahili.*

1. People with no fixed home who wander from place to place in search of food and water lead _____ lives.
2. _____ is the religion founded by the prophet Mohammed.
3. The _____ people lived along the East African coast.
4. The first great trading empire of West Africa was _____.
5. A _____ is an African oral historian.

REVIEWING THE FACTS

1. Why did a great civilization rise in Egypt?
2. Why can ancient Egypt be called a land of "firsts"?
3. Why did Egypt annex Kush?
4. How did Kush come to rule Egypt?
5. What were the highlights of Kush society?
6. What happened to Kush?
7. How did East Africa become an important center of trade?
8. Why did Arabs come to East Africa?
9. What factors led to the rise of ancient Ghana?
10. How did Ghana's rule come to an end?
11. What caused the rise and fall of Mali?
12. What caused the rise and fall of Songhay?
13. What kingdom rose to power in central Africa?
14. What was the basis of Zimbabwe's wealth?

CRITICAL THINKING

1. MAKING COMPARISONS Compare the rise of empires in East Africa and West Africa. What similarities did they have? What differences?
2. INFERRING How did Mansa Musa's journey to Mecca demonstrate the wealth of ancient Mali?

UNDERSTANDING PREJUDICE

1. Among the first "outsiders" to Africa were Arab traders. Why is it often easy for people to be suspicious of "outsiders"—even to hate them? What contributions can "outsiders" make?
2. A *stereotype* is a fixed idea about someone or something. How is Africa often portrayed in movies or news reports today? Do you think such coverage results in negative or positive stereotypes about Africa? If negative, what examples from African history can you use to refute such stereotypes?

SLAVERY BECOMES A SYSTEM

(1400–1800)

[Nigeria]—Here a most sorrowful scene imaginable to be witnessed!—Women, some with three, four, or six children clinging to their arms, with the infants on their backs, and such baggage as they could carry on their heads, running as fast as they could through prickly shrubs...while they were endeavoring to disentangle themselves...they were overtaken and caught by the enemies with a noose of rope thrown over the neck of every individual, to be led in the manner of goats tied together, under the drove of one man.

I was thus caught—with my mother, two sisters (one an infant about ten months old), and a cousin.

The last view I had of my father was when he came from the fight, to give us the signal to flee.

Samuel Ajayi Crowther's *Biography*

Samuel Ajayi Crowther was a teenager in Oyo, Nigeria, in 1821 when he was kidnapped, right out of his own family compound. Like countless others, he was forced into slavery and taken to America. His story was the story of millions of African-Americans.

SECTION ONE   AFRICAN SLAVERY DEVELOPS

VOCABULARY heathen *asiento* Middle Passage

In 1619 a Dutch ship brought some 20 African captives to Jamestown, where they became indentured servants. They were the first Africans in the English colonies.

MAIN IDEA By 1500 Europeans had established a thriving slave trade in Africa. Demand for slaves in the Americas would greatly increase the demand for slaves.

OBJECTIVES As you read, look for answers to the following questions:
1. What motivated Europeans to head south to Africa?
2. Why were slaves needed in the Americas?

When, exactly, did slavery begin? No one knows for sure. Ever since people in animal skins first settled in communities, there have been disagreements, sometimes over who owned what, sometimes over religion, culture, or family. Battles invariably erupted. What did the victors do with the captives from those battles? Shake hands and send them home? Unfortunately, the folks who won were not that broadminded. They usually made one of two choices: they killed their captives or made them slaves.

The Rationale for Slavery

Down through the ages, both alternatives have been all too common. Well-to-do people in ancient India and China kept captives as slaves. The ancient Hebrews practiced slavery as well. In fact, thousands of years before Christianity, warring nations took their captives and made slaves of them. In fact, in ancient Rome, the noted statesman Cicero is said to have complained in a letter to a wealthy slaveowner friend that "of all his slaves the *British* were the ugliest and most stupid."

So, you see, as the ancient Greek philosopher Plato once suggested, *all* of us are probably descended from slaves, in one way or another!

Slavery was always based on a desire by the slave-owner to reap a profit from the cheap labor of his slaves. Let's also keep in mind that in medieval Europe, average people were often little more than "slaves" themselves. Free in name only, families often worked as "serfs" all their lives, tilling a small patch of land from which the lord of the manor took most of the profits. So, it's no surprise that when these same former serfs (who had been bought and sold themselves) got to America for a new start, they thought nothing of buying and selling Africans.

Europeans Develop the Slave Trade

As early as 1440, European traders began to single out Africans for slavery. Many of these traders even tried to justify slavery by claiming that somehow black people were inherently "inferior" to whites. Why? Because of their dark skin color and their different customs. Ironically—at the same time these inferiority claims were being made—many African people were rising to heights of great distinction among European kings, queens, and nobility! (More on that later.)

In Europe during the 11th through the 13th centuries, under the banner of Christianity, rulers sent thousands of their top soldiers to the Middle East. Their aim was to recover the "holy land" from the Muslims. The Christians aimed to conquer those lands and subdue the **heathens** (meaning anyone who practiced another religion).

**heathen:
to a European Christian, anyone
who practiced another religion.**

Through interchanges such as this, as well as caravans through the African deserts (Chapter 1), Europeans were exposed to all sorts of exotic new things like silks, spices, and gold. These only served to entice their monarchs to find out more about those "lands out there."

Soon, everybody wanted to get in on the act. The inland desert routes were extremely dangerous, so a few explorers began to think about sea routes.

Portugal Heads South

By 1420, Portugal's Prince Henry became so obsessed with the riches of distant lands that he set up a school for sea captains to encourage exploration. So obsessed was he, that he became known as "Henry the Navigator." Finally, after more than fifteen years, Prince Henry convinced a few of his seamen to overcome their fear that if they sailed past a certain point, they would fall off the edge of the world.

Cautiously the seamen began to sail south. They didn't know where they were going. But they knew they wanted to find a water route to exotic foreign lands. They were actually hoping to get to India and China, but they discovered the lucrative trade with Africa along the way.

The Arrival of African Captives in Europe

At first, the Portuguese only traded goods politely with a few local rulers. But, eventually, someone decided to bring back a few of the Africans for the European kings to see. By the time Prince Henry died in 1460, the Portuguese were bringing back almost 1,000 African captives each year to work on their farms.

At the same time, local African rulers were getting in

on the act. They routinely traded their local war prisoners to Europeans. In exchange, they received small household goods, silk and cotton cloth, or liquor.

All Europe Hopes to Profit from the Slave Trade

In Europe, meanwhile, news spread after 1492 of Christopher Columbus's voyage to the New World. From then on, competition really started to heat up as European nations sought get-rich-quick opportunities. So much so, that the Pope, who wielded tremendous political as well as religious power in those days, intervened.

Sadly, the Pope did not use those powers to great humanitarian ends. Did he, as a religious leader, condemn the institution of slavery? No. Instead, the Pope, a Spaniard, "organized" it! His infamous decree, called the **asiento**, incredibly "gave" Africa, along with most of Asia and Brazil, to Portugal. The rest of the New World went to Spain. So the two nations immediately vied to see who could get the most explorations under way.

It wasn't until the end of the 1500s that Holland, England, and France, began to get in on the slave trade in a big way. Spain, not allowed to build trading forts in Africa under the *asiento*, finally made side deals with these other countries to establish slave trade routes to and from Africa.

By 1600, there would be no stopping the wholesale free-for-all of traders from all over Europe. Like some greedy real estate developers today, they did not see how they were destroying lives in the process. They saw only the quick profits they could make by throwing together settlements in the New World to be worked by the Africans they captured.

Africa Depopulated

Horribly, from 1500 to 1808, as many as 50 *million* African people were dragged from their homes and families and forced onto slave ships. And what's even worse, only 15 to 20 million of those 50 million captured actually survived the **Middle Passage**—the devastating trip across the ocean.

Olaudah Equiano was one who survived. In 1756 Equiano was only 11 years old. He lived in the West

asiento:
the Pope's plan to divide the world between Spain and Portugal.

Middle Passage:
the brutal voyage taken by slave ships across the Atlantic from Africa to the New World.

African kingdom of Benin. Equiano was playing in his backyard with his sister one day. He was never to see his home again:

> One day, when only I and my dear sister were left behind to mind the house, two men and a woman got over our walls, and in a moment seized us both.... They stopped our mouths and ran off with us into the nearest wood.... The next day proved a day of greater sorrow ... for my sister and I were separated while we lay clasped [weeping] in each other's arms....
>
> I cried and grieved continually, and for several days I did not eat anything but what was forced into my mouth....
>
> When I looked around the [slave] ship [when I arrived at the coast] and saw a large furnace boiling and a multitude of black people chained together ... I no longer doubted my fate.... I fell motionless on the deck and fainted. [Later] I asked if we were not to be eaten by those white men with horrible looks, red faces, and loose hair....
>
> I received such a salutation in my nostrils ... with the stench and crying together, I became so sick and low that I was not able to eat.... I now wished for the last friend, death, to relieve me.... I would have jumped over the side, but I could not.... The crew used to watch us very closely ... and I have seen some of these poor African prisoners most severely cut for attempting to do so, and hourly whipped for not eating. This indeed was often the case with myself....
>
> I had never seen among my people such instances of brutal cruelty, and this not only shown toward us blacks but also to some of the whites themselves. One white man in particular I saw ... flogged so unmercifully ... that he died as a consequence of it; and they tossed him over the side as they would have done a brute....
>
> The hold was so crowded it almost suffocated us.... The shrieks of the women and the groans of the dying rendered the whole a scene of horror almost inconceivable....

African captives

"The shrieks of the women and the groans of the dying rendered the whole a scene of horror almost inconceivable...."
—Olaudah Equiano

33

> At last we came in sight of the island of Barbados.... We were sold after their usual manner.... Without scruple, are friends and relations separated, most of them never to see each other again.

South American Slave Trade

Many of the slaves were brought across the Atlantic to work the farms and plantations of Spain's new colonies. These included the countries we now know as Mexico, Chile, Peru, Equador, and Colombia. At first, the Spanish invaders had tried to force the native Indians to work for them, but the Indians died in large numbers under the brutal treatment. Further, there were simply not enough Spaniards who wanted to live in these new outposts and do the backbreaking work of clearing and settling the land.

The Spanish found that only Africans were strong enough to do the work. In addition, most of the Africans were skilled farmers and craftsworkers whose talents were recognized and appreciated in the Americas. Black slaves became the critical factor in enabling the Spanish to explore and conquer their new frontiers.

Highlighting a Hero—Brother Porres

In Peru, Martin de Porres was born in 1579. First a surgeon's apprentice and a doctor and finally a Dominican friar, he spent years helping the poor, opening Peru's first orphanage. By the 18th century, Pope Gregory XVI had officially "blessed" Brother Porres. He was to become known as the first black saint.

Caribbean Slave Trade

As the slave trade became firmly established, the Caribbean islands played a key role. Because islands like Haiti had similar climates and living conditions to Africa, slave traders would go there first to sell their new captives. They would exchange them for slaves who had already worked there for a while. Then, they would sell these "seasoned" slaves, often to farms and plantations in North America.

SECTION ONE REVIEW ~~~~~~~~~~~~~~~~~~~~~~~~~~~~

1. VOCABULARY Write a sentence for each of the following terms: heathen, asiento, Middle Passage.

2. RELIGION What part did religion play in arousing European interest in the Middle East?

3. HISTORY Why didn't the Europeans simply enslave American Indians and not bother with Africans?

4. GEOGRAPHY Why were slaves from Africa first brought to the Caribbean islands?

5. CRITICAL THINKING What happened in 1492? Of what importance was that to Africa?

SLAVERY COMES TO AMERICA

SECTION TWO

VOCABULARY indentured servant

MAIN IDEA During the 1600s and 1700s slavery took hold in the English colonies.

OBJECTIVES As you read, look for answers to the following questions:
1. When and how did Africans first arrive in North America?
2. How did the system of indentured servitude work for whites? For blacks?
3. What English colony originally banned slavery?

Africans have been in the Americas for hundreds of years. In fact, they arrived in the New World almost a century before the first colonists from England settled at Jamestown or Plymouth.

Spaniards Bring the First Africans to America

In 1526 Lucas Vasques de Ayllon established a Spanish colony in what we know now as South Carolina. According

35

to his records, he led a party of 500 Spaniards and 100 African slaves.

It was not until 1562 that the British entered the slave trade. In that year Sir John Hawkins sailed in search of slaves. "Partly in trade and partly by violence," he captured hundreds of Africans, 300 of whom he sold at a "great profit" in the Caribbean. At first, Queen Elizabeth called his exploits "detestable" and predicted that they would "call down the vengeance of heaven upon the undertakers" if any more Africans were "taken by violence." But after the queen received her share of the bounty from several more trips, she appears to have changed her tune and knighted Hawkins for his "success." The British were on their way to becoming major players in the slave trade.

Africans Arrive at Jamestown

In 1618, British settlement of North America was just beginning. The tiny community of Jamestown, Virginia, had only existed for eleven years. Explorer John Rolfe, who married the famous Indian maiden, Pocahontas, was in town when two vessels entered the harbor. On board were African captives. The ships did not actually land their captives in Virginia, however. The acting governor, a Captain Argall, had just gone back to England. So the ships sailed on with their cargo to the Earl of Warwick's Caribbean plantation.

A year later, a Dutch slave ship came to Jamestown. Evidence is contradictory on the exact events. Some reports say the crew sold fourteen Africans as slaves. Other accounts say there were twenty Africans who were sold as servants and then freed shortly after their arrival. From correspondence of the day, it does seem that the Dutch ship was in "dire need of provisions" and bartered its human cargo for food.

However they arrived, by 1776, just before the American Revolution against Great Britain, the number of African slaves had soared to 10 percent of the entire American population. In some areas, Africans outnumbered Europeans. Most lived and worked in the South, from Maryland to the Carolinas, where planters grew tobacco, rice, and sugar cane for export back to Europe.

Indentured Servitude for Whites and Blacks

In the 1600s, many whites in America were not better off than Africans. These were people who sold their labor, usually for four to seven years, in exchange for passage to the colonies in America. (Some were actually kidnapped in Europe and sent off to America.) These **indentured servants**, like their black counterparts, received no pay, usually only getting food and clothing. However, following the European custom, they were freed at the end of their period of servitude. After that, they could, in theory, enjoy the same rights as other whites. If they were clever and had learned a skill, they could start working for wages. Some lucky ones were even given a start by their former masters in the form of some land, tools, and "seed money" to begin planting their own first crops. Not a few of them eventually bought indentured workers or slaves of their own.

This indentured servant system had one major flaw. Often, white servants ran away from their master before their years of servitude were up. They moved to another region and blended in with the population, thus giving the master a poor return on his investment.

So, the colonists ended up relying more and more on the cheap labor of Africans. These black people were much more vulnerable in the New World. Far from their homelands, not speaking English and, because of their skin color, unable to blend in easily with other colonists, they found themselves isolated and without rights.

indentured servant: a person who exchanged usually four to seven years of labor for passage to America.

The Legalization of Slavery

By 1661, the colonial legislature in Virginia voted to have African servitude last a lifetime. In fact, it later added provisions to ensure that a slave's children would remain slaves as well. What a return on their investment, the colonists snickered gleefully. For one price, slaveowners had the free labor of generations. Similar slavery laws soon spread to many other colonies.

Georgia, which was not founded until 1732, originally did *not* permit slavery. Its founder, James Oglethorpe, wanted no alcohol or slaves to disturb the hardworking thrift of the debtors and "worthwhile prisoners" he hoped would start a new life in Georgia. Oglethorpe envisioned fathers, mothers, and children working together to grow crops needed in England as well as developing silkworms for lavish fabrics. But by 1750, the influence of Georgia's neighbors was too great. Georgian colonists demanded their own booze and slaves. They began smuggling whiskey from across the border in South Carolina and "leasing" black labor for 100-year stints. Ten years later, one-third of the 9,000 Georgia residents were African-Americans.

The Role of New England

The 1700s also saw white New Englanders profiting greatly from the slave trade. Many built and operated the ships used in capturing and transporting the slaves. By 1767, New Englanders had even set up 90 distilleries to make the rum that they used to barter for slaves. A male African captive was worth approximately 130 gallons of rum.

Business grew so busy that New England slave pirates began sailing directly into their own ports with the African captives, not bothering to take them to the Caribbean first for a period of training. Boston and Salem, Massachusetts, as well as Newport, Rhode Island, became hubs of the American slave trade.

SECTION TWO REVIEW ∿∿∿∿∿∿∿∿∿∿∿∿∿∿∿

1. **VOCABULARY** Write a sentence for the following term: indentured servant.

2. **HISTORY** When and how did Africans arrive in Jamestown?

3. **ECONOMICS** Why did slavery replace the system of indentured servitude for Africans in America?

4. **HISTORY** In what way was the founding of Georgia different from that of other English colonies?

5. **CRITICAL THINKING** What obstacles did newly arrived Africans face in America?

AFRICAN ACHIEVEMENTS IN THE NEW WORLD AND IN EUROPE

SECTION THREE

VOCABULARY mulatto Moor

MAIN IDEA Even during the slave era, black people made important accomplishments in America and in Europe.

OBJECTIVES As you read, answer the following questions:
1. What role did Africans play in exploring North America?
2. Who were some notable Europeans of African ancestry?

To justify the evils of slavery, white people on both sides of the Atlantic increasingly viewed all black people as inferior. But solid evidence of African achievements before, during, and after the slave trade explodes the myth of inferiority.

African Explorers: First in the New World?

You may be surprised, but evidence exists that Africans may have sailed to the New World long before Christopher Columbus! Take Mexico, for example. Huge stone sculptures with obvious African features have been found there. Might they have been carved by people from Africa?

There is further evidence that some 200 years before Columbus, African explorers might have reached the Americas. In the early 1300s Abu Bakiri II, ruler of Mali, ordered 200 ships and supply boats to be built and outfitted for a two-year voyage. The mighty African ruler dreamed of reaching lands beyond his continent. He sent off the ships with the order that they not return until they had crossed the ocean or run out of food. Only one came back, saying that the others had been lost at sea. So Bakiri decided to lead a second expedition himself. He and his ships never returned. Some historians think that one or more of the ships may have reached South America.

When he arrived in the New World, Columbus himself reported that he received small gold slabs from the Indians in Hispaniola that were just like those that came from West

Africa. When questioned, the Indians even used the same name the Africans used, "guanin." And, in fact, they explained to Columbus that they had received the guanin "from black merchants that came to us from the southeast" (the direction of West Africa). Finally, after his third trip to the New World, Columbus personally reported "the presence of [blacks] there."

Africans Take Part in Spanish Explorations

There is no doubt that skilled Africans played important roles on many European expeditions to the New World.

Pedro Alonso Nino, for instance, was a member of Columbus's crew. Records, although scanty, indicate that he was a **mulatto** (a person of mixed white and black ancestry), and may well have been a free man. Spanish records indicate that by 1501, Spain routinely hired black men as part of the exploration teams in its colonies.

When Vasco Nuñez de Balboa crossed the Isthmus of Panama to discover the Pacific Ocean in 1513, records indicate some 30 black men were crewmembers. And others accompanied Hernando Cortès in 1519 when he conquered the Aztec Indians in Mexico. One black member of Cortès's crew is credited with planting and harvesting the first wheat crop in the Americas.

Other Spanish explorers, like Francisco Pizarro, took black men with them on their explorations in South America. In fact, Africans took part in *every* major Spanish expedition.

North Africans Called Moors Conquer Spain

At the same time, Africans in Europe were also proving that their birthplaces or the color of their skin did not make them in any way inferior to whites. As early as 711 A.D., North Africans known as **Moors** conquered Spain. There they remained for hundreds of years, not forced back to Africa until 1492.

Because of intermarriage between these Arabs and black-skinned Africans, the term "Moor" eventually became another word for "black" in Europe. Have you heard of

mulatto:
a word from the Spanish, meaning a person of mixed white and black ancestry.

Moor:
term once used in Europe referring to any dark-skinned person; from the North African conquerors of Spain.

40

Shakespeare's *Othello*? He was a fictional example of a Moorish general living in Venice. In that famous play, Othello married an Italian woman.

Africans in European Society

The greatest influx of Africans into Europe came as a result of the Europe-Africa slave trade which was described earlier. In fact, in 1474, Spain's King Ferdinand and Queen Isabella named a well-known black man of the day, Juan de Valladolid, as "mayoral of the Negroes" of the city of Seville.

The Africans from south of the Sahara, darker-skinned than the North African Moors, soon became popular in fashionable Europe. Every court had to have one. Within a few years, there was a smattering of Europeanized Africans throughout Europe. This happened at the same time that slave ships were beginning to take African captives to the Americas to work on plantations like animals.

Highlighting a Hero—Duke Alessandro De' Medici

In Italy from 1510 to 1537, a black man made his mark in society. His father was none other than Pope Clement VII, Cardinal de' Medici. His mother was a beautiful black servant woman.

This dashing gentleman's name was Duke Alessandro de' Medici. He was known as "The Moor." At the time, it was not uncommon for children born out of wedlock to inherit important titles and lands. So, Alessandro de' Medici became the first reigning Duke of Florence. The Medicis would go on to become one of the most illustrious families in European history, known for their brilliance at politics and court intrigue.

Highlighting a Hero—Father Benedict

From 1524 to 1589, also in Italy, a black monk named Father Benedict, the son of African slaves, came to be revered by Pope Pius IV. In time, he became father superior of a particularly austere and self-denying Catholic order of

41

monks. Although he could neither read nor write Latin, Father Benedict memorized entire Bible chapters and preached from them. Leading Catholic clergy consulted him on biblical passages. Before he died on April 4, 1589, so many people, rich and poor alike, loved Father Benedict that they traveled from "distant countries" to receive his blessing. He was hailed as a saint but refused formal titles and honors.

Highlighting a Hero—Abraham Hannibal

Russia was another country where the nobility admired Africans. In the 1730s, while blacks in colonial America were being called "subhuman," one of Russia's greatest generals was an African. This great general's name was Abraham (Ibrahim) Hannibal.

Hannibal was kidnapped as a boy from Africa in about 1692. Instead of being thrown onto a slave ship headed for America, he was sent to Turkey. From its capital, Constantinople, young Hannibal was taken to Russia. Peter the Great, the ruling czar (emperor of Russia), was delighted by the obviously intelligent boy. He immediately adopted and lavished gifts upon him at court.

In 1735, when Peter the Great died, a relative, Prince Menshikov, tried to bribe the popular Hannibal. He wanted Hannibal's help badly. Menshikov desperately wanted to get his daughter married to Peter II, heir to the throne. During the years that followed, court intrigues raged as Menshikov and other pretenders scrambled for the throne.

Hannibal was caught in the middle because of his relationship with the late czar. In the end, he had to be smuggled out of the capital, St. Petersburg, or risk assassination. He spent the next twelve years as commander of a Russian village, Revel.

After his exile, one of the Russian princesses, Elizabeth, succeeded to the throne. She rewarded Hannibal for his loyalty by giving him ten villages and the thousands of peasants who lived in them.

Hannibal continued to serve the Russian court with distinction. In 1752, because of his great engineering skills, Hannibal was asked to head a special Russian commission to settle a border dispute with Sweden. Hannibal handled this and other assignments with such distinction that he eventually became commander-in-chief of the Russian army.

Hannibal and his wife, a German noblewoman, had eleven children. His eldest son, Ivan, became governor of the Ukraine. One of his grandchildren, Alexander Pushkin, became one of Russia's most famous writers and poets. Hannibal died immensely rich in 1782.

Highlighting a Hero—Alexander Pushkin

The great Hannibal's grandson, Alexander Pushkin, would become even more famous than his illustrious grandfather. Pushkin was born in 1799. By the time he was fifteen, this young genius had become Russia's leading poet. He is remembered today because he was the first major writer in his country to write in Russian, rather than in fashionable French or Latin. Because of this daring act, the entire Russian language gained legitimacy. Up until then, it had been used mainly by peasants. As one Russian historian, Professor I. Luppol, put it, "Pushkin created the Russian literary language. He was the founder of modern Russian literature and made humanity the richer for his immortal works.... [He] is our ... Shakespeare."

"Pushkin created the Russian literary language."
—Russian historian on Alexander Pushkin

Highlighting a Hero—Chevalier De St. Georges

In France, at the same time, another man of African ancestry would become an immensely popular literary and military figure. Named Chevalier de St. Georges, he lived from 1745 to 1799. He became the trend-setter in the French court during Louis XVI's reign. Not only was he a top violinist, pianist, and composer, but he was the top swordsman, marksman, and military commander of his day.

Chevalier de St. Georges set the new fashion trends. His taste in clothes was so superb that whenever the tall, handsome figure appeared at court, whatever he was wearing immediately became the fashion.

Monsieur Jean de Beauvois, a court contemporary described him:

As soon as St. Georges appeared in any circle, a murmur, to which all had long been accustomed,

43

circulated through the room. . . . Men, the most distinguished in nobility . . . came forward to shake his hand. In an instant he had become the lion of the assembly.

In spite of his good looks and fabulous talents, St. Georges is said to have been modest and courteous, bringing his mother, a former West Indian slave, to court to be introduced.

For years, one of his chief admirers was Queen Marie Antoinette herself. This was the era of the French Revolution, however. And, although raised as an aristocrat, St. Georges remembered the humble island of Guadeloupe in the West Indies where he was born in 1745 to a black slave woman and the governor of the island, the Marquis Jean de Boullogne.

So it was that, despite his friendships at court, St. Georges became a leader of the fight for the common man in France. He organized an all-black military regiment in the Caribbean and led them to several military victories. However, in spite of his idealistic work, the revolutionary crowds still almost guillotined him along with Marie Antoinette and the other noblemen at the end of the revolution.

But St. Georges' popularity won out. On June 12, 1799, when he finally did die from illness, St. Georges was so popular that news of his death dominated the French headlines. Biographers remember St. Georges as having "rare character" and giving generously to the poor.

Highlighting a Hero—Alexandre Dumas

Also in France, two other black men of great significance were Alexandre Dumas, father and son. Dumas, the father, was born in Haiti in 1762, the son of a black slave woman and the French Marquis de la Pailleterie. After moving to France, Dumas became such a brilliant swordsman that he dueled three men at once. And won!

Within just a few years, Dumas came close to being named commander of the entire French army instead of Napoleon Bonaparte. As it happened, the French government, in 1793, was frantic to end the violence that had marked the French Revolution. In his *Memoirs*, Dumas writes that French government officials sent for both Napoleon and him to end the conflict.

Napoleon happened to be just one day's ride away from Paris, while Dumas was two days away. Had it been the other way around, Dumas, not Napoleon, might have been named commander-in-chief of the entire French army.

Napoleon Bonaparte went on to make Dumas commander of his cavalry and governor of the French province of Treviso. And the two great soldiers vowed to become godfathers to each other's sons.

Unfortunately, their relationship ended in a dispute over a battle in Egypt. Dumas died in 1806 before they could reconcile. However, Alexandre Dumas's name is on the Arch of Triumph in Paris, which Napoleon commissioned to be built.

Dumas's son, Alexandre, was born in 1802. A genius at an early age, he became a self-taught writer. He went on to become one of France's, and indeed, the world's, greatest novelists. By the time of his death in 1870 he had written such classic works as *The Three Musketeers*, *The Count of Monte Cristo*, and *The Black Tulip*.

Highlighting a Hero—George Bridgetower

Across Europe, in the country of Poland, an African was to become a hero during the same time period. He was George Augustus Polgreen Bridgetower. Born in 1789 of an African father and either a German or Polish mother, Bridgetower become one of the greatest violinists ever known.

The famous composer, Beethoven, was one of Bridgetower's fellow musicians. Beethoven praised him highly, and even wrote a sonata for him which they performed together. Bridgetower became an idol in Vienna, Rome, and Milan. Called "The African Prince," he died in London in 1860.

The very next year Abraham Lincoln was sworn in as President of the United States, ushering in the end of American slavery. Until then, many Africa-Americans, still laboring in bondage, would make invaluable contributions to their new homeland, whether they received credit or not.

45

SECTION THREE REVIEW

1. VOCABULARY Write a sentence for each of the following terms: mulatto, Moor.

2. HISTORY What did Columbus discover that suggests Africans had arrived in the New World before him?

3. BIOGRAPHY Who was Abraham Hannibal, and what were his accomplishments?

4. BIOGRAPHY Who was Chevalier de St. Georges, and what were his accomplishments?

5. CRITICAL THINKING Why is it not impossible to believe that Africans might have reached South America before the Europeans? (Consider the location of the two continents.)

CHAPTER TWO REVIEW

VOCABULARY

Write the numbered sentences on a separate sheet of paper. In each sentence fill in the blank with one of these terms: *heathen, indentured servant, Middle Passage, Moors, mulatto.*

1. Christians once called a person who practiced another religion a _____ .

2. The _____ was the brutal voyage taken by slaveships from Africa to the Americas.

3. An _____ was someone who exchanged his or her labor for passage to America.

4. The word _____ referred to a person of mixed white and black ancestry.

5. The _____ were the North African conqerers of Spain.

REVIEWING THE FACTS

1. What motivated Europeans to head south to Africa?
2. Why were slaves needed in the Americas?
3. When and how did Africans first arrive in North America?

4. How did the system of indentured servitude work for whites? For blacks?

5. What English colony originally banned slavery?

6. What role did Africans play in exploring North America?

7. Who were some notable Europeans of African ancestry?

CRITICAL THINKING

1. **ANALYZING** How did Olaudah Equiano's account of the Middle Passage make real the horrors of the slaves' voyage to North America?

2. **MAKING COMPARISONS** How were indentured servants like slaves? How were they different?

UNDERSTANDING PREJUDICE

1. How do you think the institution of slavery affected the way European-Americans treated African-Americans?

2. Some people point out that certain African kingdoms were involved in the slave trade and greatly profited from it. They say, then, that blacks are as much to blame for African slavery as whites. Do you agree or disagree? Explain your answer.

SLAVERY TAKES HOLD IN AMERICA

(1700–1850)

They dragged you from homeland,
They chained you in coffles,
They huddled you spoon-fashion in filthy hatches,
They sold you to give a few gentlemen ease....

The strong men keep a-comin' on
The strong men git stronger.

They point with pride at the roads you built for them,
They ride in comfort on the rails you laid for them.
They put hammers in your hands
And said—Drive so much before sundown.

You sang:
Ain't no hammah
In dis lan'
Strike lak mine, bebby,
Strike lak mine.

The strong men keep a-comin' on
The strong men git stronger.

Strong Men, Sterling Brown

Strong men and strong women they were. Those who had survived the Middle Passage were now making new lives in distant, hostile lands. Those lives were not easy ones. And worse was to come. For decades, white Americans remained uncertain about slavery. Should they put an end to it? Should they leave it in place? How strict should the slave system be? Then, after the United States won its independence from Great Britain, slavery became firmly and cruelly entrenched. The reason? The rise in importance of cotton in the South. Through all this, as you will read, African-Americans began taking the first steps on the long road toward freedom.

By 1750, 40 percent of the people in the Southern Colonies were of African descent. Most lived a hard life of forced labor, usually as field hands.

AFRICAN-AMERICANS HELP THE UNITED STATES GROW

SECTION ONE

VOCABULARY northern colonies southern colonies indigo Parliament Boston Massacre American Revolution War of 1812

MAIN IDEA Despite the active role they took in the fight for American independence, most African-Americans remained in bondage after the Revolution.

OBJECTIVES As you read, answer the following questions:
1. How did slavery vary in the English colonies?
2. What role did black people play in the wars against the British?

49

To understand the role of African-Americans, slave and free, in the development of America, we have to remember that America is located on a vast, sprawling continent. By 1700 the North American continent was characterized more by great regional differences than by similarities.

Early America—A Patchwork of Colonies

Early America was a patchwork of independent colonies. The English colonies were on the eastern seaboard. The **northern colonies** were Connecticut, Rhode Island, Massachusetts, New Hampshire, New Jersey, Pennsylvania, and Delaware. During early colonial times, there was actually no colony of New York. It was a Dutch colony called New Netherlands. Then, the English took it over, changing the colony's name in honor of the Duke of York.

northern colonies: the English colonies of Connecticut, Rhode Island, Massachusetts, New Hampshire, New York, New Jersey, Pennsylvania, and Delaware.

Slavery was minor and mild in the northern colonies, especially in New Netherlands before the English took over. Slaves who belonged to the Dutch East Indies Corporation were even allowed to own small plots of land. A number of slaves were freed when they became elderly. But after the English arrived, the few rights of slaves and even free African-Americans were kicked away. Free black people had to be inside by a 9:00 P.M. curfew, for example.

Slavery took hold most firmly in the **southern colonies**— Georgia, North Carolina, South Carolina, Maryland, and Virginia. Because of its rich land, the South became the site of many large plantations. Many of those plantations were run like the large estates of feudal lords in Europe. Their owners became, in fact, much like the lords that they, themselves, had worked for. They spent as much of their own time as possible imitating the nobility of the Europe they had left. These planters had hunts and horse races, and they entertained lavishly. They could do so because they only spent pennies a day for the upkeep of their workers.

southern colonies: the English colonies of Georgia, North and South Carolina, Virginia, and Maryland.

On the plantations the slaves were treated like beasts of burden. They were flogged unmercifully to make them work in the fields from sunrise to sunset, with only a 15-minute break, six days a week. The fate of many was death from exhaustion and malnutrition.

Even so, it is not true to think that the South was made up solely of large plantations like those in the movie *Gone*

With the Wind or on television. Actually, the vast majority of farms in the South were small, one-family operations, much like those in the North. The only reason those in the South were able to afford one or two slave families was that the warm climate made it cheaper to feed and clothe slaves.

The Spanish, meanwhile, controlled much of California, New Mexico, and Texas. Florida was a Spanish possession also. The French territory was in Canada and along the Mississippi River. To the south, the French owned Louisiana, including New Orleans.

So, the accomplishments and treatment of African-Americans varied dramatically according to what region they were in. Wherever they lived, however, it is clear that America's development as a country was due in part to African-Americans' forced labor.

The Growing Need for Slaves

When America started out, the number of slaves was small, both in the North and the South. The smallest number of slaves by far was found in New England. In 1700 there were only about 1,000 slaves there.

But by 1708 Virginia alone was importing 1,000 slaves each year. By 1765 the black population of South Carolina was more than twice that of whites, 90,000 slaves compared to 40,000 whites. Why were there so many more slaves in the South? The planters in that region, working the fertile soil, made their money largely by selling their crops back to England. Among other goods, they sold tobacco, rice, cotton, and a popular blue-black dye called **indigo**. As the demand for their crops grew, planters hurried to buy more land. Then they looked for more slaves. It became a vicious cycle.

indigo:
a plant used to make a black-blue dye.

British Policy and Slavery

In spite of the profits that southern planters made from the slave trade, they feared being outnumbered by African laborers. They decided, on at least two separate occasions, to restrict or even ban the entry of new slaves into America. This did not mean that the planters wanted to do away with slavery. But they did want to control the number of new slaves coming into their areas.

However, because the Crown refused to agree to such laws, Britain policy must bear part of the blame for slavery. In fact, after 1713 the British interfered more and more directly with their American colonies when it came to the slave trade. This was one of the irritants that would eventually lead to the American fight for independence.

Why did the British do this? Because after 1713 they began making more money from the African slave trade. In that year, the British won important concessions as a result of a war against Spain. They got, among other things, the infamous *asiento* for 30 years. (You'll recall that this was the decree made by the Pope "dividing" up the world, thus allowing a monopoly of the slave trade.) This meant that the British Crown was now getting a hefty percentage of the slavery action in America. As a result, the British encouraged their colonists to buy more slaves.

The Growing Dispute with Great Britain

By the mid-1700s, with the number of slaves mounting, white farmers and their families began to live in real fear for their lives. At the same time, colonists disliked the British Crown telling them to continue the slave trade. So, the slave trade was actually one of the reasons for the coming fight with Britain.

There were, of course, other reasons as well.

As African-American slaves toiled to help the American colonies grow, so did the British colonies toil to keep the British empire growing. By 1770 the British had chased the French out of most of North America. Spain also was less of a threat. As a result, the colonists were growing impatient with having to pay heavy taxes to maintain the empire. They had to pay, in fact, up to 20 percent to the British Crown on everything they produced.

The Americans also disliked having to ship their products to England on English ships before they could be sold elsewhere. But the colonists were powerless; they had no voice in the British **Parliament**. Still, they sent many petitions, trying to change the king's mind.

Instead, King George III sent more British troops to

Parliament: the law-making body of England.

keep the rebellious colonists in their place. Cries of "No taxation without representation!" sounded, and the Americans came to hate the very sight of redcoated British troops marching through their streets.

Highlighting a Hero—Crispus Attucks

By March 5, 1770, tensions were high in Boston. On that day a group of men defied the British soldiers with nothing more than sticks and stones. The redcoats opened fire, killing five Americans. The first to die in the **Boston Massacre** was one of the leaders of that early "revolutionary" group. He was none other than a tall, commanding black man named Crispus Attucks. The 47-year-old had escaped slavery twenty years before. He had managed to gain an education and had a keen grasp of the political conditions of the day. Earlier, Attucks had written a defiant letter to the British-appointed governor of the colony, Thomas Hutchinson:

> Sir, you are chargeable . . . with our blood. . . . You acted, cooly, deliberately, with all that premeditated malice, not against us in particular, but against the people in general, which, in the sight of the law, is an ingredient in the composition of murder. You will hear further from us hereafter.

Some conservative colonists thought of Attucks and his band as "rabble." But many Bostonians, including some of the city's leading citizens, honored him and his compatriots for bravery in Boston's Faneuil Hall.

The Role of Black Revolutionaries

The conservative Massachusetts colonists were not the only white people to have mixed feelings about the role of blacks in the revolutionary effort. Other colonists, mainly in the South, were scared stiff at the prospect of arming slaves. They issued orders "excusing" African-Americans from bearing arms. Still, many northern whites argued that if slaves were to fight for America's freedom, they should earn their own freedom at war's end.

Boston Massacre:
an incident in 1770 that started when angry colonists taunted British soldiers who then fired into the crowd, killing several colonists including Crispus Attucks.

"Sir, you are chargeable . . . with our blood. . . ."
—Crispus Attucks

53

**American Revolution:
the fight for independence by
England's American colonies
(1776–1783).**

African-Americans on the Patriots' Side

In 1776 fighting broke out in earnest. The **American Revolution** (1776–1783) had started. In the early years of the war, American patriots suffered many setbacks. Clearly, the few thousand rebels who had volunteered to fight the British would not be able to win the war on their own. Various white officers began to eye the large number of black men who were available.

So, black men were—sometimes openly, sometimes secretly—allowed to sign up and fight for America. Some whites even went so far as to "rent" free black men, hiring them to go fight in their place. And some white slaveowners often sent their own slaves to take their place in combat, rather than risk their own necks.

Massachusetts was one of the first states to enlist black troops. In the beginning, a militia act in Massachusetts had excluded "Negroes, Indians and mulattoes." But on January 6, 1777, another act called for "raising every seventh man to complete our quota." Except for the pacifist Quakers, who refused to fight at all, no exceptions were allowed.

Massachusetts eventually had a separate black regiment which proudly called itself "The Bucks of America." They even had a black commander, Colonel Middleton. By 1778, Rhode Island also had an all-black regiment, which was promised freedom for its service. In other regiments, black soldiers fought alongside whites.

In New York, the legislature created two all-black regiments in 1781. The desperate politicians offered the ultimate enticement—freedom to black soldiers after their service:

> Any such slave . . . who shall serve for the term of three years or until regularly discharged, shall, immediately after such service or discharge, be, and is hereby declared to be, a free man of this State.

Black Recruits on the British Side

The British joined in. They sent word throughout the colonies, particularly in the South, that if slaves escaped and signed up with them, the king would guarantee their freedom. On June 30, 1779, Sir Henry Clinton, commander-in-chief of the British forces, issued a proclamation to black slaves:

> I do promise to every Negro who shall desert the rebel standard, full security to follow within these lines, any occupation which he shall think proper.

As many as 25,000 slaves from South Carolina and Georgia escaped to the British side. John Adams, a colonial leader and later the second President of the United States, described the situation on September 24, 1775:

> Mr. Bullock and Mr. Houston from Georgia say that if 1,000 regular troops should land, 20,000 Negroes would join it from the two Provinces [of Georgia and South Carolina] in a fortnight [two weeks]. The Negroes have a wonderful art of communicating [information] among themselves; it will run several hundreds of miles in a week or a fortnight.

Later, with the help of the British, some 4,000 South Carolina slave-soldiers and their families joined 4,000 others from nearby Georgia and 6,000 from New York. They left America to start new lives in Canada, Jamaica, Nassau, and Europe. At war's end, at least one group, calling themselves "The King of England's Soldiers," even set up an armed camp in the woods of Georgia. They held out as an independent mini-state for several years.

African-American Heroes of the Revolution

However they were recruited, many African-Americans fought with great distinction throughout the American Revolution.

On June 17, 1775, for example, the Americans faced the British at the Battle of Bunker Hill. At the crucial moment, faced with the superior strength of the British army, a black man named Peter Salem stepped forward and shot British Major Pitcairn, thus rallying the Americans into action. A second black man, Salem Poor, also fought heroically in that battle.

James Armistead

The Marquis de Lafayette was a famous French volunteer who served during the war as a trusted aide to George Washington. Lafayette later recalled the service of James Armistead, a black spy in the American army. He said that Armistead had provided all-important information that enabled the American troops to defeat the British at the final great battle of the war, the Battle of Yorktown.

Many other blacks also distinguished themselves in battle. For instance, in one battle an all-black regiment fought successfully to save its white senior officer, Major Samuel Lawrence. He had been surrounded by the British. And a black man, Mark Starlin from Virginia, became captain of the revolutionary gunboat, *The Patriot*.

Calls for Freedom

As brilliantly as African-Americans maneuvered on the battlefield, so did they speak out eloquently for their freedom at the war's end. Many slaves themselves had already petitioned the various New England colonial governments for their freedom, based on the revolutionary ideal of "all men created equal." In 1774, black people sent these stirring words to the Massachusetts legislature:

> Your petitioners [understand] that we have in common with all other men a natural right to our freedoms without being depriv'd of them by our fellow men. . . .

In that same year, Abigail Adams worriedly wrote from Boston to her husband, John Adams. She told him word had leaked out that black slaves were drawing up a petition to the British governor, negotiating for their freedom. Said Mrs. Adams:

"I wish most sincerley there were not a slave in the Province [Massachusetts]."
—Abigail Adams

> I wish most sincerely there were not a slave in the Province [Massachusetts]. It always appeared a most [unfair] scheme to me to fight ourselves for what we are daily robbing and plundering from those who have as great a right to freedom as we have.

Thomas Jefferson, a Virginia slaveowner, may have shared Mrs. Adams' misgivings. In a letter to an American commander after the war, Jefferson described the actions of the British general, Lord Cornwallis:

Lord Cornwallis destroyed all my crops, he burned all my barns, and carried off all the horses capable of service. He carried off also about 30 slaves. *Had this been to give them freedom, he would have done right*; but it was to consign them to inevitable death from the smallpox and putrid fever, then raging in his camp. He treated the neighborhood in somewhat the same style. On the best information I could collect, I supposed that the state of Virginia lost, under Lord Cornwallis's hand, that year, about 30,000 slaves; and that, of these, 27,000 died of the smallpox and camp fever; and the rest were partly sent to the West Indies, and exchanged for rum, sugar, coffee, and fruit; and partly sent to New York, from whence they went, at the peace, either to Nova Scotia or to England. From this last place, I believe, they have been lately sent to Africa.

In 1776 Jefferson had tried to put antislavery language into the Declaration of Independence:

[The King of England] has waged cruel war against human nature itself, violating its most sacred rights of life and liberty in the persons of a distant people who never offended him, capturing and carrying them into slavery in another hemisphere, or to incur miserable death in their transportation thither.

Southern slaveowners, however, were determined to maintain the slave system. They managed to delete the passage from the Declaration. And so, by the end of the Revolutionary War, America was free from British domination. For most of the country's 500,000 African-Americans, however, "freedom" was just a word.

The War of 1812

The British tried once again, in 1812, to take charge of their former American colonies. And, once again, the white state legislatures in the United States found themselves appealing to blacks for help.

War of 1812:
the war fought in 1812 to preserve American independence from Great Britain.

As the **War of 1812** dragged on, two black battalions did such a superb job in the January 3, 1815, Battle of New Orleans that General Andrew Jackson made them the following promise:

> The President of the United States shall be informed of your conduct on the present occasion and the voice of the representatives of the American nation shall applaud your valor.

At the end of the War of 1812, some African-American slaves were granted their freedom. Sadly, others found themselves sold back into slavery.

And so it went throughout America's early years. In all too many cases, freedom was a right reserved only for whites. It would take another half-century and the Civil War before freedom would come.

SECTION ONE REVIEW

1. VOCABULARY Write a sentence for the following words: northern colonies, southern colonies, indigo, Parliament, Boston Massacre, American Revolution, War of 1812.

2. GEOGRAPHY What countries held colonies in what is now the United States? In what part of the present-day United States did slavery take hold most firmly?

3. BIOGRAPHY Why do we remember Crispus Attucks as one of the great heroes of the American Revolution?

4. HISTORY Why, during the time of the American Revolution, did some white Americans favor putting an end to the institution of slavery?

5. CRITICAL THINKING Why can it be said that the Americans' fight for independence only resulted in partial victory?

≶≶≶≶≶≶≶≶≶≶≶≶≶≶≶≶≶≶

THE RISE OF "KING COTTON"

≶≶≶≶≶≶≶≶

SECTION TWO

VOCABULARY Industrial Revolution cotton gin slave codes

MAIN IDEA Following the American Revolution slavery might have died out altogether had it not been for another revolution—the Industrial Revolution. With the rise of the textile industry in Europe, cotton became "king" in the American South. No longer did white southerners talk of ending the slave system. Instead, they sought to keep it firmly—and brutally—in place.

OBJECTIVES As you read, look for answers to the following questions:
1. How did the Industrial Revolution affect the slave system?
2. What was slavery like in America?
3. How was the slave system kept in place?

During the American Revolution the South suffered heavy losses. Markets in Europe for American crops were cut off. The war also interrupted the slave trade. In addition, many white Americans began to question the slave system. The colonists were fighting for their freedom from Great Britain. Should not black Americans be free too? Didn't the Declaration of Independence say that all people "are created equal"? Most northern states agreed, putting an end to slavery.

Antislavery feelings spead through the South as well. George Washington, for example, willed his slaves to his wife with the stipulation that they would be freed on her death. But many white southerners feared what would happen if they freed all the slaves.

Industry and the Rise of Cotton

The need for fresh African captives might have leveled off and maybe even died down altogether had it not been for

59

Industrial Revolution:
a shift from hand tools to
machines and large-scale factory
production, beginning in England
in the late 1700s and spreading
to America.

cotton gin:
a machine invented by Eli
Whitney in 1793 for cleaning
cotton quickly.

the **Industrial Revolution**. This period of rapid industrial growth started in Great Britain in the late 1700s. It involved the invention of machines that could process goods at an unheard-of rate.

The Industrial Revolution brought a great surge to the English textile industry. In 1765 the Spinning Jenny was invented to spin cotton yarn. Four years later, the water frame came along to speed cotton-thread processing. Then, in 1785 a mechanical loom was developed to weave cotton threads together into fabric. From now on, hard-to-grow crops like cotton could be quickly woven into cloth. Textile owners could make fortunes—and so could big landholders in America.

A most important advance was made in South Carolina in 1793. In that year a young Yale graduate named Eli Whitney went to teach on a southern plantation. Within six months, he had built a device which, powered by a horse to turn a wheel, could clean seeds from cotton balls 50 times as fast as a single man. Whitney had invented the **cotton gin**.

Now vast quantities of cotton could be grown, harvested, cleaned, and shipped to the world's markets to be made into cloth. Within the next 50 years, the American South would surge in cotton production. By 1850 it was supplying three-fourths of all the cotton in the world. Manning the entire enterprise were slaves.

Long past were the days when some white southerners had tried to stop the slave trade. Now cotton was "King," and any criticism of slavery was seen as an attack on the South itself.

Growth of the Domestic Slave Trade

The demand for cotton and the new technology to produce it proved to be an unbeatable combination in the South.

Plantations became, even more than they had been before, self-sufficient little "kingdoms." Now, on the plantation, some slaves would work in the fields, while others would be used for new construction projects. Still others might manufacture anything from clothes and shoes to furniture or even bricks for their fellow slaves.

A few large plantation owners, more than ever, dominated and shaped the political and social forces of the day. This, despite the fact that they made up only a small part of the actual population. It's important to remember that, much like the large corporations of today, a few influential people controlled almost everything. Three-fourths of all whites in the South did not own slaves or make any profit from their labor. Most plantations were fairly small, employing five slaves or less.

In 1860, shortly before the Civil War, there were about 8 million whites in the South. Only 384,884 owned slaves! And of those, 200,000 owned five or fewer. So, out of 8 million people, only 84,000 had more than five slaves. That's roughly equivalent to having one corporation in a single office tower owning most of the slaves, and controlling America because of it.

The South, dominated by a handful of powerful planters, increased its imports of new African captives dramatically in the 1800s. In 1790 there were fewer than 790,000 slaves in America. By 1860, there were almost 4 million. Almost half, nearly 2 million, lived in the "Cotton Kingdom." Virginia, Alabama, and Mississippi took the lead for states with the largest numbers of slaves. By 1860, Mississippi topped the list for cotton production, followed by Alabama, Louisiana, and Georgia.

African Slave Trade and Domestic Slave Trade

Here we must note the difference between two kinds of slave trade. First was the African slave trade, meaning the transportation of slaves directly from Africa. Second was the domestic slave trade, meaning the buying and selling of slaves from state to state in America. We must also distinguish both of these terms from slavery itself, meaning the actual employment of slaves.

As you have read, some frightened slaveowners, against British wishes, had pushed for laws to prohibit the African slave trade even before the American Revolution. In 1783 Maryland actually passed a law banning the African slave trade. In 1786 North Carolina briefly had laws to impose heavy fines on it. And a year later, South Carolina enacted a law (which was repealed six years later) outlawing the African slave trade.

In 1807 the British abolished the African slave trade. After losing the American Revolution they were no longer making big profits from it. By the end of the same year, under a clause in the Constitution, the United States had done the same. The United States abolished the African trade as part of a compromise between North and South at the Constitutional Convention in Philadelphia in 1787. One factor in this agreement was the fear of importing proud Caribbean slaves who had already organized large-scale rebellions.

In the North, efforts were made as early as 1780 to abolish slavery itself. In that year, Pennsylvania passed a law stating that blacks after that date would become free when they became 28 years old. In 1783 Massachusetts abolished slavery, and in the following two years Connecticut and Rhode Island passed laws calling for its gradual end. In New York, a law abolishing slavery was put on the books in 1799. In New Jersey, the first attempt came in 1786. Its law was finally passed in 1804.

All of this legislation looked great on the books. The only problem is that it was largely ignored. Even in New England, home of the most vocal antislavery crowd, many slaveowners continued to sell their slaves to customers in other states. And many slaveship captains simply turned pirate, smuggling their now illegal "cargoes" from Africa and the Caribbean into secret coves along American shores under cover of darkness.

A Boom in the Domestic Slave Trade

The laws did slow down the African slave trade. But this scarcity of new slaves meant a boom in the domestic trade. In fact, by 1815 the domestic slave trade had become one of the country's major industries. Breeding slaves became as profitable for some farmers as working them in the fields. And the cost of slaves already in America skyrocketed.

Business firms advertised "lines" of slaves, along with "lines" of farm implements for them to work with. Real estate brokers became adept at selling not only a farm, but the slaves that went with it. Sleazy "agents" would buy slaves from farm to farm and sell them for profit in a neighboring state. Even the newspapers largely cooperated with the system, advertising and sometimes even brokering slave sales.

Slave Auctions

Slave auctions became as common as used car sales today. The nation's capital, the District of Columbia, was the site of one of the country's most notorious slave auctions. Practically in view of the Capitol, there were slave "pens" where men and women alike were stripped naked and locked up so they could be inspected in public.

Although many slave traders denied it publicly, African-American families were routinely separated for sale, despite the horrible consequences to the slave families. Some especially cruel traders actually "specialized" in selling little children, helpless and alone.

Slave auction

Classes of Slaves: Field Hands

There were four classes of slaves. All classes faced hard labor. However, the most difficult class to belong to was that of the "field hand." Field hands, men and women alike, did backbreaking work. They hauled, plowed, sowed, and reaped from about 5:00 in the morning until about 8:00 at night with only a short 15–20 minute break. This, they did six days a week, all year long, with only a few days off for Christmas.

Even in winter, many had no shoes and one or two thin cotton outfits to wear. Their food consisted of a small bag of corn meal, a tiny heap of meat scraps, and what few vegetables they might have grown in the backyards of their quarters. They slept on straw like the livestock. And, for all practical purposes, they were treated on a par with the cattle and pigs.

Here's an excerpt from the autobiography of a respected escaped slave from Maryland, Henry Bibb. His poignant story disproves any notion that African-Americans were "sub-human" and had no feelings.

[My] dear little daughter was called Mary Frances. There was no one to take care of poor little Frances,

"Who can imagine what could
be the feelings of a father and
mother, when looking upon their
infant child whipped and tortured
...where they could afford no
protection."
—Henry Bibb

while her mother was toiling in the field. [Our] unmerciful old mistress...I have known to slap little Frances...until her little face was left black and blue. One summer's day...her little face was bruised...with the whole print of Mrs. Gatewood's hand. This print was plainly to be seen for eight days after it was done. Who can imagine what could be the feelings of a father and mother, when looking upon their infant child whipped and tortured...where they could afford no protection.

On this same plantation I was compelled to stand and see my wife shamefully scourged and abused by her master so violently and inhumanly that I despair in finding decent language to describe the bloody act of cruelty. My happiness was all blasted....I loved my wife and child.

Bibb managed to escape from the plantation. Later, when he could go back to the South, he spent three years searching for his beloved wife, Malinda, but she had been sold and could not be found.

Classes of Slaves: Industrial Workers

The next class of slave was that of the "industrial" slave. Usually males, they were sent to work in the factories that sprang up after the Industrial Revolution. They processed the crops. They dug in mines where noxious fumes and cave-ins made it too dangerous for whites to want to work. They labored on railroads or other construction gangs or they unloaded ship cargoes.

In the 1850s there were 52 tobacco factories in Richmond, Virginia, alone, empoying a total of 3,400 slaves. The work was gruesome and difficult. As one eyewitness put it, "Some dozen slaves, stripped to the waist (it was very hot), were tugging and heaving at long iron arms which turned screws, accompanying each push and pull by deep-drawn groans."

In 1850 a brick plant in Biloxi, Mississippi, owned 116 male and 37 female slaves who produced 10 million bricks each year.

In New Orleans in 1833, the Pontchartrain Railroad

bought 30 black workers. The owners calculated that, over the next five years, they would save $50,000 in wages they would have had to pay white workers to do the same work.

Classes of Slaves: House Workers

The third class worked in the plantation house itself. Among slaves, it was often referred to as the "big house" or "Pharaoh's house," making a biblical reference. In some respects, life here was often less taxing. Still, it entailed long hours of cooking, cleaning, sewing and so forth. Songs like this one, for example, were sung by sorrowful slave mothers who had to neglect their own children in order to take care of a white child.

> Hushaby, don't you cry,
> Go to sleepy, little baby,
> When you wake, you shall have
> All the pretty little horses.
>
> Way down yonder in the meadow,
> There's a poor little lambie;
> The bees and the butterflies
> Pickin' out his eyes,
> The poor little thing cries,
> "Mammy."
>
> *All the Pretty Little Horses*

Even slave children were not spared hard work. While still practically tots, little slave children were often forced into the fields, to help pick up odds and ends, or run errands. In cotton mills, heartless owners forced children to work for long hours at the looms and spindles. And in the plantation houses, children ran errands, helped clean, or were companions (in the social class of "pets") to the white owner's children.

Classes of Slaves: Breeders

The fourth class, much smaller, consisted of men and women, often as young as 13 or 14, who became "breeders." They were forced, not unlike some prostitutes, to have sex with whomever the master wanted. In addition, the women had then to bear these children. This they were forced to do year after year. And they rarely got to keep their own children. Their little ones were roughly snatched away and sold, never to be seen again.

In New Orleans, this class was given a different twist. The most beautiful young slave girls, usually part-white, part-black, were sold privately at lavish balls called cotillions to become the permanent mistresses of wealthy white men.

No matter how lenient the situation of some slaves seemed to be, they had one thing in common with their brothers and sisters in the field. None of them had control over their own lives. And it was this very human desire to decide their own destiny which prompted African-Americans everywhere to seek to escape from slavery.

Imposing the Slave System

To keep the slave system firmly in place, white legislators enacted a series of **slave codes** and other regulations. These efforts to control African-Americans through fear and intimidation were much like the repressive South African and Eastern European systems of recent days.

The slave codes regulated all aspects of slave life. In each state, the idea was the same—slaves were *property* to be handled at the owner's discretion. They were—literally—not considered people!

These amazing regulations included concepts like these: Slaves had no rights under law. They could not sue anyone who had wronged them, for example. Slaves could not even "own" their own ideas. They could not take out a patent for something they had invented, for instance. This would lead to some whites simply stealing many inventions by blacks, taking all the credit and the profits from them.

A slave could not own *anything*, other than a few personal belongings. Slaves could not hit a white person, even to defend themselves.

Slaves could not travel freely, for the most part, for fear of their escaping. Nor could they be taught to read or write, for the same reason.

Slaves could not legally marry or have custody of their own children.

slave codes:
laws passed in the South to restrict the conduct and activities of slaves.

66

A slave could be murdered. The crime was merely considered like that of killing someone's dog or cat. All the killer had to do was repay his "value" to the owner.

The slave codes were not uniformly enforced, by any means. Slaveowners, like feudal lords, wanted to discipline their slaves in their own way. But overall, most slaves had to endure concentration camp-like conditions throughout their lives.

Black Americans Keep Their African Culture Alive

To keep their true African culture alive in America in spite of slavery, most African-Americans had to seem docile. But in secret, they actively maintained many traditional customs. This first-hand account was told by a former slave, Mrs. Ann Parker:

> My mother, Junny, was a queen in Africa. They kidnapped her and stole her away from her throne and fetched her here to Wake County in slavery.
>
> Yes, she was a queen, and when she told them [slaves] that she was, they bowed down to her. She told them not to tell it, and they don't tell, but when they are out of sight of the white folks, they bow down to her and do what she says.

Many Africans managed to hang onto their proud traditions of art and culture as well. Some, when given the chance to make quilts, wove designs from their country of origin.

Even African words and names survived brutal slavery brainwashing. You've heard of a "tote bag"? Well, to "tote" is an African word for "carry." And what about a word we all use everyday? "OK." It may well have come from an African term, "yaw kay," which means "all right." Here are a few others:

"Hipi" is an African word. We use "hip," like the Africans of old, to mean a person who is in fashion, up with the times. "Cat" is an African word. We say "cat" to mean a "man," as the Africans did. And "juba" is an African word which developed into "jubilee" and "jubilant." Some of the more lenient plantation owners would let their slaves have a party once a year, usually on New Year's Day. To cele-

67

brate, the slaves shared in vigorous "juba dancing," accompanied by, among other things, a banjo. The banjo is similar to a stringed African instrument, the "banzar."

The Role of Religion

How did white southerners justify their evil system? One way was through religion.

From the first, slave traders had used—and abused—Christianity to justify their brutal slave schemes. They claimed that since Africans were not Christians, they were somehow less than "human." These whites even went so far as to suggest that slavery—with all its horrors—was good because it gave black people a chance to find out about God. So in 1444, when the Portuguese captured their first victims in Africa, they promptly baptized them, even as they enslaved them!

Once African captives were sold, their owners often tried to brainwash them into believing that it was their "fate" and "God's will" to be in bondage. Frederick Douglass, who later became famous for speaking out against slavery, recalled in 1838 that as a young man he was taught to recite a "Slave Catechism":

> Who gave you a master and a mistress?
> —God gave them to me.
> Who says you must obey them?
> —God says that I must.
> What book tells you these things?
> —The Bible.
> How does God do all his work?
> —He always does it right.

Slaveowners droned on, quoting passages from the Bible that stressed meekness and a "heavenly" reward. A Virginia bishop was quoted in 1856 as preaching:

> Having thus shown you the chief duties you owe to your great Master in heaven, I now come to lay before you the duties you owe to your masters and mistresses here upon earth. And for this you have one general rule, that you ought always to carry in

your minds, and that is to do all service for them as
if you did it for God himself.

Slaveowners walked a thin line with Christianity, however. They did not want their slaves to learn too much
about the Bible, because many of its passages concerned
slavery and freedom. How could they explain the Hebrews
fleeing from oppression when black people were supposed
to be content with theirs?

Also, the slaveowners were outnumbered by their
slaves. As a result, they were reluctant to let them gather
together in large groups, even for prayer meetings. Uneasy
and fearful, they could never be sure if their slaves were
using the time to plan revolts. (This, in fact, did happen, as
we will see later.)

Despite restrictions, African-Americans did manage to
get together and sing hymns with hidden messages. These
and other songs showed the slaves contempt for their condition and their resolve to change it:

One o' dese mornin's—it won't be long,
You'll look for me an' I'll be gone.

African-American Churches

The formation of African-American churches helped a great
deal in the antislavery freedom movement. Whites refused
to let African-Americans practice their traditional religions.
Instead, many slaveowners imposed Christianity on black
people as a means of mind control, hoping that fear of God
would keep them in line.

Before the early 1800s there were occasional churches,
mostly in the North, where African-Americans might be
allowed to worship. But even then, they had to sit in a
special balcony, away from the white parishioners. One
black American Revolutionary war hero, Lemuel Haynes,
even became a pastor in white churches in Vermont for
twenty years. But he was definitely an exception. Most
whites didn't want blacks learning to read the Bible or
holding large prayer meetings. They feared this would lead
to slave escapes and revolts.

So there arose black churches, for black people only. In

the South, for example, black people started independent Baptist churches. The earliest in Virginia was in Petersburg in 1776, in Georgia at Savannah in 1779, in Mississippi in Mound Bayou in 1805, and in Boston in 1809. Black churches from other denominations cropped up in the North as well as the South. Their ministers and the congregations would form the core of important black freedom organizational efforts.

Highlight a Hero—Morris Brown

In 1817 the Reverend Morris Brown's African Methodist Church in Charleston, South Carolina, had more than 1,000 members. Today, Morris Brown College in Atlanta, Georgia, is named after that early black religious pioneer.

SECTION TWO REVIEW

1. VOCABULARY Write a sentence for the following words: Industrial Revolution, cotton gin, slave codes.

2. TECHNOLOGY How did the cotton gin speed up cotton production?

3. HISTORY When and why did Great Britain abolish the African slave trade? The United States?

4. HISTORY What were the four classes of slaves in America?

5. CRITICAL THINKING How did the Industrial Revolution affect African-Americans?

SECTION THREE   BLACK ACHIEVEMENTS IN THE SLAVERY YEARS

MAIN IDEA In spite of all the prohibitions against education, many African-Americans learned to read and write English well. Some became authors; others gained success in business.

OBJECTIVES As you read, look for answers to the following questions:
1. What obstacles did African-Americans have to overcome to gain an education?
2. Who were some successful African-American businessmen and businesswomen?
3. What were some of the literary achievements of African-Americans?

In Africa, many black people in their traditional societies had been highly educated before being captured and forced to the United States. Here, they were separated from their friends and relatives and thrown together with strangers. This meant a tremendous struggle to learn a foreign language and customs in hostile surroundings.

Many slaveowners, however, were afraid to teach their black workers to read or write. They feared the power of education. Despite the difficult situation, some black people amazingly managed to learn. Without books or paper, often teaching themselves at night, by a single sputtering candle, they learned how to read and write English.

Over the years, this incredible fortitude paid off. Against great obstacles, a system of black education slowly evolved.

African-American Schools

Some black people took matters into their own hands. Paul Cuffe of Massachusetts was one such person. Born in 1759, the enterprising Cuffe taught himself arithmetic and navigation. By the age of 20, he had his own small boat and his own tiny trading company. As a sea merchant, his travels took him to the Caribbean and as far away as England, Russia, and Africa. By the time he was 47, he owned a shipping fleet consisting of a schooner, two brigs, and smaller boats. He also owned a great deal of land and property.

When Cuffe had just turned 21, he demonstrated the courage and zeal which would characterize his life. In 1791 he tried to have a school built for his children and other black youngsters. The white people in his town of New Bedford were violently opposed. So, he built the school on his own land, at his own expense. He could see that it was the only way his children would get an education.

71

Meanwhile, in Boston in that same year, a free black named Prince Hall ran up against the same obstacle. Like Cuffe, Hall owned land, was able to vote, and had fought in the Revolutionary War. To get around the difficulty many African-Americans had in getting an education in Boston, Hall started a school in his own home. In 1797, he spoke out eloquently about the need for African-Americans never to give up their dreams and to educate themselves, if necessary:

> Let us not be cast down under these and many abuses we at present labor under: for the darkest is before the break of day. Although you are deprived of the means of education; yet you are not deprived of the means of [thinking].

In 1830 a black man named John Melvin moved to Cleveland, Ohio, from Virginia. After establishing his own transportation business with a boat he was able to purchase, Melvin determined to help other less fortunate African-Americans. He helped set up the first school for black children in Cleveland and in several other cities in Ohio. He also helped establish the First Baptist Church in Cleveland. There he persuaded fellow white churchgoers to do away with segregation in the church, thus managing to get free seating for all.

In South Carolina, in 1829, Daniel Payne, a free black man, opened a school in Charleston. Each pupil paid 50 cents a month. Because his own education had been limited, Payne struggled to teach himself subjects like geography, Greek, Latin, and zoology. He managed to buy some of the necessary textbooks. Sometimes he had to make his own:

> But as I could never get hold of any work on [zoology], I had to make books for myself. This I did by killing such insects, toads, snakes, young alligators, fishes, and young sharks as I could catch. I then cleaned and stuffed those that I could, and hung them upon the walls of my schoolroom. . . .
>
> My enthusiasm was the inspiration of my pupils. At the end of five years I had accumulated some fine specimens.

"[T]he darkest is before the break of day."
—Prince Hall

72

Some whites helped. Even in the South, a handful of whites agreed to teach African-Americans to read and write in the years before cotton became "king." For example, in Charleston, South Carolina, Alexander Garden set up a school for slaves in 1743. Its schoolmasters were two young black slaves, Andrew and Harry. The school was a great success, educating up to 60 slaves at a time. Garden praised Harry, the black schoolmaster, as a genius. The school continued until 1764, when Harry died.

As time went on, however, white southerners grew even more fearful of education for blacks. State legislatures passed more and more laws that banned teaching blacks to read and write.

Still, the thirst of African-Americans to gain an education would continue. The first black men to graduate from college in America were John B. Russworm and Edward Jones. Russworm received his degree from Bowdoin College in Maine in 1826, as did Jones from Amherst College in Massachusetts.

Two other black men would go on to receive degrees from universities in Europe. Dr. James McCune Smith received a medical degree from Glasgow University in Scotland and Reverend James W. C. Pennington became a Doctor of Divinity at the University of Heidelberg in Germany.

African-American Poets and Authors

Lucy Terry was the first African-American we know of who wrote poetry that still exists today. A remarkable woman, she was kidnapped from Africa as a baby and brought to the town of Deerfield, Massachusetts. Naturally, she was sensitive to any brutal treatment whites inflicted. So, when she saw a group of Indians being massacred near Deerfield in 1746, she decided to write about it.

Ten years later, Terry married Abijah Prince, a former slave and a landowner. He bought his wife's freedom.

Lucy Terry, now Lucy Prince, continued to be the most eloquent black woman of her era. When her son, Cesar, was denied admission to Williams College, she herself went to appeal to the Board of Trustees. And, years later, when some of the Prince family land was threatened by a neighbor, she personally argued her case all the way to the U.S. Supreme Court. Supreme Court Justice Samuel Chase is said to have praised her, and she won her land case.

Phillis Wheatley, a young slave woman of Boston, was actually the first African-American to have her works published. Her first poem appeared in 1770, and she became a sensation in society. The impression she created was so great that she was made a member of the all-white Old South Meeting House in Boston.

Phillis Wheatley had learned to read and write English just a year and a half after being kidnapped in Africa and brought to America in 1758. She was taught by Mary, the daughter of her wealthy master, John Wheatley.

Phillis Wheatley's book of poetry was published in London in 1773 after John Wheatley took her there because of her frail health. Hailed as an African-American genius, Wheatley saw her book reprinted a dozen times.

After returning to colonial America, Wheatley wrote another poem, this one praising the newly appointed commander-in-chief of the American revolutionary army, George Washington. On February 28, 1776, Washington wrote to Wheatley:

> Thank you most sincerely for your polite notice of me, in the elegant lines you enclosed . . . the style and manner exhibited a striking proof of your poetical talents.

Washington invited Wheatley to his Cambridge, Massachusetts, headquarters. He thanked the young woman and gave her a tour of his command post.

Phillis Wheatley's poetry also came to the attention of Benjamin Franklin, the great American scientist and thinker. He too praised her. But in spite of her fame, Wheatley did not forget that she had been stolen from her African home. In another poem, she wrote:

> I, young in life, by seeming cruel fate
> Was snatch'd from *Afric's* fancy'd happy seat:
> What pangs excrutiating must molest,
> What sorrows labour in my parent's breast?
> Steel'd was the soul and by no misery mov'd
> That from a father seiz'd his babe belov'd

Such, such my case. And can I then but pray
Others may never feel tyrannic sway?

Among the noted black authors of this period, Olaudah
Equiano (page 33) learned to write English after being
captured from his homeland in Nigeria. His heartrending
account of being torn away from his family was published
in London in 1793. Equiano's autobiography was so popular
that it went through eight editions.

Phillis Wheatley

Black Successes in Business

Across America, a handful of African-Americans managed
to gain fame in business. In New York, a black businessman
named Thomas Downing owned and managed a popular
restaurant on Wall Street from 1820 to 1866. During that
time, Downing loaned the then-enormous sum of $10,000 to
the owner of the New York *Herald*, James Gordon Bennett.
Downing's loan saved the paper from bankruptcy.

And, during the bitter winter of January 1842, Downing
saved the entire Wall Street area when fire broke out. The
fire hoses froze because of the icy weather. Downing
shrewdly instructed the firemen to use his huge supply of
vinegar instead, thus saving the financial district.

Later, in that year, when the famous English writer,
Charles Dickens (of "A Christmas Carol" fame) visited
America, Downing received the grand sum of $2,200 for
managing the reception in his honor.

On the West Coast in 1841, a brilliant young businessman and merchant seaman, William Alexander Leidesdorff,
sailed his 106-ton schooner in San Francisco. Only 21, the
enterprising young man set up a sailing trade between San
Francisco and Hawaii. By 1846, he was able to build San
Francisco's first hotel.

In 1845 Leidesdorff was appointed American vice con-
sul of California. Three years later he was on the first San
Francisco school board. Black civic leaders like Leidesdorff
fought an uphill battle, however, when it came to efforts to
allow minority children to go to school with whites. Not
until 1872, for example, would the Oakland school board
agree to allow black children into its system.

During the same period, Mary Ellen Pleasant (known as

Mary E. Pleasant

"Mammy" Pleasant) was the most extraordinary black woman of her day. Brilliant and educated in Boston as a young slave, Pleasant secured her freedom and then married a wealthy free black who was active in antislavery activities. After his death in 1849, she moved to California where she used her $50,000 inheritance to open a boarding house and start several businesses, including other real estate ventures. She became so well-respected that leading businessmen of the day came to her for advice.

All this time, Pleasant was helping runaway slaves who had fled the South. In addition, when word reached her that John Brown was organizing a slave revolt (Chapter 5), she personally gave him $30,000 to finance it.

In 1864, after being pushed off a San Francisco streetcar, Pleasant hired an attorney to fight for the right of African-Americans to sit on streetcars with other riders. As a result, African-Americans were allowed to use the city's public transportation system freely.

Biddy Mason, born a slave in Georgia, was brought to southern California along with her three children, by Robert Smith. Smith settled in San Bernadino in about 1854 and lived there for three years. Then, when he tried to move to Texas, the California government freed Mason and her children, since they had been living in a nonslave state for so long.

Mason and her children moved to Los Angeles where she became a nurse and a successful real estate investor. She spent her spare time helping the needy in prison and in poor neighborhoods, even supplying food for many homeless families after a flood. She died an honored citizen.

SECTION THREE REVIEW

1. HISTORY Why did most slaveowners oppose teaching African-Americans to read and write?

2. HISTORY Why do you think black people were so eager to gain an education?

3. BIOGRAPHY Why is Phillis Wheatley remembered as a great African-American hero today?

4. **ECONOMICS** Why were achievements in business in this era by African-Americans so noteworthy?

5. **CRITICAL THINKING** Read again Phillis Wheatley's poem on page 74. What deep emotions does that poem reveal?

BRAVE AFRICAN-AMERICANS HELP OPEN AMERICA

SECTION FOUR

MAIN IDEA In spite of the horrors of slavery, African-Americans used their special skills inherited from generations of careful training in Africa to blaze new trails for America.

OBJECTIVES As you read, look for answers to the following questions:
1. What role did African-Americans play in exploring the Southwest?
2. What role did African-Americans play in exploring the Midwest?
3. What role did African-Americans play in exploring the West, including California?

From the early days of exploration, African-Americans had been active participants in opening up North America. In the 1530s, for example, a black man named Estevan helped discover areas from present-day Florida to Arizona and New Mexico.

Estevan and the Southwest

Estevan, born in Morocco, first came to the New World with the Spanish explorer Cabeza de Vaca. He later became famous for his knowledge of the many Indian tribes in southwestern America. In 1539, Estevan led an expedition in New Mexico among the Zuñi Indians. This expedition opened the way for eventual European settlement of the Southwest. Unfortunately, Estevan was not given credit as an important American pioneer during his own day.

Estevan is best-remembered for his search for a fabled

77

town in the Southwest where the streets were said to be made of gold. Friar Marcos de Niza, supposedly in charge of the expedition, did not actually venture into the Indian territory but sent Estevan instead. Estevan sent back a series of wooden crosses, the last as tall as a man. These crosses indicated his progress in searching for the legendary town. Although no town with streets of gold was never found, Estevan's explorations helped open up the Southwest for the Spanish.

The Midwest

In the Midwest, perhaps the best-known explorer was Jean Baptiste Pointe DuSable, a striking black man who had gone to school in Paris. He originally came to America to explore the area of the Midwest known then as New France. He eventually settled along the Chicago River, marrying an Indian woman. His holdings grew and grew until he had built a large home, complete with barn and stables, as well as a smokehouse, bakehouse, and dairy. What did his Midwestern oasis grow into? None other than the city of Chicago. He was most fondly remembered by the Indians. As they joked, "The first white man to come to Chicago was a black man!"

Nearby, in Michigan, a similar story was being told about black explorer and trapper Pierre Bonza. His son, George, went on to wealth with the American Fur Company. George Bonza was even picked as an Indian interpreter by Michigan's governor, Lewis Cass.

"The first white man to come to Chicago was a black man!"
—Indians on Jean Baptiste Pointe DuSable

The West

The explorers Lewis and Clark, who were credited with mapping much of the Louisiana Territory, were accompanied by their African-American servant, York. In Lewis's diary, he described York as a first-rate hunter, swimmer, and fisherman. York even is said to have worked with the famous Indian guide, Sacagawea, in interpreting for the two whites on the trip. So grateful were the explorers that they freed York at the end of their two-and-a-half year journey.

James Beckwourth was another African-American who hit the trail for the western frontier. He became a chief of the Crow Indian tribe and was named "Morning Star." He even successfully led his adopted brethren into battle against the whites. Beckwourth was also successful as a scout. He discovered an important pass through the Sierra Nevada mountains to California.

To the north, George Washington Bush, a free black who had fought bravely for the United States during the War of 1812, was one of the founders of Oregon. Bush Prairie bears his name today. In 1844 Bush and his family led white families on the difficult journey through the Columbia River country. So grateful were the many settlers helped by the Bushes, that the new Oregon government granted the Bush family a 640-acre homestead. Ever-generous, even after they became wealthy, the Bush family gave away part of their crops to less fortunate white settlers.

James Beckwourth

African-Americans Help Found Los Angeles

On September 4, 1781, 26 of the original 46 settlers of the settlement now known as Los Angeles were black, some of whom were freeborn. (The settlement was originally named *Nuestra Senora la Reina de Los Angeles de Porciuncula*.) Beginning in 1746, black people were issued deeds to land in California by the Spanish government. And one black settler, Francisco Reyes, was elected mayor of Los Angeles during the 1790s. Free black people also helped settle San Jose, Santa Barbara, San Francisco, and Monterey. By 1800, black people made up 20 percent of California's population.

Highlighting a Hero—Pio Pico

Forty-five years later a mulatto named Pio Pico became governor of the California territory. (California, not yet part of the United States, was under Mexican control.) Saddled with tremendous debts, California was in a sad state when Pico took over. He fought valiantly to create stability. He enforced laws against illegal shipping. He advised citizens to produce their own food and sell it locally. He revitalized the territorial assembly and petitioned the Mexican Congress for reforms that would promote home rule. He granted land to Californians to encourage the economy.

In spite of his untiring efforts, Pico was unable to get along with his military counterpart, Commandante Jose Castro. While they argued, American troops entered California. In August 1846 both Castro and Pico went into exile in Mexico.

SECTION FOUR REVIEW

1. **HISTORY** What areas of America did Estevan explore?

2. **BIOGRAPHY** What city did Jean Baptiste Pointe DuSable found?

3. **GEOGRAPHY** What important discovery did James Beckwourth make?

4. **HISTORY** What role did an African-American play in the founding of Oregon?

5. **CRITICAL THINKING** Why may it have been easier for blacks to rise to positions of authority in the West than in other regions of America?

CHAPTER THREE REVIEW

VOCABULARY

Write the numbered sentences on a separate sheet of paper. In each sentence fill in the blank with one of these terms: *cotton gin, northern colonies, Parliament, slave codes, southern colonies.*

1. In England's _____, there were relatively few slaves.
2. The invention of the _____ meant that the South could produce huge quantities of cotton.
3. The absence of American representation in _____ led to the colonies' fight for independence.
4. Plantations in the _____ required large numbers of slaves.

5. Laws passed to restrict the conduct and activities of slaves were known as _____ .

REVIEWING THE FACTS

1. How did slavery vary in the English colonies?
2. What role did black people play in the wars against the British?
3. How did the Industrial Revolution affect the slave system?
4. What was slavery like in America?
5. How was the slave system kept in place?
6. What obstacles did African-Americans have to overcome to gain an education?
7. Who were some successful African-American businessmen and businesswomen?
8. What were some of the literary achievements of African-Americans?
9. What role did African-Americans play in exploring the Southwest?
10. What role did African-Americans play in exploring the Midwest?
11. What role did African-Americans play in exploring the West, including California?

CRITICAL THINKING

1. MAKING A JUDGMENT If you were an African-American living in South Carolina in 1779, which side would you have fought for? What it have made a difference? Explain your answer.
2. COMPARING What was the difference between the African slave trade and the domestic slave trade? How did the slowing down of the first affect the second?
3. INFERRING As you have read, three-fourths of the white people in the South owned no slaves. Does this mean they were antislavery? Explain your answer.

UNDERSTANDING PREJUDICE

1. Why were white colonists at first reluctant to let African-Americans join in the revolutionary effort? Was their reluctance justified?
2. In this chapter you read that "most slaves had to endure concentration camp-like conditions throughout their lives." What does this sentence refer to? What peoples were forced to suffer in concentration camps during World War II?

CHAPTER FOUR

AFRICAN-AMERICANS RESIST SLAVERY

(1500–1860)

Brethren! Arise! Arise! Strike for your lives and liberties! Rather die freemen than live to be slaves. Let your motto be resistance!
> Henry Highland Garnet, Antislavery Address

Were many African-Americans determined to escape to freedom? Darned right. Individually, in small groups, by the hundreds, by the thousands, African-Americans, outraged at being kidnapped from their homeland, made attempt after attempt to escape. From the moment they were taken, captives used their wits and will to make their way back to Africa. Some made it. Many who did not preferred death to captivity.

Those in America were equally determined to find a way to end slavery. Some took part in revolts. Others escaped to freedom in the nonslave North or in Canada. All were united in their hatred of the cruel slave system.

SECTION ONE   SLAVE REVOLTS

VOCABULARY mutiny Amistad Revolt Palmares Haiti Nat Turner's Rebellion

MAIN IDEA Resistance to slavery in North and South America often took the form of revolts and rebellions.

OBJECTIVES As you read, look for answers to the questions on the next page:

In 1831 Nat Turner led a famous rebellion against slavery, sending shock waves through the South. Here, the defiant Prophet Nat is captured.

1. **How did captives on slaveships try to resist their oppression?**
2. **What were some of the notable slave revolts in South America? In the Caribbean? In North America?**
3. **What effects did the slave revolts have?**

If care not be taken, they will mutiny and destroy the ship's crew in hopes to get away. To prevent such...we visit them daily, narrowly searching every corner between decks, to see whether they have...any pieces of iron or wood or knives.

mutiny:
a rebellion against superior
force.

This diary entry, written by a slaveship crewman, reveals how much the slave traders feared shipboard **mutinies**. And those mutinies were frequent. Many took place as the slaveships lay just off the coast of Africa, awaiting the arrival of more captives. Some took place on the high seas.

Revolts Aboard Slave Ships

In 1759 Captain Daniel Cooke reported on an uprising of African captives aboard a slaveship, the *Perfect*. The 100 Africans aboard the *Perfect* somehow got out of their shackles and killed the ship's captain, along with ten other crew members. Then, in spite of an entire hour's worth of gunfire from another slaveship, the Africans sailed the *Perfect* back to shore and burned it.

Highlighting a Hero—Cinque

The *Perfect* episode was just one of many famous slave mutinies. Another, led by a proud African warrior named Cinque, took place in 1839. The Spanish schooner on which Cinque was held captive was called the *Amistad* which, ironically, means "friendship."

On August 26, 1839, U.S. Navy crewmen in the harbor of New Haven, Connecticut, were astounded to find the *Amistad* floating into port. Only two Spaniards were left on board alive. The 41 Africans who had overcome the slavers and tried to steer back to Africa were led by Cinque. They gave themselves up voluntarily.

A professor from nearby Yale University was able to locate a black sailor who spoke Cinque's language. And, in what became one of the most celebrated court cases of U.S. history, the noble Cinque told the story of his group's capture, torture, and beating at the hands of the Spanish slave smugglers.

The **Amistad Revolt** sharply divided whites throughout the United States. So controversial was it, that the case went before the U.S. Supreme Court. Former President John Quincy Adams defended Cinque and his freedom fighters. On March 9, 1841, nearly two years after the Africans' cap-

Amistad Revolt:
the famous shipboard revolt led
by Cinque in 1839 which resulted
in freedom for the African
freedom fighters.

84

ture and revolt, Adams stood before the Supreme Court and argued in the Africans' defense. The high court finally freed Cinque and his brave band. In 1842 Cinque and his group returned to Africa.

The *Creole* Revolt

The year 1841 saw another celebrated African shipboard revolt. On this occasion, 130 captives overcame the captain of the *Creole* and took the ship to the British islands of the Bahamas. There, under British law, the Africans were free. Despite hot debate in the United States, the British upheld the Africans' rights. Still, the British government eventually agreed to pay a fee to the American plantation owners for whom the African cargo was originally bound.

Cinque

Slave Revolts in South America

No matter where slavery took hold in the New World, Africans resisted it. The first revolts against slavery in the Americas took place in the first colonies, those of Spain and Portugal.

As early as 1502, when Spanish explorers first began to visit the New World, the Spanish governor of Mexico issued the following complaint. The Africans, he said, had "fled among the Indians and taught them bad customs and never would be recaptured."

Escape was one form of revolt. So was actual warfare. In the Brazilian city of Rio de Janeiro, a statuesque Ashanti warrior from Ghana named Quobah led a slave revolt. The fierce freedom fighters were never captured, although Portuguese troops just managed to save the city and drive them into the mountains. There the African freedom fighters established their own republic in northeastern Brazil and called it **Palmares**. For 67 years, utilizing their skills from their homeland, the Africans set up their own courts and markets. They even traded with neighboring towns. As many as 200,000 people lived in Palmares and followed the laws and customs of Africa.

The Portuguese army failed 25 times to invade Palmares. Finally, in desperation, the Portuguese govern-

Palmares:
the republic set up by Africans in northeastern Brazil in the 1600s.

85

ment sent massive numbers of troops to the area. They finally overcame the republic in 1697. The Africans' leader, Zambi, is said to have hurled himself over a cliff, rather than give in to the enemy. Many of his warriors followed suit.

In the Dutch colony of Surinam, a band of Africans fought successfully against their former owners for 36 years! In 1761, the Dutch governor signed a peace treaty with them, declaring the former slaves free.

Again in 1772, other African freedom fighters took up arms in Surinam. This time an African leader called "The Baron" organized his warriors along military lines. His "Black Rangers" fought so successfully that they nearly took control of the entire colony.

Slave Revolts in the Caribbean

Haiti:
the Caribbean island on which a successful slave revolt in 1791 shocked slaveholders throughout the Americas.

One of the most famous slave revolts in history took place in **Haiti**, on the Caribbean island of Hispaniola in 1791. Its impact would be felt around the world. Using drums as a signal, the slave leaders made careful plans for the uprising. Then, on August 22, 1791, the fateful night arrived. At midnight, more than 100,000 slaves rose up with the precision of an army raid. They burned 1,200 coffee and 200 sugar plantations and threw the owners into the flames. The slaves, joined by thousands of free Africans, ransacked the colony for three weeks straight.

Highlighting a Hero—Toussaint L'Ouverture

The revolt in Haiti became a full-fledged revolution when, from the midst of the smouldering ashes there emerged one of the most brilliant leaders the world has known—Toussaint L'Ouverture. Toussaint realized that, following the revolt, the black people of Haiti had to find a way to maintain the independence they had fought so hard for. Sleeping only two hours a night, Toussaint used his natural genius to mold the black rebels into a disciplined fighting force. And, amazingly, for the next ten years, Toussaint and his black army outfought and outthought the armies of France, Spain, and England.

Under Toussaint's able administration, Haiti repaired roads, rebuilt buildings, and restored friendly relations with the remaining white residents on the island. In fact, in one parade, white planters and their wives and children threw flowers after the black general.

Finally, Toussaint trusted one Frenchman too many. Instead of a meeting with a French general, Toussaint found himself overpowered. The French feared the black general's power so much that they shipped him all the way to France. There they locked him in a mountain tower until his death in April 1803.

Even after he died, the effects of Toussaint L'Ouverture's independence struggle had profound repercussions in America. Slaveowners and their families lived in fear that the same thing was going to happen in the United States.

And Napoleon was ultimately outfoxed by the black general, even in death. In 1803, Napoleon lost 30,000 troops to Toussaint's successor, Jean-Jacques Dessalines. So frustrated was Napoleon, that he gave up on his New World venture, selling the entire Louisiana Territory to the United States. At $15 million, the sale came to four cents an acre, the greatest buy the young country had made. It doubled the size of the United States.

Slave Revolts in North America

One historian who has studied slave revolts in North America found that there were more than 250 revolts and conspiracies during the 300-odd years of slavery. If we include innumerable small and individual escapes, then we can see that African-Americans were constantly trying, in one way or another, to gain their freedom.

The first slave rebellion in North America came as early as 1526. That was the year some 500 Spaniards and their 100 African captives tried to start a colony in present-day South Carolina. Within months of their arrival, several slaves managed to escape to the local Indians, who also hated the Europeans for their intrusions and killings. Shortly thereafter, the Spaniards, discouraged and ill, abandoned the colony, leaving the Africans with their new Indian allies.

Highlighting a Hero—Gabriel Prosser

Most of the best-known slave revolts took place in the period after cotton took hold in the South. Many were inspired by the success of the Haitian Revolution.

In Virginia on August 30, 1800, the white inhabitants of Richmond faced danger. Led by 24-year-old Gabriel Prosser, thousands of slaves were prepared to take the town by force. Quoting the Bible, Prosser and his family skillfully slipped from plantation to plantation to inform black slaves everywhere.

Two factors kept Prosser's plan from succeeding. First, the night of the planned attack, torrential rains washed out roads and bridges, making it impossible for the slaves to get into town. Second, on the very day of the rebellion, two slaves lost their nerve and told their master, who alerted the governor and the army.

Before Prosser could regroup, troops arrested him and 34 of his men. On October 7, 1800, Prosser said, before he was hanged, "I have nothing more to offer than what General Washington would have had to offer, had he been taken by the British."

"I have nothing more to offer than what General Washington would have had to offer, had he been taken by the British."
—Gabriel Prosser

Highlighting a Hero—Denmark Vesey

In 1800, a lucky slave in Charleston, South Carolina, bought a raffle ticket and won $1,500. With the winnings he purchased his freedom. Denmark Vesey was his name.

Vesey had seen the worst, for his master had been a slave trader. So incensed was he from that painful experience, that even after he became a free carpenter, he used his time and money to encourage his fellow African-Americans to find a way to win their freedom. Finally, in 1821, after studying the French Revolution as well as the Haitian Revolution, Vesey decided to lead an uprising in South Carolina. For the next year, he carefully chose his associates, including an African woman said to possess special powers.

A tactical genius, Vesey organized his 9,000 freedom fighters into commando units. To try to cut down the risk of discovery, not one unit knew the entire plan. The strike date was set for July 16, 1822. As fate would have it, three months before the appointed night, an overeager recruit mentioned the plan to a black house servant. Out of loyalty to his white master, the servant revealed the plan. Then, just days before the strike date, another slave let more information slip. Frantic South Carolina authorities arrested Vesey and 131 suspects. (Among them were four white men who had aided the plot.) They hanged 47 of the revolutionary leaders, including Vesey. The men died proudly, urging the slaves they left behind to keep up the fight.

Highlighting a Hero—Nat Turner

In Southampton County, Virginia, African-American freedom fighters came the closest to duplicating Toussaint L'Ouverture's success in Haiti. They were led by the brilliant, Bible-inspired Nat Turner. After living a monk-like existence of "fasting and prayer," Turner had mystical visions. He interpreted them to mean that he had to "deliver his people from bondage."

And sure enough, on August 21, 1831, Prophet Nat and six of his band began their revolt. Killing whites on farm after farm, their numbers swelled as other slaves joined them. The next day, however, Turner and his fighters were outnumbered by a force of white soldiers. Frightened by **Nat Turner's Rebellion**, the whites killed more than 100 black people, many of whom had nothing to do with the revolt, during the three months that Turner eluded their capture. He was finally tracked down, brought to trial, and hanged on November 11, 1831.

Prophet Nat was dead, but his fiery spirit of freedom lived on in the hearts of black people everywhere. Meanwhile, several states in the South passed new laws to restrict the slaves. As a result, slaves lost any freedom of movement they might have had. These strict laws failed, however, to prevent rebellions, and the fear of slave uprisings continued to terrorize the white South.

**Nat Turner's Rebellion:
a 1831 slave revolt in Virginia
that frightened white
southerners.**

Seminole Wars with the Indians

In the Southeast, entire families of African-Americans escaped to Spanish Florida in the early 1800s, which at that

Runaway slave

time did not permit slavery. And the Indians living there often willingly accepted African-Americans into their tribes, because they hated the whites for trying to enslave them. By 1816, for example, the U.S. government ordered General Andrew Jackson to attack and take back an abandoned British fort that runaway African-Americans had made into a command post. These black people were aided by the Seminole Indians. When Jackson crossed into the Seminole region and shelled the fort, the Seminoles and the former slaves fought back furiously.

By 1835, a second Seminole war erupted after a U.S. agent kidnapped the famous chief Osceola and his wife, a half-black, half-Indian woman. But Osceola escaped, only to return with a force of Indian warriors who captured and killed the U.S. agent. The second Seminole War did not end until 1843. The cost? To black people, 500 African-Americans were seized from Florida and forced back into slavery. To the United States government, the price tag was as much as $20 million.

SECTION ONE REVIEW

1. VOCABULARY Write a sentence for each of the following words: mutiny, Amistad Revolt, Palmares, Haiti, Nat Turner's Rebellion.

2. BIOGRAPHY Why is Cinque remembered as a great African hero?

3. HISTORY What effect did the revolt in Haiti have (a) On slaveowners throughout the Americas? (b) On American territorial growth?

4. HISTORY What steps did white southerners take to put down Nat Turner's Rebellion? What measures did southern legislatures take after Nat Turner's Rebellion was over? Why?

5. CRITICAL THINKING List some of the obstacles facing brave African-American heroes like Gabriel Prosser or Nat Turner. What does this suggest about the determination of African-Americans to resist slavery?

GREAT ESCAPES

VOCABULARY Fugitive Slave Act abolition Underground Railroad

MAIN IDEA Another way thousands of African-Americans resisted slavery was to escape north to freedom.

OBJECTIVES As you read, answer the following questions:

1. What were some of the ways by which slaves escaped ?

2. What roles did such heroes as Harriet Tubman and Frederick Douglass play in the antislavery movement?

Besides taking part in slave uprisings, large numbers of slaves courageously escaped their oppressive condition.

Highlighting a Hero—Harriet Tubman

Harriet Tubman was one of the greatest freedom fighters who ever lived. Had she been born in another era, in another place, she undoubtedly would have been covered with medals. As it was, she was hunted by fearful slaveowners, with a price of up to $40,000 on her head.

Tubman was born on a Maryland plantation in about 1823. By the time she was 25 years old, she could no longer bear the oppression around her. Even though she was married, she had to escape. So, one night, with two of her brothers, she left the plantation. Frightened, the brothers turned back. But Harriet Tubman pressed on to freedom.

An extraordinary woman with nerves of steel, Tubman found out that there were other free blacks as well as some whites who would help more slaves to escape. So, she fearlessly returned to the South—nineteen times—to guide other African-Americans to safety. On one trip, she even managed to get her aged parents out. Over the long years, she did not mind spending nights in swamps or in the false bottoms of wagons in order to help save one more life.

In 1850 Congress passed the **Fugitive Slave Act**. This

Fugitive Slave Act:
a law passed in 1850 requiring people in free states to help capture escaped slaves.

91

meant that whites could capture blacks in the North "suspected" of being runaway slaves and receive a cash reward for it. Even this did not stop the fearless Harriet Tubman. She took her charges and traveled northward all the way to Canada! Once there, she would often stay for weeks or months until she could arrange work for the ex-slaves. Then, she was off again, back into the "enemy camp" to free more slaves.

All told, this amazing revolutionary helped more than 300 slaves escape to freedom.

Individual Escapes

Henry Brown of Richmond, Virginia, found his own way to escape. In 1848 he ingeniously folded himself into a tiny two-by-three foot box! With just a few air holes and a pouch of water, Brown had himself mailed to Philadelphia and freedom!

The fearless young man almost died on the journey. A white friend had written "This Side Up" on the box, so that during transport Brown would not be on his head and choke to death. But in spite of this precaution, a careless baggage handler threw Brown's box *wrong side up* onto the train! For two agonizing hours, the blood rushed to Brown's head. He wanted to scream and beat on the crate to be let out. But he didn't dare: "The veins on my temple seemed ready to burst. I made no noise, however, determining to obtain victory or death."

Miraculously, another baggage handler came along and set the box right side up, just when Brown was about to suffocate. Brown, still nailed in the box, managed to survive. The next day, Brown's box was delivered to friends in Philadelphia.

> One of them rapped upon it, and with a trembling voice, asked, "Is all right within?" to which I replied, "All right." At length the cover was removed, and I arose, and shook myself.

Other African-Americans used their ingenuity to escape too. Witness this account. A slave on a Virginia plantation brought a young man named Thomas Jackson pine knots

"I made no noise, however, determining to obtain victory or death."
—Henry Brown

for his fire so he could prepare for his military school exams. In exchange, Jackson taught the young slave to read and write. The slave was then able to write a pass saying that he was a free man. He successfully escaped to the North and the young white man passed his exams. Jackson would go on to become a famous southern leader during the Civil War—General Thomas "Stonewall" Jackson.

Highlighting a Hero—Frederick Douglass

As a ten year old, a slave named Frederick Douglass managed to learn to read and write. His teacher was his owner, Mrs. Lloyd. Young Frederick had even taught a few other slaves in a small Sunday school, until the class was broken up one day by whites who feared the youngsters were planning a revolt.

While still barely in his teens, Frederick and five friends first tried to escape. He later recalled the failed effort:

> Betrayed! Five young men guilty of no crime save that of preferring liberty to slavery were literally dragged fifteen miles to jail. I wished myself a beast, a bird, anything rather than a slave.

Angered, Frederick's slave master, Colonel Lloyd, sent him to a nearby farm. Lloyd hired a sadistic slave overseer, Edward Covey, to "break" the proud, bright, young man. So every week, for six months straight, Covey would beat and brutally kick young Frederick as he tried to work in the fields. Then, just turned sixteen, young Frederick vowed to fight back. Every time Covey tried to hit him, he punched him back, knocking him down. Covey soon gave up. Young Frederick learned:

> When a slave cannot be flogged, he is more than half free. Men are whipped oftenest who are whipped easiest.

A few years later, Frederick's master hired him out as a dockside worker unloading boats in the Baltimore harbor. His master took all of his pay, even though Frederick was beaten and kicked in the face by jealous white dockworkers

"I wished myself a beast, a bird, anything rather than a slave."
—Frederick Douglass

93

while he tried to work. He decided, "I will run away. I will not stand it. I have only one life to lose."

So, with his heart set on freedom, Frederick Douglass borrowed a sailor's clothes, an "official looking paper" with an eagle on it, and escaped to New York on September 3, 1838. The 21 year old joined his sweetheart, a free young black woman from Baltimore, and the two were married.

As precious as it was to him, Frederick Douglass went on to risk his freedom as he became a popular speaker in the North for the **abolition** of slavery. In appearance after appearance, he told shocked white audiences of the brutality he and his fellow slaves had endured.

abolition:
the movement to abolish (or put an end to) slavery.

The Underground Railroad

Across the United States, from New York to San Francisco, a network of free blacks and whites who opposed slavery grew into a secret revolutionary organization. It became known as the **Underground Railroad**. Its "stations" were the homes and barns of the sympathizers who would hide escaped slaves, give them food and shelter, and then smuggle them farther northward to another station. The "conductors" were those brave freedom fighters like Harriet Tubman who knew they were risking their own lives to do this.

Underground Railroad:
a secret network of people who helped runaway slaves escape, often to Canada.

According to one estimate, by 1858 some 3,000 people were involved in the Underground Railroad in one way or another. They are said to have guided about 75,000 slaves to freedom between 1851 and 1861, when the Civil War broke out.

SECTION TWO REVIEW

1. **VOCABULARY** Write a sentence for each of the following words: Fugitive Slave Act, abolition, Underground Railroad.

2. **BIOGRAPHY** How many slaves did Harriet Tubman lead to freedom?

3. **BIOGRAPHY** How did Henry Brown reveal the lengths to which African-Americans would go to escape slavery?

4. **CRITICAL THINKING** Why can it be said that escaping from slavery was a form of rebellion?

5. **CRITICAL THINKING** What do you think were some of the dangers faced both by the "conductors" on the Underground Railroad and by those they wanted to help?

FREE BLACKS

SECTION THREE

VOCABULARY free black altruistic

MAIN IDEA In the years before slavery was banned in the United States, large numbers of African-Americans found different ways to gain their freedom.

OBJECTIVES As you read, look for answers to the following questions:
1. How did African-American slaves gain their freedom?
2. Who were some notable free blacks?

According to the 1850 census, 196,016 free African-Americans lived in the North and 238,187 in the South. Admired by their brothers and sisters still in slavery, these **free blacks** were barely tolerated by whites, who feared the example they might set for slaves.

Free blacks, however, did not have an easy time of it. Slave traders often resorted to kidnapping free blacks in the South, in the border states, and even on the streets of the nation's capital. Then they sold them back into bondage. Denied rights such as voting or getting an education, free black people nevertheless persevered and progressed.

free black:
an African-American not held
in bondage.

Steps to Freedom

African-American slaves used every means they could to gain their freedom. The most common way—and the most dangerous—was to escape to the North or to Canada. Another method was for slaves to work extra hours, put aside part of their earnings, and buy their freedom. Then there

95

were slaves, like Benjamin Bradley of Annapolis, Maryland, who were so bright that they came to the attention of antislavery sympathizers who lent them the money to purchase their freedom. Bradley's freedom cost $1,000, all of which he paid back to his supporters. The following is from a letter written to the man who lent the last $122 for Bradley:

> [At] sixteen, [Bradley] showed great mechanical skill. With a piece of gun-barrel, some pewter, a couple of pieces of round steel, he constructed a working model of a steam engine.
>
> His master soon afterwards got him the place of a helper in the department of Natural and Experimental Philosophy in the Naval Academy at Annapolis. [Bradley] sold his first steam engine to a midshipman. With the proceeds, and what money he could lay up (his master allowing him $5 a month out of his wages), he built an engine large enough to drive the first cutter of a sloop-of-war at the rate of sixteen knots an hour.

Black Literary Societies

Once free, African-Americans made their mark in society. Between 1828 and 1846, for example, free African-Americans formed 46 literary societies as far north as Buffalo, as far south as Baltimore, and as far west as Detroit.

In Philadelphia, in 1828, a prominent black man named William Whipper, along with several friends, started the "Reading Room Society." Their goal was to avoid being "idle spectators to the movement being carried on by nations to improve themselves." The Reading Room was actually an early library where the group pooled their books and encouraged discussion and debate on topics of the day.

One of the most ambitious literary societies was New York City's Phoenix Society, organized in 1833. Members launched an ambitious fundraising project of $10,000 to build a library/museum for "colored youth." Lectures on science brought out as many as 500 eager listeners.

Some of the literary societies lasted as long as ten to twelve years. They formed an important bridge in the ever-expanding network of efforts to create an educational system from which African-Americans could really benefit.

Black Achievements in the Arts

In 1853 Williams Wells Brown wrote the first novel published by a black American. It was called *Clotel, or the President's Daughter*, and was read with great interest. So was Martin Delany's novel about black unity, *Blake*. And the Reverend James W. C. Pennington was the first black author to write a history of African-Americans. His *Textbook of the Origin and History of the Colored People* appeared in 1841.

Pennington was himself an escaped slave from Maryland, and as we mentioned earlier, one of the first black people to received a higher education degree.

Pennington wrote movingly of his own escape to freedom and of the terror of leaving his family and friends for the unknown:

Reverend James W.C. Pennington

> The emotions of that moment I cannot fully depict. Hope, fear, dread, terror, love, sorrow, and deep melancholy were mingled in my mind together. But the hour was come, and the man must act, or forever be a slave.

With only a piece of bread in his pocket, young Pennington set off on Sunday, the slaves' only day of rest. Once captured on the road to Pennsylvania, Pennington managed to escape a few days later, and hungry, exhausted, miserably lonely, but determined, he kept walking toward his destination. Finally, when he thought he might starve, he came upon a field and was able to eat a little corn. Later, he was lucky enough to be given directions to a Quaker home, where the family oppposed slavery.

Pennington was amazed at being treated as a human being. The father of the family told him, "Come in and take thy breakfast, and get warm." Wrote Pennington:

> These words spoken by a stranger, but with such an air of simple sincerity and fatherly kindness, made an overwhelming impression upon my mind.

97

"Had he turned me away, I must have perished. Nay, he took me in, and gave me of his own food, and shared with me his own garments."
—James W.C. Pennington, on his Quaker saviors

They made me feel, spite of all my fear and timidity, that I had found a friend and a home. Had he turned me away, I must have perished. Nay, he took me in, and gave me of his own food, and shared with me his own garments.

Other blacks made their marks in the arts too. Writers like George Moses Horton and Frances E. W. Harper wrote poetry, hoping to keep their fellow freedom fighters inspired.

Edmonia Lewis gained renown in New York as a black sculptress, while Elizabeth Taylor Greenfield was highly acclaimed as a concert singer of classical music.

Perhaps the greatest black stage artist of the era was the actor, Ira Aldridge. Aldridge was born in Maryland in 1807, the son of a minister in New York. Instead of following his father's profession, the young Aldridge soon became a member of a local theater company. A British theater manager met him in New York and hit upon the idea that Aldridge might do well in England, where antislavery sympathy was now high.

Despite an argument with his would-be mentor, Aldridge did get to London. He tried to find work as an actor, but was turned down so many times that he returned to America in 1830, dejected. But once back, things there were even worse. So, Aldridge mustered his determination and sailed for London again. This time he stayed. And he won. He became a star, playing choice roles such as Shakespeare's Othello to huge, admiring crowds. In April 1833, for instance, he played Othello at the prestigious Theatre Royal in Covent Garden.

Aldridge's tall, handsome looks, his deep, powerful voice, and his incredible stage presence are said to have made audiences weep. One leading actress, Madame Malibran, enthused, "Never in the whole course of my professional career have I witnessed a more powerful and interesting performance."

Another important thing to remember about Aldridge is that he was a great success in roles that, up to that point, had been reserved for whites. He played Shakespeare's King Lear and Macbeth, for example, receiving estatic praise from literary bigwigs such as the noted French critic, Theophile Gautier. Said Gautier, "King Lear's own daughter, Cordelia, would have taken him for her father."

Aldridge performed to acclaim all over Europe, as far as Russia, where he became friends with the famous writer Tolstoy, who wrote *War and Peace*. King Frederick William IV of Prussia awarded Aldridge his country's Gold Medal of Science and Arts.

Aldridge's place in Europe was so secure that he still holds a position of special honor at England's Royal Shakespeare Theatre at Stratford-on-Avon. A chair was named in his honor, and he is remembered today as one of the world's great Shakespearean actors of all time.

Highlighting a Hero—Benjamin Banneker

One of the most dramatic examples of an achievement by a free African-American was the great city planner, scientist, astronomer, and mathematician, Benjamin Banneker. Banneker was the grandson of a white indentured servant and an African man. While still a teenager, the brilliant young Banneker built the first clock made entirely of American parts. Later, Banneker became involved with astronomical research. He gained fame in 1789 when he predicted a solar eclipse "with astonishing accuracy."

By the time Banneker had reached his forties, he was chosen to be one of a special team of three men to design Washington, D.C. Thomas Jefferson, with whom he had corresponded, had recommended him for this prestigious job. Banneker worked with a white engineer, George Ellicott, and a French engineer, Pierre L'Enfant. The elite team surveyed the land which had been donated by Maryland and Virginia. Then L'Enfant had a disagreement with the American government and returned to France, taking some of the most important city plans with him. Banneker and Ellicott used their considerable abilities to reconstruct the plans totally from memory! The two went on to choose sites for the White House, the Capitol, and other important structures.

Banneker then retired to his Maryland farm where, for the next ten years, he published an *Almanac*. This publication became as important in many American farming homes of the day as the telephone directory is to us today.

Although highly regarded by white society, Banneker never forgot the millions of African-Americans still held in bondage. In 1791, for example, he boldly chastised Thomas Jefferson about his views on slavery. How could Jefferson, who had just fought in the Revolutionary War to free America from the British, suddenly turn a deaf ear when it came to freedom for black people? Banneker gave Jefferson a piece of his mind:

> You were then impressed with proper ideas of the great violation of liberty to which you were entitled by nature; but sir, how pitiable is it to reflect that . . . you should at the same time . . . detain by fraud and violence, so numerous a part of my brethren under groaning captivity and cruel oppression, that you should at the same time be found guilty of that most criminal act, which you professedly detested in others.

Frightened perhaps by the persistent efforts of outspoken critics like Benjamin Banneker, the Maryland legislature voted in 1803 to forbid free African-Americans like him from voting in elections. (Black people still had the "privilege" of paying taxes, however!)

Highlighting a Hero—Paul Cuffe

Paul Cuffe of Massachusetts, a brave free black man, as we have seen, did win the right in his state to vote and to inherit property. When Cuffe was just 21, the authorities in Dartmouth, Massachusetts, where he lived, informed young Cuffe that he would have to start paying taxes. Cuffe called the bluff of the white civil servants. Why, he asked, should he pay taxes if he had none of the privileges of citizenship?

Cuffe refused to pay his taxes. The state of Massachusetts sued him and finally forced the money out of him. But this only served to fuel the flame of Cuffe's burning desire for equality. At the very next session of the state legislature in 1780, Cuffe drew up a petition asking for the right to vote and inherit property.

The legislators denied the gutsy petition in that session. But come next session, the persistent Cuffe was right there, submitting the petition again. This time, amazingly, it passed and "all the free coloured people of the state, on paying their taxes, were considered, from thenceforth, as entitled to all the privileges of citizens."

This was a major political triumph, but by 1788 a backlash had set in. Whites in Massachusetts feared that more black people would be attracted to their state because of the rights its black citizens enjoyed. So, the state legislature prohibited new black arrivals from staying in Massachusetts for more than a two-month period of time.

Highlighting a Hero—Norbert Rillieux

One of the greatest inventors in America of the era was Norbert Rillieux (ree-YOH), a black man in Louisiana. He was an engineer and contractor who invented the "vacuum-pan," a revolutionary new way to refine sugar from cane. So prominent was he, that, as often was the case when whites wanted to praise black achievement, the white press often omitted the fact that he was black in its coverage of him.

Free Blacks Who Owned Slaves

It sounds amazing, but it's true. There were free black people who actually owned slaves. They fell into two categories. First, there were black people who owned small businesses or farms of their own and used slaves as workers. Second, and in the majority of cases, there were individuals who owned someone for an **altruistic** reason. For example, a husband might buy family members in order to free them. In some cases, however, a free black husband purchased a wife and only freed her after he was sure he liked her as a wife! One black shoemaker in Charleston, South Carolina, resold the new wife he didn't like for a $50 profit. But most of the time, family members were freed soon after being bought.

altruistic:
showing a selfless concern for others.

The majority of black slaveowners lived in southern towns and cities. But even they had a hard time after Nat Turner's Rebellion, when repression against African-Americans, slave and free, reached a fever pitch.

And so it went. Time and again, African-Americans managed to drive a wedge into the system, only to find it

101

close around them again. Each time, however, the number of white sympathizers grew. The abolition of slavery became the hot topic of the mid-1800s. How long could the United States tolerate the chains that bound millions of African-Americans?

SECTION THREE REVIEW

1. VOCABULARY Write a sentence for each of the following words: free black, altruistic.

2. HISTORY What were some of the ways by which slaves could gain their freedom?

3. BIOGRAPHY Why do we remember Benjamin Banneker?

4. BIOGRAPHY Why did Paul Cuffe refuse to pay his taxes?

5. CRITICAL THINKING Does it surprise you to learn that some black Americans actually owned slaves? Does this change your view of slavery in any way?

SECTION FOUR

THE BACK-TO-AFRICA MOVEMENT

VOCABULARY colonization Liberia

MAIN IDEA The idea of sending blacks back to Africa was widely debated during slavery days.

OBJECTIVES As you read, look for answers to the following questions:
1. What Americans favored sending black people back to Africa?
2. Why did most African-Americans oppose the plan?
3. How did Liberia come into being?

For a number of people, black and white, one answer to the slavery question was for African-Americans to return to Africa to live. Many reasoned that black people could take the skills they had learned in America and construct model societies with the best of both worlds.

Paul Cuffe and Colonization

As early as 1714, one white New Jersey resident proposed sending black people back to Africa, a move called **colonization**. And in 1777 a Virginia state legislative committee, headed by Thomas Jefferson, was at work on a plan for the resettling of black people in Africa.

Everything was just talk until 1815 when Paul Cuffe, the enterprising black sailing magnate, took 38 African-Americans to Sierra Leone, a British colony in West Africa. Cuffe got moral support from his friends and fellow black businessmen, James Forten and John Russworm. These men believed, as Forten put it, that African-Americans "will never become a people until they come out from amongst the white people." They planned an all-black shipping line that would secure the economic footing for the new African colony.

colonization: the sending of people of African descent to another country, preferably in Africa.

"[African-Americans] will never become a people until they come out from amongst the white people."
—James Forten

White Advocates of Colonization

In December 1816, a group of northern whites formed the American Colonization Society. Their aim was to finance any African-Americans who wanted to go back to Africa. The Society's members included such well-known whites as Frances Scott Key, author of "The Star-Spangled Banner." They lost no time in publishing a journal, *The African Repository*, and in petitioning Congress to get land in Africa where black people could be sent.

Free African-Americans Oppose Colonization

From the start, most free African-Americans rejected the idea of going back to Africa. In 1817, 3,000 free black people in Philadelphia held a huge convention to voice their opposition to colonization. James Forten, apparently having changed his mind, was there. So was the militant abolitionist black minister, Richard Allen. The convention called the colonization idea an "outrage, having no other object in view than the benefit of the slaveholding interests of the country." Free African-Americans opposed colonization for three reasons.

First, they argued, black people had contributed greatly to the development of America without getting payment or recognition. Now, when the number of free black people was at its height, wouldn't it be better to own property and develop businesses right here in America?

Second, many African-Americans objected to the American Colonization Society's degrading view of black people in America. The Society had publicly stated that African-Americans were "notoriously ignorant, degraded and miserable, mentally diseased [and] broken-spirited." It said they would "wander unsettled and unbefriended" or "sit indolent, abject and sorrowful" if they were not sent back to Africa. Further, the Colonization Society did *not* propose freeing slaves. Its members merely wanted to get rid of the black people who were without a "master." Most even opposed educating African-Americans or giving them more rights in the society. It was useless, they argued, to give black people "a higher relish for those privileges which they can never attain."

Third, African-Americans opposed colonization because they did not approve of simply dumping black people in distant locations. They saw such a move as being filled with complications. For instance, since black people had been robbed of their original heritage, how could they go back to just *any* African country? Culturally, socially, and politically, how could African-Americans blend into African societies after being away for several hundred years? And what would they do for money once they got there? Would the entire venture be funded indefinitely by the American government? Was such a notion economically feasible?

The Founding of Liberia

The Colonization Society wasted no time in pushing bills through Congress to purchase land in West Africa. Backed by powerful white legislators, the United States established an American colony called **Liberia**. (By 1847, Liberia would become a "free" republic, under the "protection" of the United States.)

White colonists immediately started sending black people to Liberia. By 1830, 1,420 African-Americans had arrived in Liberia. Most were free, though some had been slaves

Liberia:
country in West Africa settled by black Americans starting in 1821.

104

who were hastily freed and then put right on ships bound for the new colony. In all, the American Colonization Society sent about 12,000 black people to Africa. Most were free black people from the South.

SECTION FOUR REVIEW

1. **VOCABULARY** Write a sentence for each of the following words: colonization, Liberia.

2. **BIOGRAPHY** Why did Paul Cuffe favor colonization?

3. **ETHICS** On what grounds did most African-Americans oppose colonization?

4. **HISTORY** What African country was founded as a home for American blacks?

5. **CRITICAL THINKING** If you were an African-American living in the United States in 1820, would you have favored or opposed colonization? Why or why not?

CHAPTER FOUR REVIEW

VOCABULARY

Write the numbered sentences on a separate sheet of paper. In each sentence fill in the blank with one of these terms: *free blacks*, *Fugitive Slave Act*, *Haiti*, *Nat Turner's Rebellion*, *Underground Railroad*.

1. The successful slave revolt on the Caribbean island of _____ shocked slaveholders throughout the Americas.

2. The most famous slave revolt in America, _____, took place in Virginia in 1831.

3. The cruel _____ required people in free states to help capture runaway slaves.

4. The _____ helped African-Americans escape slavery.

5. African-Americans not held in bondage were known as _____.

REVIEWING THE FACTS

1. How did captives on slaveships try to resist their oppression?
2. What were some of the notable slave revolts in South America? In the Caribbean? In North America?
3. What effects did the slave revolts have?
4. What were some of the ways by which slaves escaped to freedom?
5. What roles did such heroes as Harriet Tubman and Frederick Douglass play in the antislavery movement?
6. How did African-American slaves gain their freedom?
7. Who were some notable free blacks?
8. What Americans favored sending black people back to Africa?
9. Why did most African-Americans oppose the plan?
10. How did Liberia come into being?

CRITICAL THINKING

1. **INFERRING** What was the importance of the slave revolt on Haiti?
2. **ANALYZING A QUOTATION** What did Frederick Douglass

mean when he said, "Men are whipped oftenest who are whipped easiest." Do you agree with Frederick Douglass? Why or why not?

3. **EVALUATING** What is the main idea of this chapter?

4. **ANALYZING AN ARGUMENT** Many defenders of slavery in the South said that there has never existed a wealthy society in which one portion of the society did not live on the labor of others. Do you agree with this justification of slavery? Why or why not?

UNDERSTANDING PREJUDICE

1. How did most white people view Indians in the early 1800s? (Consider the story of the Seminole Wars.) How are Indians viewed today?

2. What obstacles did Harriet Tubman have to overcome? To what extent did she succeed?

3. How does an idea such as colonization indicate the failure of groups to put aside their prejudices and work out their differences?

STEPS TO FREEDOM

(1850–1865)

In 1814 William Trail escaped to Indiana from Maryland with the help of a forged slave "pass." He was captured and forced to go back to his master. He escaped again. Again, he was recaptured. Resolutely, Trail escaped a third time! Finally, he managed to win his freedom in the courts. After tremendous effort, Trail moved to Union County, Indiana, where he became a well-to-do farmer.

It was clear. African-Americans had had enough. Throughout the 1800s, in larger and larger numbers, they escaped. Any way they could. Anywhere they could.

After the prohibition of slavery in the North, more and more slaves went there to start new lives, despite everything that was against them. Still, tensions were rising. Those tensions would lead to war between the North and South in 1861 and, finally, to the end of slavery.

SECTION ONE

THE COMING CONFLICT

VOCABULARY secede Compromise of 1850 Kansas-Nebraska Act popular sovereignty Republican Party Dred Scott case

MAIN IDEA By 1860 rising tensions between the North and South brought the United States to the brink of war.

OBJECTIVES As you read, look for answers to the following questions:
1. Why did the question of admitting new states to the Union divide the United States?
2. Describe the impact of the Kansas-Nebraska Act, the Dred Scott case, and John Brown's raid.

Recruitment posters like this one urged African-Americans to enlist on the Union side in the Civil War. By war's end about 200,000 African-Americans served in the army or navy.

America was growing. As the eastern half of the country filled with people, pioneers looked westward for expansion. As we have seen, the Haitian Revolution led to the Louisiana Purchase, thus doubling the size of the entire United States. But southern planters were worried. How could they take advantage of the new territory?

The Search for New Slave States

The South desperately needed to expand slavery. Many farmers had worked their original plantation acreage to death, in much the same way they did their slaves. Season after season, the owners planted the same crops which, after a few years, depleted the soil.

Did they care? No. They simply looked farther west for more cheap land to buy and more cheap slave labor to work it. If the planters didn't expand to new regions every few years, they would not be able to grow anything. The fear of sitting on vast tracts of dead, unusable land with thousands of slaves to feed, haunted the planters.

In 1844 the *Jacksonville Reporter*, an Alabama newspaper, saw a solution to the problem: "Under the circumstances, the addition of Texas with its slaves is the only means of saving the South."

So, the leading question in American politics was asked: Would each new state come into the Union as "slave" or "free"? The southern planters lobbied furiously in Washington, D.C., for any new state to have the "right" to be a slave state, if its people so desired.

And, in fact, in 1845, Texas officially joined the Union as a slave state. However, to appease the North, which opposed the entry of more slave states, the federal government allowed Iowa to became a free state in 1846. It did the same thing with Wisconsin in 1848.

The Compromise of 1850

The South was frantic. What could it do? Then in 1848 the United States defeated Mexico in the Mexican War. In the peace treaty, Mexico gave up almost half its land to the United States. The new American territories included present-day California, Nevada, Utah, and parts of Arizona, New Mexico, Colorado, and Wyoming.

Immediately, southern political leaders demanded the admittance of the new territories to the Union as slave states. In a last desperate gesture, the southern states even threatened to **secede** from the United States and form their own country if their demands weren't met.

"Let them secede!" countered the North scornfully. Sentiment there held that American slavery had largely outlived its usefulness. The *Cleveland Plain Dealer* stated bluntly, "Rather than see slavery extended one inch beyond its present limits we would see this Union split apart."

Members of Congress wrung their hands. After all, the United States was still a young country. How could they preserve this fragile newborn Union? Things were getting out of control—fast.

"The addition of Texas with its slaves is the only means of saving the South."
—*Jacksonville Reporter*, 1844

secede:
to withdraw formally from membership.

"Rather than see slavery extended one inch beyond its present limits we would see this Union split apart."
—*Cleveland Plain Dealer*

110

Worried congressmen called on a respected senator, Henry Clay from Kentucky, to work out a compromise. On January 29, 1850, Clay proposed a plan called the **Compromise of 1850**. Under this compromise California would join the Union as a free state. This meant that the South would give up the requirement that if one state were admitted into the United States as "free," then the next one had to come in as a "slave" state. In addition, the slave trade was abolished in Washington, D.C.

To please the South, Congress passed a tougher Fugitive Slave Law (Chapter 4). This new law allowed bounty hunters to go North, capture runaway slaves, and return them to the South. Further, anyone caught helping a runaway could be jailed or fined.

Compromise of 1850:
an agreement by which (1) California was admitted to the Union as a free state, (2) the territories were allowed to decide whether to permit slavery, (3) the slave trade was ended in Washington, and (4) a strict Fugitive Slave Law was enacted.

The Kansas-Nebraska Act

No sooner had the Missouri Compromise calmed things down for a while, than the **Kansas-Nebraska Act** of 1854 heated them up again. In it, Congress allowed Kansas and Nebraska to become territories. Both territories had been part of the Louisiana Purchase, however, and under the terms of an earlier compromise—the Missouri Compromise of 1820—they had been closed to slavery. Now the Missouri Compromise was being thrown out in favor of a new principle—**popular sovereignty**. In other words, the people of the territories would have the power to decide whether to allow slavery.

Kansas-Nebraska Act:
a law passed in 1854 that allowed the residents of Kansas and Nebraska to decide whether to permit slavery.

Much like the abortion issue of today, popular sovereignty bitterly divided the nation. So angry were the antislavery forces that in 1854 they formed a new political party, one that would have an "unalterably antislavery" point of view. That new party was none other than the **Republican Party**. It quickly gained support across the North.

popular sovereignty:
the principle that the voters living in a territory should decide for themselves whether to allow slavery.

Southerners, incensed at the rise of the Republicans, renewed their call for more slave states. Some even demanded that the African slave trade be opened up again.

Republican Party:
a political party formed in 1854 in opposition to slavery.

The Dred Scott Case

The pro- and antislavery pots boiled furiously on America's political stove. Then, in 1857, a case came before the

111

Dred Scott case:
a Supreme Court decision
declaring that slaves had no
rights of citizens and that
Congress could not forbid
slavery in the territories.

Supreme Court that was to have landmark significance. It came to be known as the **Dred Scott case.** The case dealt with Dred Scott, a Missouri slave who had been taken by his owner to Illinois and then to Minnesota Territory. When Scott returned to Missouri, a slave state, he sued for his freedom. He argued that living in a free territory had made him free.

In a blow to freedom lovers everywhere, the Court rejected Dred Scott's argument. It said that (1) Dred Scott could not sue because, under the Constitution, he was not a citizen. The Court went on to say that (2) Congress had no right to forbid slavery in the territories. Only when a territory became a state could it decide whether to allow slavery.

Antislavery forces were enraged. Did this mean that the highest court in the land was on slavery's side? They did not intend to wait much longer to find out. They immediately began to round up all the candidates they could to run for political office under the new Republican Party. If the Republicans became strong enough, perhaps they could keep slavery in check.

White Antislavery Sympathizers

In America in the 1850s, whether you were directly involved with slavery or not, you had an opinion about it. It was *the* hot issue. Some whites were against slavery on principle. In 1831 William Lloyd Garrison, a white abolitionist in New England, founded the country's leading antislavery newspaper, *The Liberator.* In the first issue, Garrison made his position clear. He declared:

"I WILL BE HEARD"
—William Lloyd Garrison

> I *will* be harsh as truth. . . . I am in earnest—I will
> not [mislead]—I will not excuse—I will not retreat
> a single inch—AND I WILL BE HEARD.

Over the years, Garrison worked hard for an end to slavery. He and other northern antislavery advocates chipped in to pay for lecture tours for black speakers like Frederick Douglass. They also contributed toward the freeing of as many slaves as they could.

There were also many whites who resisted slavery, not

out of respect for black people, but because they did not like slavery as a system. They felt it was as degrading for white people as for black people, in that neither could live normal lives.

Congressman David Wilmot was one such person. So was Abraham Lincoln, a young Illinois lawyer. They both argued publicly that slavery "disgraced" the entire work ethic. How could ordinary whites continue to toil day by day, they asked, when next door to them a slaveowner might move in. That slaveowner could idle his days away because, unlike his neighbors, he had slaves doing all his work for him.

John Brown

John Brown's Raid

Some whites were willing to take radical measures to help black people regain their freedom. One of the most famous was John Brown, who shocked the nation to the brink of war.

John Brown had for years banded with other whites in aiding the antislavery movement. He had helped slaves escape from Missouri and had corresponded regularly with black abolitionists like Frederick Douglass.

By 1859 John Brown could stand slavery no longer. He decided that the only way for black people to be free was by force. So he came up with a plan to raid the federal arsenal at Harpers Ferry, Virginia. After seizing the weapons inside, Brown planned to slip into as many plantations as possible, arm the slaves there, and kill the slaveholders.

On the night of October 16, 1859, after months of secret planning, Brown struck. Along with a band of eighteen followers, he broke into the federal arsenal. The first part of his plan worked. Unfortunately, the second did not. Brown and his men were discovered before they had reached more than a few farms. An enormous manhunt tracked the band down.

On December 2, 1859, John Brown was hanged. But he was dedicated to his cause until the end:

I pity the poor in bondage that have none to help them; that is why I am here; not to gratify any personal animosity, revenge or vindictive spirit.

113

"You may dispose of me easily, but this question is still to be settled—the Negro question—the end of that is not yet."
—John Brown

You may dispose of me easily, but this question is still to be settled—the Negro question—the end of that is not yet.

In one stroke, John Brown's raid forced all white Americans to focus on the black/white issue. Whites who were already hostile to black people became more hostile. White southerners were stunned by Brown's attack. On the other hand, many northerners viewed Brown as a hero. Bells tolled and guns fired in salute the day Brown was executed. Many whites decided to vote for whomever the Republicans put up for President—as long as he would do something about slavery! That man happened to be Abraham Lincoln. Lincoln was to become President of one of the biggest powderkegs the world had ever seen.

SECTION ONE REVIEW

1. **VOCABULARY** Write a sentence for each of the following words: secede, Compromise of 1850, Kansas-Nebraska Act, popular sovereignty, Republican Party, Dred Scott case.

2. **GEOGRAPHY** Why did the South look west for new states?

3. **POLITICS** What were the terms of the Compromise of 1850? How did it most directly affect African-Americans?

4. **CONSTITUTIONAL GOVERNMENT** Why did the Dred Scott case so anger antislavery forces?

5. **CRITICAL THINKING** Why did compromise between the North and South no longer seem possible by the late 1850s?

SECTION TWO   BLACKS IN THE NORTH IN THE 1850s

VOCABULARY discrimination

MAIN IDEA Black northerners resisted the slave catchers who pursued fugitives in the 1850s.

OBJECTIVES As you read, look for answers to the following questions:
1. What was the effect of the Fugitive Slave Law on African-Americans living in the North? How did they react?
2. How did African-Americans protest discrimination in the North?

> Make me a grave where'er you will,
> In a lowly plain, or a lofty hill;
> Make it among earth's humblest graves,
> But not in a land where men are slaves.
> "Bury Me in a Free Land," Frances Harper

As the poet Frances Harper wrote, African-Americans wanted freedom. But by the year 1850, tensions between pro- and antislavery forces were making life almost impossible for black people in the North. They were constantly watched, checked on, and pursued—the result of the Fugitive Slave Law. Across the North, African-Americans took measures to defend themselves.

Black Freedom Fighters and the Fugitive Slave Law

As the slave catchers dragged fugitives back south, black leaders shouted, "Enough!" Martin R. Delany, a free black from Boston, spoke regularly at abolitionist gatherings throughout the North. He urged African-Americans to defend themselves:

> We must act according to our desperation. Let no man consent to be a slave. Let no man be taken from the North alive. . . . What little we do enjoy is too precious to be yielded up without a struggle. Let us die for it, if need be.

He added:

> If any man approach [my] house in search of a slave, if he crosses the threshold of my door, and I do not lay him a lifeless corpse at my feet, I hope the grave may refuse my body a resting place.

"Let no man consent to be a slave. Let no man be taken from the North alive."
—Martin R. Delany

115

And the young, militant David Walker, like the Black Panthers in the 1960s, openly called for black people to use any means necessary to defend their freedom:

> Can our condition be any worse?...Can they get us any lower? Where can they get us? They are afraid to treat us worse, for they know well, the day they do it they are gone.
> ...They want us for their slaves, and think nothing of murdering us in order to subject us to that wretched condition—therefore, if there is an attempt made by us, kill or be killed.

"Can they get us any lower? Where can they get us? They are afraid to treat us worse, for they know well, the day they do it they are gone."
—David Walker

Like many others, Harriet Tubman was determined to fight the Fugutive Slave Law any way she could. And fight she did.

In Troy, New York, in early 1850, word reached Mrs. Tubman that a man named Charles Nalle was being hustled off to the U.S. Commissioner's office to be sent back into slavery. Without another word, Mrs. Tubman rushed to the office herself. The ever-brilliant strategist, she told several little boys to run outside through the gathering crowd, yelling "fire."

Confusion mounted. Then, when the federal marshal brought the hapless man out, Mrs. Tubman threw her own sturdy body on the officer. With superhuman strength, she managed to keep the officer down on the ground while friends pulled the black man into the crowd. They tied Harriet's bonnet on the man's head, so he became unrecognizable in the fracas and was able to escape.

Black Self-Protection Groups

One year later, in 1851, another famous incident showed how far African-Americans would go in order to protect their own.

William Parker, a free black man living in Christiana, Pennsylvania, organized a mutual protection society against slave catchers. The group, like many others in northern cities, agreed on a plan to alert one another if a bounty hunter was seen in the vicinity. They were even prepared to beat or drive out of town those free black people in their midst, who, for money, would betray their own neighbors to the white bounty hunters.

On September 9, 1851, a Maryland slaveowner named Edward Gorsuch pounded on Parker's door, demanding that four black people staying with the Parkers be turned over to him. Gorsuch had brought fifteen burly men with him, including his son, to intimidate the stalwart freedom seekers.

Parker's wife blew a horn for help, and the melee was on. The intruders shot at Parker, who fired back. By the time the shooting was over, Gorsuch lay dead and his son seriously wounded. The blacks had won the day!

However, a crowd of angry whites later returned to the Parker home in a fury. Parker and two of his friends were forced to flee to Canada, in order to avoid arrest and re-enslavement.

But the mob still demanded vengeance. They eventually seized two white Quaker abolitionists and several black people and arrested them for treason. Such was the ugly, terrifying atmosphere that blacks and white abolitionists alike were forced to stand up to. It can be likened to the reign of terror of Adolf Hitler in Germany as he had Jewish people dragged from their homes to their deaths during World War II.

When William Parker and his companions fled with nothing but the shirts on their backs, Frederick Douglass sheltered them in his home in Rochester, New York, until they could make their way farther north. Douglass later wrote:

> I could not look upon them as murderers. So I fed them, and sheltered them in my house. Had they been pursued then and there, my home would have been stained with blood.... The mountains in Pennsylvania were being searched.... The hours they spent at my house were therefore hours of anxiety as well as activity.... I remained at home myself to guard my tired, dust-covered, and sleeping guests, for they had been harassed and travelling for two days and nights.... Happily for us the suspense was not long, for it turned out, that very night a steamer was to leave for Toronto, Canada.

The "Jerry Rescue"

In October 1851 another famous black freedom fighter, William Ward, risked his own freedom to save an escaped slave named "Jerry." Ward, a former slave himself, lived in Syracuse, New York, where he had served for a time as pastor of a white church. Ward and the Reverend Samuel J. May managed to get into the prison where Jerry was being held prior to being sent back to slavery in Missouri. Ward recalled:

> Though chained, he could not stand still. He implored us who were looking on in such strains of fervid eloquence as I never heard before nor since from the lips of a man, to break his chains, and give him that liberty which the Declaration of Independence assumed to be the birthright of every man, and which, according to the law of love was our duty towards a suffering brother.

Meanwhile, a crowd had gathered outside the courthouse. Ward passionately spoke in the helpless man's defense, knowing Jerry would not get a fair trial. The crowd began throwing stones into the courtroom. One stone narrowly missed the judge, who quickly adjourned Jerry's hearing. An hour later, the freedom fighters, black and white, managed to break down the jailhouse door, douse the lights, and grab Jerry. The federal marshal became so frightened that he "fled in female clothing"!

Soon thereafter, angry whites, in retaliation, hauled several of Jerry's rescuers into court on charges of treason. William Ward himself was forced to flee to Canada.

Other former slaves living in Syracuse also risked their freedom in what became known as the Jerry Rescue of 1851. One was the Reverend J.W. Loguen. Risking everything, Loguen publicly wrote to William Lloyd Garrison, the prominent white abolitionist and editor of the anti-slavery newspaper, *The Liberator*. In his letter, Loguen disagreed with Garrison's philosophy that, in spite of their horrible circumstances, African-Americans should be completely nonviolent in their response to the slave catchers and bounty hunters who hunted them daily.

Several of the wives of these stalwart freedom fighters,

in brave, stony defiance themselves, sent the prosecutor of the Jerry Rescue 30 pieces of silver, calling them "wages of iniquity and treachery." They also sent Jerry's chains, which Ward had helped file off, to the President of the United States, Millard Fillmore. They sent the chains in a beautiful mahogany box.

Early Protests Against Unfair Treatment in the North

Free African-Americans not only did what they could to resist the slave catchers that roamed the North. They also began to protest against **discrimination**—unfair treatment— that they suffered because of their race.

discrimination: an unfair attitude based on prejudice toward a particular group of people.

Most people today think that the first protests against blacks' having to sit at the backs of buses came in Montgomery, Alabama, during the civil rights movement that began in the late 1950s. Those were the memorable days, as you will read in Chapter 9, when Rosa Parks refused to give her seat to a white person. But in the 1850s, right in New York City, Elizabeth Jennings fought officials of a horse-drawn trolley line who wanted her to wait until the "colored" car came along.

Mrs. Jennings and a friend wanted to go to church. The conductor, a recent Irish immigrant, told the black women to get off the trolley they had just boarded. Elizabeth Jennings told what happened next:

> I told him I was a respectable person, born and raised in New York, and did not know where he was born. He took hold of me and I took hold of the window sash. He pulled me until he broke my grasp. I took hold of his coat and held onto that. He then ordered the driver to fasten his horses and come and help him put me out of the cars. Both seized hold of me by the arms and pulled and dragged me down on the bottom of the platform, so that my feet hung one way and my head the other, nearly on the ground.

"I told him I was a respectable person, born and raised in New York, and did not know where he was born."
—Elizabeth Jennings

When the driver could not force Mrs. Jennings from the trolley, he drove her to the nearest police station. The officer there sided with the trolley operator. He dared Mrs. Jennings to take her case to court.

119

That's exactly what she did. Elizabeth Jennings boldly sued the Third Avenue Railroad Company. And she won! She received $225 in damages (a large sum in those days). And, most importantly, she won the right for all black New Yorkers to ride the trolley line.

Black Freedom Conventions

Throughout the 1800s free black people, wherever they were, stood up to take action against slavery. Now, with the Fugitive Slave Law placing all free blacks in danger in the 1850s, antislavery conventions met across the North.

In 1852 delegates gathered at a Boston convention called "Negro Adherents of the Free Soil Party." One participant was the Reverend J. B. Smith from Rhode Island. He spoke of his own father, who had died while trying to escape from slavery. "He believed," said Smith, "that resistance to tyrants was obedience to God."

In 1854 African-Americans held a huge antislavery convention in Philadelphia. They resolved to fight slavery in the South as well as unfair practices in the North. They said, "We advise all oppressed to adopt the motto, 'Liberty or Death'."

So even before the Civil War began, brave African-Americans made their own declaration of war, a war against a tyrannical system that refused to recognize them as human beings.

"We advise all oppressed to adopt the motto, 'liberty or Death'."
—Philadelphia antislavery convention, 1854

SECTION TWO REVIEW

1. **VOCABULARY** Write a sentence for the following word: discrimination.

2. **RELIGION** What part did northern clergymen play in resisting the Fugitive Slave Law?

3. **VALUES** What was the Reverend J.W. Loguen's disagreement with William Lloyd Garrison?

4. **BIOGRAPHY** What victory did Elizabeth Jennings win for African-Americans in New York City?

5. CRITICAL THINKING In what way did the Fugitive Slave Law affect every black northerner?

THE CIVIL WAR—FREEDOM WON

VOCABULARY emancipation Confederacy Civil War border states Emancipation Proclamation

MAIN IDEA The Civil War began when southern slave states tried to set up their own country. It ended with the defeat of the South and the freeing of the slaves.

OBJECTIVES As you read, look for answers to the following questions:
1. What effect did Lincoln's election have on the South?
2. What was the attitude of the North regarding the enlistment of African-Americans?
3. What was the impact of Lincoln's order freeing the slaves?

Nobody in America really wanted a civil war. But, little by little, the North and South edged closer to conflict. Could the country go on like this, half-slave and half-free? The tension of the two opposing forces tore the country at the seams.

Lincoln's Election

Abraham Lincoln's election as President in 1860 was the final match that lit the fuse. The election of a Republican shocked the South. White southerners thought it terrible that a U.S. President should have any antislavery sentiments at all.

Lincoln would go down in history as the man who "freed the slaves," but he was never really a radical abolitionist at all. He sincerely thought that slavery made it hard for the average white guy to make a decent living.

In the years before he became President, Lincoln did not favor the immediate **emancipation**, or freeing, of all slaves. He favored a gradual approach, which included the

emancipation:
freedom from slavery.

121

government paying slaveowners who freed their slaves. Further, he suggested that all black people, once they were free, should be sent to Africa to live. In speaking on racial matters, Lincoln once expressed a view held by most white people of the time:

> I am not, nor ever have been, in favor of bringing about in any way the social and political equality of the white and black races—that I am not, nor ever have been, in favor of making voters or jurors of Negroes...; there is a physical difference between the white and black races which I believe forbids the two living together on terms of social and political equality...and I as much as any other man am in favor of having the superior position assigned to the white race.

Lincoln, however, could never forget the sight, one day in 1841, of slaves in chains on the Ohio River. As Lincoln wrote to a Kentucky friend:

> You and I had together a tedious low water trip on a steamboat from Louisville to St. Louis. You remember as well as I do that from Louisville to the mouth of the Ohio, there were on board ten or a dozen slaves shackled with iron. That sight was a continual torment to me, and I see something like it every time I touch the Ohio or any other slave border.

It was this tug and pull of morality that was to keep him pushing, however hesitantly, along the antislavery path.

The South Secedes

Soon after Lincoln's election, seven southern states seceded from the Union. They were South Carolina, Georgia, Alabama, Florida, Louisiana, Texas, and Mississippi. The seven states formed what they called the **Confederacy**.

Lincoln, not officially President until his inauguration in March 1861, could only watch in frustration. Meanwhile,

Confederacy:
the southern states that seceded from the Union and formed a separate nation.

President James Buchanan made a half-hearted effort to negotiate with the southerners, asking them to rejoin the Union. They would not. He then decided that the rebel states should not have the use of U.S. facilities, like post offices or forts.

The First Shots

By the time Lincoln was finally sworn in as President, southerners had taken control of several federal forts in the South. U.S. troops had refused to leave Fort Sumter in South Carolina, however. The fort stood on an island in Charleston Harbor. Though its location made it easy to defend, the troops were low on food. Lincoln made the fateful—though cautious—decision to send food, but no other relief, to Fort Sumter.

When Confederate leaders learned of Lincoln's decision, they suspected that troops might follow. On April 12, 1861, they began firing on Fort Sumter. After more than 30 hours of cannonfire, the Union forces surrendered. The **Civil War** had begun.

The fighting at Fort Sumter led four more southern states to leave the Union. Within a few days, Virginia, Arkansas, Tennessee, and North Carolina had joined the Confederacy. Meanwhile, northern troops quickly occupied the **border states** of Maryland, Kentucky, and Missouri. In those slave states, on the dividing line between the North and South, loyalties were sharply divided.

Civil War:
the war between the Union and the Confederacy (1861–1865).

border states:
slave states occupied by the North at the beginning of the Civil War.

Preparing the Union Army

Men of color, to arms!...There is no time for delay! The tide is at flood that leads to fortune. Better even to die free than to live as slaves.
A call to arms by Frederick Douglass

"Men of color, to arms!"
—Frederick Douglass

With the outbreak of fighting, Lincoln began to organize the Union army. From the moment he called for volunteers, gallant black men were ready to join. As Frederick Douglass put it, "Longing for the end of the bondage of my people, I was ready for any political upheaval which should bring

123

about a change in the existing condition of things." But the U.S. Secretary of War said absolutely no. Black men could not join the armed forces.

During the first year of the war, President Lincoln compromised. He allowed a few black men to join the army, but only as cooks, hospital orderlies, or other servants. Lincoln was hoping for a speedy, negotiated truce that would not force him to give black men guns, something many whites feared.

But the war did not go well for the Union. From the beginning the North lost important battles, like the Battle of Bull Run. Further, many whites in the North did not want to fight at all, saying they would not risk their lives for slaves. These sentiments would lead, in 1863, to draft riots in New York City by angry mobs of whites, many of them poor immigrants.

Frustrated by Lincoln's hesitancy, some Union generals went ahead and took black men into their ranks anyway. And some black men, on their own, began fighting for their liberty and their honor.

Highlighting a Hero—William Tillman

In June 1861 a free black man named William Tillman worked as a cook aboard the American sailing ship, *S.J. Waring*, when it was captured by the Confederate ship, *Jeff Davis*. Tillman learned that the southerners planned to sell him into slavery upon reaching port.

One night, Tillman single-handedly overpowered his captors and piloted the ship into New York Harbor, flying the U.S. flag. Tillman received $6,000 as a reward for capturing the schooner and was publicly commended: "To this colored man was the nation indebted for the first vindication of its honor at sea."

The Enlistment of Black Troops

Union forces continued to fare badly. Finally on July 17, 1862, the U.S. War Department approved the enlistment of up to 5,000 black men in areas of the South where fighting was heaviest. Then, in 1863 the House of Representatives passed a bill allowing the recruitment of black soldiers. Massachusetts and Rhode Island began recruiting efforts right away, with Frederick Douglass and other black abolitionist leaders acted as recruiting agents.

Douglass shrewdly explained that there were three reasons African-American men would do well to enlist:

(1) They would learn to use weapons, a skill they could use later on to defend themselves and their families, if need be.

(2) Black men could prove their courage on the battlefield and boost their own self-confidence.

(3) By acts of valor, blacks could earn medals and, at last, the right to full U.S. citizenship. Declared Douglass, "Once let the black man get upon his person an eagle on his button, and a musket on his shoulder and bullets in his pocket, and there is no power on earth which can deny that he has earned the right to citizenship in the United States."

Frederick Douglass

By the end of 1862, entire regiments of free African-American men had been formed in the parts of Louisiana and South Carolina under Union control. Two elite regiments under General Butler were called the *Corps d'Afrique* (later known as the Louisiana Native Guards). They were commanded by black officers such as Major F.E. Dumas and Captain P.B.S. Pinchback. Major Martin Delany and Captain O.S.B. Wall headed up the 104th Regiment. Within months, recruitment bureaus were also in operation in Tennessee, Maryland, and Missouri. Union officials offered $300 to each slaveowner who agreed to have his slave sign up, but warned that 30 days later, slaves would be accepted, with or without their masters' consent.

In Massachusetts, black church leaders and businessmen formed the Black Committee to recruit soldiers for the 54th Regiment of Massachusetts Volunteers (all to be of African descent). The committee quickly raised $5,000 and, incredibly, managed to collect the tremendous sum of $100,000 to establish the regiment.

Blacks on the Battlefront

Black troops faced hardships not shared by whites. They usually received lower pay, fewer supplies, and less training than whites. They also faced special dangers if taken

125

captive. The Confederate troops would either send them back to slavery or put them to death, rather than hold them as prisoners of war.

In spite of discrimination and hardship, blacks fought loyally for the Union side. More than 200,000 African-American men fought bravely in the Union army and navy during the Civil War. Officials believe the actual number to be higher, because mulatto soldiers were often thought to be white.

African-Americans were especially noted for their service in the U.S. Navy. Fully one quarter of all sailors in the Civil War were black. One heroic black sailor, Robert Smalls from Beaufort, South Carolina, singlehandedly seized a large Confederate steamboat and brought it into Union waters.

In all, black troops fought with distinction in over 250 battles. African-American soldiers and sailors won 23 Congressional Medals of Honor, the nation's highest military award.

Black Heroism in Battle

There is no doubt that black soldiers were a major factor in helping the North win the Civil War. One great example was the regiment called the 1st South Carolina Volunteers. Commanded by Colonel Thomas Wentworth Higginson, this regiment saw furious action in Florida and South Carolina. Higginson had nothing but praise for his brave men:

> It would have been madness to attempt with the bravest white troops what [was] successfully accomplished with black ones. . . . No officer in this regiment now doubts that the successful prosecution of this war lies in the unlimited employment of black troops.

Black Valor at the Battle of Port Hudson

"Take those guns!" That was the desperate command that went out to the black soldiers of the 1st and 3rd Louisiana Negro Regiments at the Battle of Port Hudson in Louisiana on May 27, 1863.

Union troops were desperately trying to take control of

that area's fort, so they could command the Mississippi River. The white troops fought hard, but they could not take the fort. They had to call in the Louisiana Negro Regiments, which included black officers like Captain Andre Callioux, described as a "splendid horseman."

Extraordinarily brave, these black soldiers burst toward the fort, despite the Confederates' firing on them, again and again. As Union general Banks reported on May 30, 1863, "No troops could be more determined or more daring. The highest commendation is bestowed upon them by all the officers in command." The fall of Port Hudson helped the North gain control of the Mississippi River, thus cutting the Confederacy in half.

Heroic Black Women in the Civil War

Black women also displayed outstanding bravery during the Civil War. Harriet Tubman herself became a Union scout, risking her life many times to go south and gather information. General Rufus Saxton praised her "remarkable courage, zeal and fidelity." Mrs. Tubman also spent two years nursing war wounded in the Sea Islands off South Carolina.

Harriet Tubman

Another heroic black nurse was Susie K. Taylor, whose husband was an officer in the 1st South Carolina Volunteers. Not only did Mrs. Taylor nurse the sick, but she taught many soldiers to read and write in her spare time. During the war, Susie Taylor also worked with Clara Barton, who would later found the Red Cross.

Sojourner Truth, a former slave and one of the most active black female abolitionist speakers in the country, raised money for black troops. In spite of her advanced age, in 1864, after meeting with President Lincoln, she agreed to nurse wounded soldiers in Freedman's Hospital in Washington, D.C.

Mary Elizabeth Bowser, a refined, educated young slave woman, spied on Confederate soldiers. Bowser, who pretended she could not read, found work as a maid in the home of none other than the Confederate president, Jefferson Davis! She is said to have gathered crucial information regarding Confederate troops which was delivered to Union General Ulysses S. Grant.

Black Nurses in the Civil War Era

In 1865 the Confederacy made its own laws to recruit black troops. But it was too late. For too long, southern whites had feared what might happen if slaves were given guns. On March 13, 1865, Jefferson Davis asked for 300,000 men, black and white. A small number of black soldiers enlisted, but the majority who wanted to fight had long since escaped to the Union side. Less than a month later, the South surrendered and the Civil War was over.

The Emancipation Proclamation

Official estimates indicate that blacks died at twice the rate of whites in the Civil War. More than 38,000 African-American soldiers lost their lives on the battlefield, and thousands more were killed when taken captive by the Confederates.

There is no doubt that the black soldiers were an important factor in the Union's defeat of the Confederacy. But the crucial question remained: What would happen to these soldiers and their families at war's end?

At the start of the Civil War, Lincoln was in a precarious position. He did not want it to seem as if the war were being fought only over slavery. He knew many whites would refuse to risk their lives for black people, to whom they felt superior. Besides, Lincoln still believed that free black people should be sent back to Africa or to one of the Caribbean islands.

Ironically, Lincoln's "on-the-fence" position would back him into a corner. After more than a year of fighting, he had no choice but to issue the **Emancipation Proclamation**. This famous order had the aim of freeing all slaves in the rebelling states.

Why did Lincoln act?

First, delaying a decision had had a terrible effect on many brave slaves in the South. Risking their lives, by the wagonload, they had started to flee to the Union side. But because of the lack of a firm federal policy, some Union officers, really proslavery themselves, actually turned these slaves back over to their masters. Or, they allowed slave

Emancipation Proclamation: order issued by President Lincoln freeing all the slaves in the states still fighting against the Union in the Civil War.

agents to come into the Union camps and take the run-aways back. Northern abolitionists, black and white, were furious. They pointed out that every slave who left the South meant one fewer person who could help the Confederate cause.

Second, Lincoln had no choice because some abolitionist Union generals, like Benjamin Butler, were already standing up for what they believed. In May 1861, Butler simply refused to give back three slaves who had escaped to his camp. And in August 1861, General John C. Fremont proclaimed martial law in Missouri. He declared that because the escaped slaves in his camp had been the property of people who were resisting U.S. laws, they did not have to be returned to their former owners. In March 1862, General David Hunter issued "certificates of emancipation" to all slaves who had been working for the Confederate army but who had come over to the Union side.

Third, Congress had begun to act without waiting for Lincoln. In August 1861 it passed a Confiscation Act, allowing the "confiscation" of slaves who had been helping the Confederacy. Further, in April 1862 Congress abolished slavery in the District of Columbia and, two months later, in all the western territories. Finally, on July 16, 1862, Congress declared in a second Confiscation Act that the slaves of anyone committing treason or supporting rebellion against the Union were "forever free."

Lincoln realized that he had to make a decision. In the Spring, and later in July 1862, he wrote and revised his own Emancipation Proclamation. But even then, he did not issue it. Only after the North turned back the South at the Battle of Antietam did he get up the nerve to issue his proclamation. Realizing that freeing the slaves would be a serious blow to the South, he declared that beginning on January 1, 1863, "all persons held as slaves within any state ...in rebellion against the United States, shall be then, thenceforth, and forever free."

When news of the Emancipation Proclamation was made public, the effect among African-Americans was electric. People everywhere foresaw the end of slavery. Lincoln also recognized the importance of his act. "If my name ever goes into history," he told a Cabinet member, "it will be for this act."

"If my name ever goes into history, it will be for this act."
—Abraham Lincoln on the Emancipation Proclamation

129

Unanswered Questions

Actually, Lincoln's Emancipation Proclamation did not free all the slaves in the United States. It freed only those slaves who were living in rebel states—slaves over whom the Union had no control.

Lincoln had left three vital questions unanswered.

First, if he were only freeing slaves in the rebel states, then what about the 830,000 slaves who were already in the Union? They were *still* in bondage!

Second, how could Lincoln hope to enforce an emancipation order in states that were in rebellion? The North would have no authority in those states until it defeated them.

Third, Lincoln gave the southern rebel states three months to issue their own emancipation proclamation. Why? The reason they went to war in the first place was to keep their slaves. So why would they turn around and free them now? (In fact, at one point, Jefferson Davis, enraged at the Emancipation Proclamation, threatened to *re-enslave* those 250,000 free black people still living in the South at the time. Fortunately, he never got the chance to do so.)

Black Response to the Emancipation Proclamation

What saved Lincoln in this situation was the bravery of southern black people. Thousands risked their lives to spread the word about the Emancipation Proclamation throughout the South. This was followed by the bravery of those slaves who put down their tools and, with just the clothes on their backs, walked away from their owners.

As for the slaves in Union-controlled states, many simply decided that the Emancipation Proclamation included them too. They put down their rakes and hoes and left. According to one report, Kentucky lost 30,000 slaves almost overnight.

Many joined the Union forces, for the Emancipation Proclamation opened the army and navy to all African-Americans, slave or free. President Lincoln said it best. Just one year after issuing the Emancipation Proclamation, he wrote that black troops had "heroically vindicated their manhood on the battlefield."

Benefits of the Emancipation Proclamation

There were three major benefits of Lincoln's Emancipation Proclamation. First, as a war measure, it weakened the fighting strength of the Confederacy. With the flight of many slaves, white southerners who would otherwise have been free to fight now had to go back home for plowing and planting.

Second, it brought new support to the Union from other countries. Britain and France, the South's major customers for cotton, had once considered helping the Confederacy. Now that the goal of the war was not only to save the Union but to free slaves, British and French sympathies turned against the South.

Third, an important legal precedent for African-Americans had been made. At war's end, in 1865, Congress would pass an amendment to the Constitution ending slavery forever.

The Emancipation Proclamation, which started as a last-ditch military measure, ended up being one of the most important documents in American history.

SECTION THREE REVIEW

1. VOCABULARY Write a sentence for each of the following words: emancipation, Confederacy, Civil War, border states, Emancipation Proclamation.

2. HISTORY Why was the Confederacy formed?

3. HISTORY Why did the Union begin to enlist black troops in 1862?

4. HISTORY How did the Emancipation Proclamation affect African-Americans in captivity?

5. CRITICAL THINKING Lincoln predicted that the Emancipation Proclamation would result in his name going "into history." Did his prediction come true? Explain.

CHAPTER FIVE REVIEW

VOCABULARY

Write the numbered sentences on a separate sheet of paper. In each sentence fill in the blank with one of these terms: *Confederacy*, *Dred Scott case*, *Emancipation Proclamation*, *popular sovereignty*, *Republican Party*.

1. The _____ was President Lincoln's order freeing the slaves.
2. When the southern states seceded from the Union, they formed the _____.
3. Antislavery forces formed the _____ in 1854.
4. Under the concept of _____, the territories could decide for themselves whether or not to allow slavery.
5. The Supreme Court's decision in the _____ dealt a blow to freedom lovers everywhere.

REVIEWING THE FACTS

1. Why did the question of admitting new states to the Union divide the United States?
2. Describe the impact of the Kansas-Nebraska Act, the Dred Scott case, and John Brown's raid.
3. What was the effect of the Fugitive Slave Law on African-Americans living in the North? How did they react?
4. How did African-Americans protest discrimination in the North?
5. What effect did Abraham Lincoln's election have on the South?
6. What was the attitude of the North regarding the enlistment of African-Americans?
7. What was the impact of President Lincoln's order freeing the slaves?

CRITICAL THINKING

1. **MAKING A JUDGMENT** Do you think another compromise could have been found to avoid the Civil War? If so, what? If not, why not?
2. **EVALUATING** What three arguments did Frederick Douglass use to urge the enlistment of black troops? Which of those

arguments do you think was most important? State reasons for your answer.

3. **ANALYZING A QUOTATION** John Brown once noted that the Fugitive Slave Law made "more abolitionists than all the lectures we have had for years." What did he mean? Why do you think this was so?

UNDERSTANDING PREJUDICE

1. After the Mexican War, Mexico gave up almost half its land to the United States. In the decades that followed, Spanish-speakers were treated as second-class citizens. Children, for example, were beaten for speaking Spanish in school. Why do you think such rules were put in force? How, on the other hand, has the situation changed today? What problems remain for Hispanic Americans?

2. Not until 1989 did the movie *Glory* tell the story of black troops fighting in the Civil War. What have been more usual roles for blacks in Hollywood films? How does *Glory* reveal a more accurate picture of black history?

CHAPTER SIX

THE RECONSTRUCTION ERA

(1865–1877)

The Civil War was far from over in 1862 when Charlotte Forten, a genteel, middle-class young black woman from Philadelphia, insisted on going south. Determined to do what she could to help her people, she found a position teaching school in Union-occupied territory. She went to the Georgia Sea Islands, just off the coast of that state. Later, she wrote:

> I never before saw children so eager to learn.... The older ones, during the summer, work in the fields from early morning...then come to school, after their hard toil in the hot sun, as bright and as anxious to learn as ever....I told them about Toussaint [L'Ouverture], thinking it well they should know what one of their own color had done for his race. They listened attentively, and seemed to understand.

For thousands of people like Charlotte Forten, the Civil War period and the decade that followed was one of the most exciting—and frustrating—eras in American history. During those years America witnessed startling changes. African-Americans became citizens of the United States, with the same right to vote and own property as whites. Two black men became United States senators. Fourteen others served in the House of Representatives.

But such gains came with a high price tag. Very high indeed. Many white southerners fought *any* black progress tooth and nail. And, in time, they would take back control of the South. Still, the lives of African-Americans would be forever changed.

HEROES OF THE COLORED RACE.

Reconstruction was a time of high hope for African-Americans. This print shows Frederick Douglass with the first two black senators, Blanche K. Bruce (left) and Hiram Revels (right).

THE POLITICS OF RECONSTRUCTION

VOCABULARY Reconstruction amnesty Thirteenth Amendment black codes disenfranchise Fourteenth Amendment Fifteenth Amendment

MAIN IDEA The rebuilding of the South brought with it constitutional amendments that extended political rights to African-Americans.

OBJECTIVES As you read, look for answers to the following questions:
1. What plans did President Lincoln have for restoring the southern states to the Union? What were his views on colonization?

135

2. What constitutional amendments guaranteed rights to African-Americans?

3. Why did Congress step in and take a firm hand in establishing Reconstruction policy?

On April 9, 1865, southern forces surrendered at the small Virginia town of Appomattox Courthouse. The South finally admitted defeat. But now the former Confederacy was in ruins. Bridges and railroads were torn up. Barns and buildings were destroyed. The federal government had to step in and organize the rebuilding of the South. Its plan to rebuild the former Confederacy is known as **Reconstruction**.

Lincoln's Reconstruction Plan

Reconstruction:
the period (1865–1877) during which the federal government sought to rebuild the states of the former Confederacy.

Even before the war's end, President Lincoln had started to put a plan into action to reconstruct the fallen South. His Proclamation of Amnesty and Reconstruction, as he outlined it in December 1863, contained four main provisions.

(1) Lincoln wanted to make it as easy as possible for the average person in the South, black and white, to get back to work. He declared that only the top Confederate officials should be barred from regaining citizenship. And even then, Lincoln did not order those top officials to be imprisoned or shot for treason.

(2) Lincoln explained that all other citizens who swore an oath of loyalty to the United States would receive **amnesty**—official pardon. Poor whites who previously had not been allowed to vote, because they did not own property, would also be allowed to do so.

amnesty:
a general pardon by a government for political offenses.

(3) Each southern state, in its entirety, could get back into the Union when as few as one-tenth of the people who had voted in the 1860 election pledged their renewed allegiance to the United States.

(4) Lincoln asked the various states if those black people who were already educated and owned some property might be allowed to vote.

Colonization of Black People After the War

By the end of the war, Lincoln's plan met with opposition. Southern planters did not like it because they were still proud and angry from the war days. Abolitionists in the North were upset too. They called for stiffer penalties against the South. They also disagreed with another of Lincoln's hopes, namely that he could somehow persuade the millions of African-Americans in the South to get on ships and leave America without compensation for the centuries of pain and strife they had endured in the United States.

Lincoln was not the only one still thinking of colonization. Indeed, on April 16, 1862, when Congress abolished slavery in the District of Columbia, it also provided $100,000 to finance "voluntary Negro emigrants." Three months later, Congress threw in another $500,000 for the venture. Additional funds were to come from the sale of confiscated southern lands. The legislators then asked Lincoln to scout around for a suitable "tropical country." They didn't care which one. It could be in Africa or the Caribbean. It could even be Brazil. Any slave freed as "war contraband" was to be offered the opportunity to go to Africa or the Caribbean right away.

In August 1862 President Lincoln spoke with a delegation of black leaders headed by E. M. Thomas. Lincoln said:

> Your race suffers very greatly, many of them, by living among us, while ours suffers from your presence. In a word, we suffer on each side. If this is admitted it affords a reason why we should be separated.

Later, he added in his Second Annual Message to Congress:

> I strongly favor colonization. . . . Reduce the supply of black labor by colonizing the black laborer out of the country and by precisely so much you increase the demand for and wages of white labor.

As time passed, the President grew frantic about what to do with freed black people. He asked one Union general:

> But what shall we do with the Negroes after they are free? I can hardly believe the South and the North can live in peace . . . if we don't get rid of the Negroes whom we have armed and disciplined and who have fought with us. . . .

"But what shall we do with the Negroes after they are free? I can hardly believe the South and the North can live in peace."
—Abraham Lincoln

137

In 1863 a white adventurer was hired, as a test, to take 5,000 black emigrants to a small island off the coast of Haiti. Only 400 people actually undertook the trip, which ended in disaster after many died from disease and neglect. Even so, at least one Cabinet member nearly persuaded Lincoln to make colonization *mandatory*.

It was only after the need for black men to fight in the army became obvious that on July 2, 1864, Congress repealed all laws about colonization.

So, when Lincoln realized he needed black people to win the war, he began to address the black situation in America. Lincoln was still not an abolitionist. He did not believe in black citizenship. That is why his Reconstruction plan contained a very tentative suggestion about letting blacks vote. In March 1864 he suggested to the Union-appointed governor of Louisiana, that maybe, just maybe, a few of the talented black people in his state might be allowed to vote. "But this is only a suggestion," he assured Governor Michael Hahn, "not to the public, but to you alone." Hahn gave the idea a resounding no.

Congress Steps in

Meanwhile, Congress was growing anxious. It wanted clear signals that the Civil War would not end with African-Americans back at square one. After all, members pointed out, Lincoln had not even mentioned the Fugitive Slave Law, which was still on the books. Nor had he addressed the laws that still restricted the freedom of black people in the Union-controlled areas of the South.

Reformers in Congress introduced seven bills, one after the other, until they finally wrangled repeal of the Fugitive Slave Law in January 1864. One more link in the chain of slavery had been severed.

But they could not rest. For one thing, they knew that the Emancipation Proclamation was merely a war order. If Lincoln failed to win re-election in 1864 or if a conservative majority took over Congress, the Proclamation might get thrown by the wayside—and the slaves' freedom with it.

Led by such tireless reformers as Thaddeus Stevens in the House and Charles Sumner in the Senate, the congressional reformers decided to launch a bold plan while there was still time. They resorted to help from the supreme bastion of the entire country—the United States Constitution. Only by going to the source and by modifying this great document, did the congressmen feel they could guarantee African-Americans their freedom. So, they proposed the **Thirteenth Amendment**. It clearly stated that slavery in the United States was forever abolished.

The congressmen then launched a whirlwind campaign to have the amendment ratified. At the same time, they pleaded with reluctant voters that Lincoln *had* to be re-elected to end the war in an orderly way. The voters agreed, returning Lincoln to office in the presidential election of 1864.

Meanwhile, the states began to ratify the Thirteenth Amendment. Maryland and Missouri were among the first southern states to agree to abolish slavery with no money paid for slaveowners. (Lincoln had initially asked that former slaveowners be paid.) In fact, Frederick Douglass' own son was able to begin teaching in a freedmen's school in Maryland, the very state where his father had been a slave.

Could it be that a real change in America was actually around the corner?

Lincoln's Assassination

With the surrender of the Confederacy, the hopes of African-Americans were high. Then, just days later, tragedy struck. On the night of April 14, 1865, a wild-eyed southerner named John Wilkes Booth shot Abraham Lincoln in cold blood while the President and First Lady were attending the theatre.

The nation was overcome with grief. In a letter written a few days after Lincoln's death, black poet Frances Harper said:

> Sorrow treads on the footsteps of the nation's joy.... Today a nation sits down beneath the shadow of its mournful grief. Oh, what a terrible lesson does this event read to us!

Even people in the South mourned the loss. Jefferson Davis himself said, "Next to the defeat of the Confederacy, the heaviest blow that fell upon the South was the assassination of Lincoln."

Thirteenth Amendment: amendment to the Constitution, ratified in 1865, that abolished slavery.

"Next to the defeat of the Confederacy, the heaviest blow that fell upon the South was the assassination of Lincoln."
—Jefferson Davis

139

Andrew Johnson Takes Office

To add to the tragedy, African-Americans found themselves faced with a new President whom they viewed with mistrust. Andrew Johnson was a southerner from a poor white family in Tennessee. (His wife had taught him to read and write after they were married.) Would Andrew Johnson—could Andrew Johnson—carry out measures designed to insure reforms for black people? At first, Johnson said that he would, because of his own hatred for wealthy whites. But, within months after taking office, his words proved him different. A new battle was on.

Among his first acts, Johnson issued the North Carolina Proclamation, offering amnesty to the same former Confederate officials Lincoln had specifically rejected. He also ignored any language regarding African-Americans in the restructuring of that state's constitution.

Johnson then came up with what he called a plan of "Restoration," rather than Reconstruction. He allowed southern states to hold constitutional conventions. At these meetings, white delegates quickly passed laws restricting the freedom of black people. Under these **black codes**, African-Americans would be subject to curfews, arrest, and humiliating treatment. How, observers asked, was this different from slavery days?

Johnson also issued a decree designed to bring as many southern states as possible back into the Union. By the time Congress reconvened in December 1865, these states had blatantly voted their former Confederate officials back into office and arrogantly sent them to Washington. Northern congressmen were shocked to discover that they would be serving alongside the Vice President of the Confederacy, 4 Confederate generals, 6 Confederate Cabinet members, and 58 Confederate congressmen! They quickly decided to do something about it.

Black People Organize for Their Rights

Meanwhile, angry African-Americans had begun to organize as well. Early in 1866, a delegation of the nation's most prominent black leaders, led by Frederick Douglass, met with President Johnson in Washington. The most the Presi-

black codes:
laws passed by southern states just after the Civil War to restrict the rights of African-Americans.

140

dent managed to do was to shake their hands. It soon became clear that Johnson planned to skirt the entire issue of civil rights for African-Americans. He declared that the issue was one for each state to decide.

George Downing, a member of the delegation, came right to the point with Johnson. Said Downing:

> We are ... native-born Americans; we are citizens. ... It has been shown in the present war that the government may just reach its strong arm into the states and demand from those who owe it allegiance, their assistance, and support. May it not reach out a like arm to secure and protect its subjects upon whom it has a claim?

Douglass followed:

> We do hope that you ... will favorably regard the placing in our hands, the ballot with which to save ourselves.

Johnson squirmed at such a direct request. Finally, he refused it outright:

> It is the people of the states that must for themselves determine this thing. I do not want to be engaged in a work that will commence a war of races.

Douglass grimly but politely pointed out:

> You enfranchise your enemies and disenfranchise your friends.

The meeting was over.

African-Americans and the Black Codes

African-Americans were also unwilling to accept the black codes that southern legislatures were passing. On May 12, 1871, an unknown young black man singlehandedly started a "sit-in" on board a horsedrawn streetcar in Louisville,

Kentucky. Riding alone, he was subjected to curses and screams by white youths, until, dragged from the car and fighting back, he was arrested. His courageous stand led scores of other young black men to follow his lead. When faced with black passengers, some streetcar drivers got off their cars and walked away. The brave young black men simply took the reins and drove themselves! The solidarity of these black youth was so strong that the Louisville streetcar company changed its policy and allowed black people to ride, admitting it was "useless to resist."

In Savannah, Georgia, a similar episode took place the next year when a group of black people, led by the Reverend James Simms, tried to ride in the same horse-drawn streetcars as white passengers. This kind of gutsy demonstration would later be repeated throughout the twentieth century, as black people, inspired by leaders such as the Reverend Martin Luther King, Jr., fought to reclaim their civil rights.

Black Conventions

During the 1860s, educated African-Americans had held conventions in the North and the South. Their aim was to put pressure on the government to guarantee the freedoms so many had fought and died for.

In 1864 and 1865 in South Carolina, black people, who were actually in the majority, organized several conventions. Naval entrepreneur Robert Smalls (who had gained recognition when he stole a Confederate ship and sailed it to Yankee lines) was there. So were black men who would go on to play an important role in Reconstruction politics, such as Robert C. DeLarge, who would serve in Congress; Beverly Nash, a former slave who had not learned to read or write until after he was grown; and Francis L. Cardozo, a free man of black, Jewish, and Indian ancestry. A Presbyterian minister, Cardozo had been educated at the University of Glasgow in Scotland. Cardozo would later serve as Secretary of State of South Carolina from 1868 to 1872, and as Treasurer from 1872 to 1876.

Cardozo bluntly demanded that the federal government turn over to freed slaves land taken from wealthy Confederates:

General Sherman . . . gave lands to the freedmen; and if it were not for President Johnson, they would have them now. . . . I say every opportunity for helping the colored people should be seized upon.

DeLarge agreed:

I know one large landholder in Colleton District who had twenty-one freedmen working for him upon his plantation the entire year. He raised a good crop but the laborers have not succeeded in getting any wages for their labor. They are now roaming to Charleston and back, trying to get money for their services. We propose to give them lands, and to place them in a position by which they will be enabled to sustain themselves.

In Louisiana, where there was a considerable population of wealthy free blacks, conventions were held as early as November 1863. Delegates appealed to the governor, asking for the right to vote. They reminded him that, as "peaceable citizens," they had paid taxes on "assessments of more than $9 million"! Was it any wonder that Lincoln had thought of this group, when requesting an "experiment" in black people being given the right to vote?

The History of Black Voting Rights

At one time, when free black people had made up just a tiny portion of the population in the southern states, they had actually had the right to vote. Voting was determined by the ownership of land, whether a person was black or white. But as soon as the numbers of free blacks grew, white men felt threatened. So, out went the vote. (Remember, at that time women could not vote, whether black or white.)

In South Carolina, in 1716, free black people, as well as Jews, were denied the vote. In Virginia, as early as 1723, free African-Americans, along with Indians, were denied the vote. In Georgia, originally, anyone who owned 50 acres of land could vote. But by 1761, that right went exclusively to whites. In Kentucky, free black men voted up until 1799 and in Tennessee, up until 1796.

"I say every opportunity for helping the colored people should be seized upon."
—Francis L. Cardozo

143

disenfranchise:
to exclude from voting privileges.

By 1812 Louisiana had **disenfranchised** black voters. Next came Alabama in 1819, Missouri in 1821, Arkansas in 1836, and Texas and Florida as late as 1845.

In the North, free black men could vote fairly consistently after 1784. But in the early 1800s, white workers grew concerned that free blacks would take away their jobs. As a result, they pushed for restrictions on black votings rights. Blacks were disenfranchised in New Jersey in 1807, got the vote back in 1820, and lost it again in 1847. In New York, after being disenfranchised, blacks with property worth at least $250 could vote in 1821. (Whites did not have a property qualification in New York.) Maine, New Hampshire, and Vermont also had property qualifications for black men. Connecticut disenfranchised black voters in 1814. Even Pennsylvania refused black men the vote after 1838.

In the West, when new states were admitted to the Union free black people could no longer vote there. This was true of Indiana, Illinois, Iowa, Kansas, Michigan, Minnesota, and Ohio from 1803 to 1861.

So, even after the Civil War the idea of granting blacks the right to vote was taboo to most white politicians. Couple that with the fact that, by 1866, President Johnson was pardoning former Confederate officers at the rate of 100 per day, and it is clear that liberalism toward African-Americans was hardly the byword of the day.

Reformers in Congress Help

The reformers in Congress knew their work was cut out for them. Their first move was to get the vote for black people in the District of Columbia. Of greater importance for the future was their refusal to seat the former Confederate officials in Congress (page 140). Instead, they voted to set up a Joint Committee on Reconstruction. The Committee would investigate conditions in the South. It would then decide whether the southern states were eligible to send representatives to Congress.

Fourteenth Amendment:
amendment to the Constitution
declaring all native-born persons
to be citizens.

The Fourteenth Amendment

Meanwhile, Congress returned to the question of black voting rights when it proposed the **Fourteenth Amendment** to the Constitution. This amendment declared that all persons born in the United States were citizens and had the rights of citizens. All citizens were to be granted "equal protection of the laws."

The Fourteenth Amendment had a greater impact than the Civil Rights Act of 1866, which Congress had passed over President Johnson's veto. It too had declared all persons born in the United States to be citizens. But now, with the Fourteenth Amendment, that right would be guaranteed by the Constitution.

The amendment stopped just short of insisting on voting rights for blacks. Such an idea was still too radical for most whites. Nevertheless, it aroused angry protests. President Johnson denounced it, campaigning against it in the 1866 congressional elections. The voters, however, rejected Johnson's arguments. They returned a heavy Republican majority to Congress.

The Reconstruction Act of 1867

Except for Tennessee, all the southern states had voted to reject the Fourteenth Amendment. In response, Congress passed the tough Reconstruction Act of 1867. It passed this bill in the face of the South's continued insolence and arrogance, and over the protests of President Johnson, who had by then publicly walked away from any civil rights guarantees for African-American people.

The law divided the former Confederacy, except for Tennessee, into five military districts. It disenfranchised most of the prewar planter class. Finally, it explained the steps by which states could rejoin the Union. States would have to (1) hold elections in which everyone, black and white alike, could vote for representatives to draw up new state constitutions; (2) approve those constitutions; and (3) ratify the Fourteenth Amendment.

Black citizens in the North and South applauded the bill. Black conventions in 1865 and 1866 had appealed to the federal government for just such help.

The law, meanwhile, had another effect on national politics. It led to further disagreements between Congress and President Johnson. Those differences grew so great that in 1868 Congress tried to remove the President from office.

The Senate's vote was just one short of the required number. A weakened Johnson remained in office.

"Forty Acres and a Mule"

Some members of Congress, known as Radical Republicans and led by Thaddeus Stevens, raised another issue at this time. They sought to have the large southern plantations, taken over by Union forces at the end of the war, distributed to black families in forty-acre segments. The measure was quite fair, they argued. The plantation owners had lost their rights to the vast acreage during the war. Besides, no one was talking about including the thousands of small southern plots owned and worked by poor whites.

"Forty acres and a mule" became the slogan of hope on the lips of the black South. But Stevens was never able to muster enough support to get this legislation enacted. Many northern representatives stopped short of allowing black men to take over lands previously occupied by whites.

"Forty acres and a mule."
—Reconstruction slogan

The Fifteenth Amendment

Fifteenth Amendment:
amendment to the Constitution
declaring that the right to vote
should not be denied on the
basis of race.

As the Reconstruction years passed, Congress proposed one more amendment to the Constitution to protect the rights of African-Americans. The **Fifteenth Amendment** declared that the right to vote could not be denied "on account of race, color, or previous condition of servitude." Black men, in brief, were guaranteed the right to vote. Approval of the Fifteenth Amendment became another condition that southern states had to meet to rejoin the Union.

It had taken five long years after the Civil War's end to get even these basic freedoms on the books for black people. Was the effort worth it? It was. These amendments gave Americans of African descent, after 200 years of slavery, the same legal rights as their white counterparts.

SECTION ONE REVIEW

1. VOCABULARY Write a sentence for each of the following words: Reconstruction, amnesty, Thirteenth Amendment, black codes, disenfranchise, Fourteenth Amendment, Fifteenth Amendment.

2. HISTORY What were the four parts of Lincoln's plan to restore the South to the Union?

3. HISTORY Why did Congress pass the Reconstruction Act of 1867?

4. CONSTITUTIONAL HERITAGE Why was ratification of the Thirteenth, Fourteenth, and Fifteenth Amendments to the Constitution important?

5. CRITICAL THINKING How do you think African-Americans would have fared if Congress had passed Thaddeus Stevens' proposed "forty acres and a mule" plan?

THE EMERGENCE OF BLACK POLITICAL LEADERS

SECTION TWO

MAIN IDEA During the Reconstruction period, African-Americans won election to high political offices.

OBJECTIVES As you read, look for answers to the following questions:
1. How did the new southern constitutions affect the lives of African-Americans?
2. Who were the first black senators? Who were some of the first black congressmen?

At the same time that laws and amendments were being enacted at the federal level, legislators across the South were working to complete the restructuring of state governments loyal to the United States. For the first time, delegations to these state conventions would include black representatives. And in spite of the vengeance of many white southerners, there would be African-Americans in *every* southern constitutional convention. In fact, in South Carolina, they formed the majority!

147

Southern Constitutional Conventions—Righting Old Wrongs

Under the new state constitutions, five major areas were improved in the lives of African-Americans.

(1) On the state level, the right for all men to vote was guaranteed.

(2) Free public schools were established.

(3) Everyone was given the right of free travel, without the "passes" that black people had been required to carry during slavery days.

(4) All people were accorded the right to a fair trial and other legal privileges.

(5) The hated black codes were formally repealed or rewritten.

Within three years, by 1870, Congress had approved the new state constitutions. In addition, the Fourteenth and Fifteenth Amendments to the Constitution were ratified. The South was re-admitted into the Union.

The new constitutions were so equitable that numerous black men were able to make their way into political office. In all, more than 600 African-Americans served in state legislatures during Reconstruction. Others served in even higher offices. These officeholders served with distinction. As one prominent white congressman, James G. Blaine, observed:

> The colored men who took their seats in both Senate and House did not appear ignorant or helpless. They were as a rule studious, earnest, ambitious men, whose public conduct ... would be honorable to any race.

Let us look at some of these outstanding Americans.

Highlighting a Hero—Hiram Revels

Hiram Revels has the honor of being the first African-American to serve as a U.S. senator. Ironically, Revels occupied the very seat once held by Confederate President Jefferson Davis.

Revels took office on February 25, 1870. This is even

148

more amazing when you consider that Mississippi sent Revels to Washington *before* the Fifteenth Amendment was adopted, giving black people the right to vote. (This amendment was not ratified until March 30, 1870.)

Revels was a very enterprising young man who had lived in several states before settling in Mississippi. Born in North Carolina in 1822, he received his early education in Indiana and later went to Knox College in Illinois. After college, he became a minister in the African Methodist Episcopal Church, traveling widely from the Northwest Territory into Kentucky and Missouri. Finally, Revels became a school principal as well as a pastor in Baltimore, Maryland.

Revels remained in Maryland for most of the Civil War. He even became a recruiter for two black regiments in that state. After a brief stint in St. Louis, where he established a school and recruited more black soldiers, he went on to Vicksburg, Mississippi, to become chaplain of a black regiment.

By war's end, Revels had done such a good job that the Union military command, which took over the Mississippi state legislature, appointed him to local office. From there, Revels' brilliance and courage on tough issues won him the support of his white political colleagues, so that by 1870 he was the first black senator in America.

Revels served only one year in the U.S. Senate, from 1870 to 1871, completing an unfilled term of office. Later, he became president of Alcorn University in Mississippi. Revels was a respected civic and religious leader in the African-American community until he died in Holly Springs, Mississippi, in 1901.

Black voters

Highlighting a Hero—Blanche Bruce

Blanche Bruce was the only other black man elected to the U.S. Senate in the 1800s—no small feat for someone born a slave. Bruce was born into bondage in Farmville, Virginia, in 1841. Young Bruce was finally able to complete a formal education at Oberlin College in Ohio.

Not even 30, the industrious Bruce decided to try his luck in Mississippi in 1868, after the Civil War. He went there and was clever enough to become a successful planter.

149

Then, eager to conquer yet another world, Bruce set his sights on politics. He held a succession of positions, starting with sergeant-at-arms of the Mississippi Senate. He next became assessor of taxes in Bolivar County, and then sheriff. After that, he was named a member of the Board of Levee Commissioners of the Mississippi River.

The height of Bruce's political career came in 1874, when he was chosen to become a senator from Mississippi. In office, Bruce not only championed African-Americans' rights, but those of such other mistreated people as American Indians and Asian-Americans. A talented businessman, he also proposed legislation to enhance trade along the Mississippi River. In February 1879, Bruce even briefly presided over the U.S. Senate.

Unfortunately, Bruce was too forthright. His strong stands, along with his courageous attacks on election frauds rampant in the South, meant that, with racial prejudice still strong, he would not get elected to another term. Bruce served in the U.S. Senate from 1875 to 1881.

Bruce's business skill, however, later earned him the position of Register of the U.S. Treasury Department. Imagine it. A man who came from a race of people that some argued was "inferior" was now signing his name to the country's currency. Bruce served as Register of the Treasury under two Presidents—Garfield and McKinley.

Highlighting a Hero—Robert Brown Elliott

Born in Boston in 1842 to West Indian parents, Robert Brown Elliott attended school in Jamaica and later in London. Upon his return to America, Elliott took a job as editor of the *Charleston Leader*. In 1868, when he was only 26, he was elected to the South Carolina state legislature. Later he served two terms in Congress.

As a congressman, Elliott courageously spoke out against giving amnesty to former Confederates. In one debate he boldly refuted Alexander H. Stephens, former Vice President of the Confederacy, who opposed political rights for blacks:

Let him put away entirely the false and fatal theories which have so greatly marred [his] record. Let him accept, in its fullness and beneficence, the great doctrine that American citizenship carries with it every civil and political right which manhood can confer.

Elliott served in Congress from 1871 to 1875. After his successful tenure in office, he moved to New Orleans where he practiced law until he died in 1884.

"American citizenship carries with it every civil and political rights which manhood can confer."
—Robert Brown Elliott

Highlighting a Hero—Jefferson Long

Jefferson Long was born a slave near Knoxville, Georgia, in 1836. An industrious young man, Long educated himself and saved enough money to open his own tailor shop.

During Reconstruction, Long's fellow Republicans soon recognized his talents, and he was elected to Congress, where he served from 1869 to 1871. Outspoken, Long courageously campaigned for the Fifteenth Amendment as well as for anti-lynch laws.

Even after he went back to his successful tailor shop in 1871, Long stayed active in politics as a delegate to two Republican Conventions in 1874 and 1880. He died in 1900.

Highlighting a Hero—Joseph Rainey

Joseph Rainey was born in 1832 in Georgetown, South Carolina. As a slave, he was made to work on harbor fortifications during the Civil War. Ingeniously, Rainey used the opportunity to escape to the West Indies, where he stayed almost until war's end.

After the war, he was elected to the South Carolina state congress, the state senate, and then the U.S. Congress. He served in Congress from 1871 until 1879.

A staunch advocate of rights for African-Americans, Rainey consistently stood up and spoke out for what he believed. Ten times he tried to get legislation passed to guarantee full civil rights for black people. Rainey even argued for civil rights for the Chinese who had been brought over to work in California and on the railroads. His reputation as a human rights advocate was such that he was the first black man to preside over the House of Representatives

151

during a noted public debate on the plight of the American Indian.

Arguing in 1871 for civil rights for African-Americans in South Carolina (where they were in the majority), Rainey proved he was also a skillful debater:

> I ask this House, I ask the country, I ask white men, I ask Democrats, I ask Republicans whether the Negroes have presumed to take improper advantage of the majority they hold in that State by disregarding the interest of the minority? They have not. Our convention which met in 1868, and in which the Negroes were in a large majority... adopted a liberal constitution, securing alike equal rights to all citizens, white and black, male and female, as far as possible. Mark you, we did not discriminate, although we had a majority.

"Mark you, we did not discriminate, although we had a majority."
—Joseph Rainey

An accomplished businessman, Rainey also fought for the creation of a steamship line between the United States and Haiti. After he left Congress, he became a U.S. Treasury agent, and then went into banking and the stock market.

Highlighting a Hero—Benjamin Turner

Benjamin Turner was born a slave in 1825 in Halifax, North Carolina. As a young boy, he was taken to Alabama where he was freed and educated. An enterprising young man, he soon became a tax collector and councilman in Salem, Alabama. He went on to become a well-to-do livery stable owner.

In September 1870, the Alabama Republicans sent Turner to Congress, where he remained from 1871 to 1873. After a party split in 1872, Turner retired from politics and continued his work in business. He died in 1894.

Highlighting a Hero—Josiah Walls

Josiah Walls was elected to Congress from Florida in 1873, serving until 1877. In office, Walls challenged many of his state's policies. For instance, he courageously denounced the discrimination in aid for education, noting the high percentage that went to whites. Walls even went so far as to call for national aid for education.

Other Black Congressmen

All in all, between 1869 and 1877, fourteen black southerners served in the House of Representatives. Besides those mentioned above, the following eight were in Congress for at least one term: Richard H. Cain, Alonzo J. Ransier, and Robert Smalls from South Carolina; Jere Haralson and James T. Rapier from Alabama; John A. Hyman, from North Carolina; John R. Lynch, from Mississippi; and Charles E. Nash, from Louisiana.

Black Governors/Lieutenant Governors

During Reconstruction, three black men served as lieutenant governor of Louisiana, and one of them even served a month and a half as governor of the state.

Oscar J. Dunn managed the incredible feat of rising from slavery to become lieutenant governor of Louisiana. An escaped slave, he had managed to educate himself before obtaining his freedom. Dunn led the fight against corruption by greedy Reconstruction politicians and gained the title of "incorruptible" among his political peers. In spite of heavy pressure against him, Dunn bravely signed the 1868 Louisiana constitution which guaranteed civil rights to whites and blacks alike.

Dunn was such an upstanding politician that, when he died suddenly in 1871 after having served as lieutenant governor since 1868, the Republicans put another black man in the position, P.B.S. Pinchback.

Pinchback was extraordinary himself, in that, to all appearances, he was white. But he openly declared himself black, even though this was inconvenient, to say the least. Born in Georgia, he was educated in Cincinnati, and served as a captain in the Union army before settling in Louisiana after the war.

Pinchback's strong moral character was amply demonstrated when he argued long and hard for equal accommodations for black people during the 1868 debates on a Louisiana civil rights bill. So well-respected was Pinchback that when the corrupt governor, Henry Clay Warmoth, was removed from office in December 1872, Pinchback served as governor for 43 days. He was succeeded by another black lieutenant governor, C. C. Antoine, who served from 1872 to 1876.

Meanwhile, Alonzo J. Ransier became lieutenant governor of South Carolina in 1870. He had been born free and, after helping draft that state's new constitution, was elected to the state senate, where he presided. Richard H. Gleaves was lieutenant governor from 1872 to 1876. Born in Pennsylvania, Gleaves was a former probate judge.

Northern Black Politicians

African-Americans also made their mark in political races in the North. Nowhere was the progress greater than in Massachusetts. That state's voters were the first in the nation to elect black legislators to office.

The first was Edwin G. Walker, son of the famous abolitionist David Walker. Just one generation after his father had appealed to black men to fight for their rights, Edwin G. Walker was elected to the Massachusetts House of Representatives in 1866. Along with Walker, voters sent Charles Mitchell to the House. Mitchell was a former typesetter for the abolitionist newspaper *The Liberator* and, later, a soldier in the Civil War. Like Walker, Mitchell served one term in office. In 1869, Mitchell was made a customs inspector in Boston.

In 1868 and 1872, John J. Smith became a state legislator; so did black attorney George L. Ruffin in 1870. In 1873, Lewis Hayden was elected to the state assembly, as was Joshua B. Smith, a prominent caterer.

Along with electoral gains, other blacks worked for civil rights in Massachusetts. William H. Lewis and Butler R. Wilson argued the case for more civil rights for African-Americans in Massachusetts. Lewis was a Harvard Law School student and Wilson a practicing attorney. Thanks to their efforts, the Massachusetts Civil Rights Act of 1885 gave Massachusetts blacks nearly equal rights with whites of the state.

SECTION TWO REVIEW 〰〰〰〰〰〰〰〰〰〰〰〰

1. CONSTITUTIONAL HERITAGE How did the new state constitutions in the South improve conditions for African-Americans?

2. POLITICS Who was the first African-American elected to the Senate?

3. BIOGRAPHY How did Blanche Bruce make history after he left the Senate?

4. CRITICAL THINKING Why do you think black officeholders were also concerned about the rights of Asian-Americans and American Indians?

5. CRITICAL THINKING What obstacles did blacks have to overcome to win election to high political office during Reconstruction?

SOCIAL REFORMS

SECTION THREE

VOCABULARY Freedmen's Bureau sharecropper

MAIN IDEA Reconstruction brought the former slaves great hopes for advancement, and some of those hopes appeared to be realized.

OBJECTIVES As you read, look for answers to the following questions:
1. What effect did relief organizations have on life in the South?
2. What organizations did African-Americans form to help themselves during Reconstruction?

With emancipation, African-Americans went to work to improve their lives. In this they were helped by various organizations. They also helped themselves.

The Freedmen's Bureau

The **Freedmen's Bureau** was this country's first large-scale relief organization. Although its name refers to freed slaves,

Freedmen's Bureau: federal agency set up to help poor southerners and to manage abandoned or confiscated southern land.

155

the organization actually helped both southern whites and blacks get on their feet after the Civil War.

Congress set up the Freedmen's Bureau just before Lincoln's death in March 1865. The Bureau's goal was to deal with the needs of black refugees during the war. Soon thereafter it was strengthened, over the veto of President Johnson to supply food, clothing, fuel, and hospital care to all needy southerners.

Freedmen's Bureau officials went to each southern state to set up branches of this emergency relief organization, in much the same way the government today provides disaster relief in times of fire or flood. They lost no time in doing what they could to stave off the hunger and destitution suffered by millions of ex-slaves who faced uncertain futures. By 1867, they had set up 46 hospitals, spending over $2 million to treat more than 450,000 people. (Actually, by the time the Freedmen's Bureau was disbanded in 1870, it had helped many more whites than blacks. One Bureau official cited a statistic as high as 64 whites to each black person fed in some southern border states.)

During this time, a great controversy arose over who could settle on abandoned or confiscated properties throughout the South. Many African-Americans wanted to start independent new lives, and had, at one point, been led to believe that the U.S. government would allocate "40 acres and a mule" to each family (page 146).

But, unfortunately, because of all the wrangling and political infighting in the nation's capital, this never came to pass. The best the Freedmen's Bureau could do was to distribute a few parcels of land.

The Bureau did help, however, in providing funds for relocating about 30,000 people to better surroundings. And Bureau officials also fought diligently to get white southerners to hire their former slaves at fair wages, under fair conditions. This, however, proved to be an uphill battle indeed.

The Rise of Sharecropping

Throughout the South, a new system of landholding grew. Wealthy southerners leased out small parcels of land to tenant farmers. Some tenants paid a wage or a small percentage of the profit from the crops. But many were poor whites or blacks who could furnish nothing but their labor. They became **sharecroppers**. The landlord provided them with food, seed, tools, and lodging. In return, the sharecroppers gave the landowner a share of the crops raised on their land. Many sharecroppers found themselves in debt to the landowners, especially when harvests were bad. When that happened they were not free to leave their land. Their fate was not that different from that of slaves.

sharecropper:
a farmer who works a plot of land in return for part of the crop.

The Freedmen's Banks

The Freedmen's Bureau also went to work in other areas. It set up bank branches throughout the South, where thrifty black workers saved diligently for years. In 1873, the Charleston branch had $350,000 deposited by 5,500 people, with accounts ranging from $.05 to $1,000.

Tragically, a scandal developed when white speculators were allowed to borrow the black depositors' funds, most of which they could not pay back. The Charleston branch failed in 1874, owing 5,296 depositors $253,168. It was a crushing blow to the efforts of black farmers and workers to become self-sufficient.

Disillusioned southerners gave names to the unscrupulous profiteers who took advantage of the confusion of Reconstruction to make money. They called white southerners who cooperated with the Reconstruction governments "scalawags," which originally meant "undersized, worthless animals." White northerners who moved south to help out—and sometimes to profit—were dubbed "carpetbaggers" because the suitcases they carried were made from carpet-like materials.

Black Education

During its five years in action, the Freedmen's Bureau did manage to achieve a good deal of success in education. It helped create about 4,200 free schools for African-American people. It employed more than 9,300 teachers, both black and white, and educated some 250,000 students.

In North Carolina, J. W. Alvord of the Freedmen's

Bureau, was impressed when he checked on one of the newly created rural schools. There he saw "a child six years old, her mother, grandmother, and great-grandmother, the latter over 75 years of age...[learning] their alphabet together."

Most of the major black institutions of higher learning were founded during this time. Howard University in Washington, D.C., was incorporated on March 2, 1867. It was named after General Oliver Otis Howard, commissioner of the Freedmen's Bureau. Congress set up this college in the District of Columbia for African-Americans seeking a higher education.

Fisk University in Nashville, Tennessee, was also incorporated in 1867. It was named in honor of General Clinton B. Fisk, assistant commissioner of the Freedmen's Bureau. Fisk became noted for its world-famous chorale, the Jubilee Singers, whose travels earned enough money for the school to build a large hall on the campus.

Other black institutions of higher learning included Atlanta University, Tougaloo College, Hampton College, Shaw College, Storer University, Morehouse College, Biddle College, and the Tuskegee Institute.

Black Self-Help

Much of the money for black education and improvement in the South came from African-Americans themselves. Former slaves in many areas built their own homes and schools after war's end.

In Hampton, Virginia, for example, over 800 freedmen organized themselves in 1866 to take over 600 acres of abandoned plantation lands. J. T. Trowbridge, a northerner, marveled at how well the village was doing:

> There was an air of neatness and comfort...which surprised me....A sash-factory and blacksmith's shop, shoemaker's shops and stores, enlivened the streets. The business of the place was carried on chiefly by freedmen, many of whom were becoming wealthy, and paying heavy taxes to the government.
>
> I found no idleness anywhere. Happiness and industry were the universal rule.

General Rufus Saxton was head of the U.S. Department of the South during Reconstruction. He personally went before Congress and the President to explain how, in many areas of the South, black people had moved swiftly to make productive use of lands abandoned by the devastated planters:

> The faith of the government has been pledged to these freedmen to maintain them in the possession of their homes, and to break its promise in the hours of its triumph is not becoming to a just government.... On some of the islands, the freedmen have established civil governments with constitutions and laws, with all the different departments for schools, churches, building roads, and other improvements.

An All-Black Town Prospers

In Mississippi, not far from Vicksburg, an ex-slave named Isaiah Montgomery devoted every ounce of his ingenuity, skill, and training to wrest an entire black town from the forest and swamp of Bolivar County.

In 1865, when times were hard in Mississippi, Montgomery and his relatives had leased the plantation lands on which they had worked all their lives. (Those lands had originally belonged to Jefferson Davis's brother, Joseph.) By the end of 1867, the Montgomerys had worked so hard that they were able to purchase the property. Several years later they were the third largest cotton producers in the entire state.

But that first dream was to come to a sad end when Joseph Davis's heirs demanded the prosperous plantation back. With the knowledge of violence against blacks fresh in his mind, Isaiah Montgomery signed over his property, worth at least $14,000, for a mere $3,500.

The next day, the Mississippi *Register* proclaimed, "A White Man in a White Man's Place. A Black Man in a Black Man's Place. Each According to the Eternal Fitness of Things."

Fortunately, Montgomery had enormous determination. He took his money and part-ownership in a sawmill,

"A White Man in a White Man's Place. A Black Man in a Black Man's Place. Each According to the Eternal Fitness of Things."
—Racist Reconstruction slogan

and bought swampland in Bolivar County, Mississippi. At the time, this was land no one wanted.

From 1886 to 1889, Montgomery and twenty other families dynamited and sawed, clearing the first 80 acres for the hearty little colony they named Mound Bayou.

Together, they bravely battled everything from swamp fever to bears, wolves, and panthers. By 1888, their village had erected a small train depot, a "general mercantile emporium," a meeting hall, and even a funeral parlor. Isaiah Montgomery, the town patriarch, built a grand, gabled cottage of his own, to underscore his position in the tiny community.

Montgomery was elected mayor. By 1893 there were 4,000 black residents in Mound Bayou, and the first 80 acres had spread to over 20,000. (The town would eventually grow to more than 30,000 acres.) Isaiah Montgomery was known as "the only Negro in the United States who could put his hands on $50,000 'cash money' in an hour's notice."

Montgomery's major shortcoming was that he remembered, perhaps only too well, his frustration at having to hand over his plantation to the Davises. So, he avoided taking an outspoken stand in politics. In fact, at the Mississippi constitutional convention, Montgomery went so far as to oppose voting rights for blacks!

Montgomery's caution was, however, understandable. As you have read, thousands of acres of land were being returned to the very white planters who, just a few years before, had been Confederate leaders—sworn enemies of the American government. But they were white, and even if they had committed treason, they were, in the eyes of President Johnson and some members of Congress, more worthy of consideration than African-American people who had fought for and sided with the Union.

Notable Individuals

In spite of white resistance, many African-Americans were able to build prosperous careers and businesses. Samuel Lowery was one.

Samuel Lowery was born on December 9, 1832, in Nashville, Tennessee. His industrious and energetic father, Peter, married a free woman, Ruth Mitchell. The couple worked so hard that they were able to save $1,000 to buy the husband's freedom. They went on to buy freedom for his mother, three brothers, two sisters, and a nephew. In time, Lowery became the first black minister of an established church in Nashville, Tennessee.

Samuel, the Lowery's only son, entered Franklin College when he was only twelve. He did very well, in spite of the prevailing climate of racial prejudice.

After the Civil War, Samuel Lowery was licensed to practice law, and by 1875 he had moved to Huntsville, Alabama, where he opened a school. Ever innovative, Lowery introduced silkworms to the area. His daughters, Ruth and Anna, helped him develop a small silk industry, at the same time that they taught sewing, knitting, and needlework to local young women. Lowery himself went north to a number of scientific conventions, introducing specimens of the silk made at his school. The silk fabric was so well-made that it won prizes at international fairs.

Samuel Lowery's greatest distinction came in 1880. He went to Washington, D.C., where he was admitted to practice before the U.S. Supreme Court. He was the first African-American to attain this distinction.

In business and other areas, African-Americans did equally well in Louisiana. Dr. James Derham had a thriving medical practice of $3,000 a year. Joseph Abeillard was a prominent architect who planned many New Orleans buildings before the Civil War. Indeed, according to state records, black people in Louisiana owned $15 million worth property in 1860.

SECTION THREE REVIEW

1. **VOCABULARY** Write a sentence for each of the following terms: Freedmen's Bureau, sharecropper.

2. **ECONOMICS** How did the sharecropper system arise? Why did it prove disadvantageous to blacks?

3. **EDUCATION** What were some of the major black colleges and universities founded during Reconstruction?

4. **CRITICAL THINKING** Do you think President Johnson was right to return land to former Confederate plantation owners? Why or why not?

5. **CRITICAL THINKING** Do you think Isaiah Montgomery was wise to found an all-black town? Are there times, in other words, when the separation of the races is justified? Or can such separation never be justified? Explain your answer.

SECTION FOUR

THE WHITE RESPONSE

VOCABULARY Ku Klux Klan

MAIN IDEA The return to power of the Democratic Party in the South signaled the demise of Reconstruction. The Reconstruction Era formally came to an end in 1877.

OBJECTIVES As you read, look for answers to the following questions:
1. What was the reaction of many white southerners to Reconstruction?
2. Why did Reconstruction come to an end?

The progress of black people during Reconstruction was just too much for many white southerners. In response, they turned to violence to restore their system of control.

As early as 1866, white mobs killed 46 black people in Memphis, Tennessee, destroying 4 churches and 12 schools. In New Orleans, whites fired right into a black political rally—with the help of the police! They continued to gun down the black activists, even those who had run into a nearby building for shelter. All in all, the police killed 58 innocent people and wounded another 100. An investigation later confirmed the role of the mayor and police in the massacre, but they were not prosecuted.

The Ku Klux Klan

In 1868 the **Ku Klux Klan** was born. Former General Nathan B. Forest, who was known for having ordered the massacre

Ku Klux Klan:
a secret organization that grew in the South after the end of the Civil War to promote "white supremacy," often by terrorizing blacks.

of hundreds of black soldiers captured during the Civil War, founded the organization.

Started as a kind of social club, the Klan soon became a terrorist group. Its members pledged to destroy the Republican Party in the South. They also wanted white southerners once again to have complete control over their states' affairs, without federal intervention. In that way they could establish "white supremacy" at all costs.

The white-robed, gun-toting, horse-riding Klansmen slaughtered any people who stood up for their freedom, including black businessmen, ministers, and even some Jewish merchants. They lynched freedmen just because they could read and write! On many occasions, black students were roused in the middle of the night to go and protect their schools from attack by angry whites. In 1866, a white northern army officer wrote about threats to a black teacher and his school in Marianna, Florida:

Ku Klux Klan members

> The teacher...was confronted with four revolvers if he did not close the school. The freedmen promptly came to his aid, and the mob dispersed.
>
> [Later], the same mob threatened to destroy the [school]....Not fewer than 40 colored men armed to protect themselves.

By 1871 the reign of terror that swept the South could no longer be ignored. In that year Ulysses S. Grant, now President, asked Congress to pass tough laws against the Klan. It did so, and federal marshals arrested thousands of Klansmen. But other members went into hiding, and the Klan never was crushed. Even today, in many southern towns and cities, Ku Klux Klan groups march in efforts to intimidate blacks over civil rights issues.

Black Progress Undermined

Little by little, white southerners began to regain control of the South. Through the use of terror, they kept black and Republican voters away from the polls.

Other factors also brought an end to Reconstruction:

(1) As the years passed, more and more former Confederate leaders gained pardons. Again able to vote and hold office, they resumed their place in public affairs.

(2) Northerners, at the same time, were losing interest in the problems of the South. The deaths of leading reformers such as Thaddeus Stevens hurt too. New northern leaders in Congress seemed more interested in the rights of businessmen than in human rights. On the social scene, white southerners began passing laws that created separate facilities for blacks and whites wherever possible, such as on streetcars and in schools.

(3) Federal officials grew tired of enforcing the Fourteenth and Fifteenth Amendments and the major civil rights laws passed by Congress. For example, southern whites used unscrupulous methods to prevent black people from voting. In Mississippi in the late 1870s, whites actually hid voting booths from black voters! They also had strange voting hours—before 7:00 in the morning, or late at night. And in many areas, whites openly menaced blacks who tried to vote, by threatening to shoot them if they exercised their ballot privileges.

Throughout the South they did these things—and got away with them.

(4) The Democratic Party regained its national strength as scandals plagued the Republican administration of Ulysses S. Grant. In the South, the Democratic Party was seen as the party of "white supremacy."

The End of Reconstruction

As the southern states were readmitted to the Union, they threw blacks and white Republicans out of office. By 1876 Democrats had seized control of all but three ex-Confederate states.

The final blow came in 1877, when President Rutherford B. Hayes withdrew the last of the federal troops from the South. With this action, the heavy door of white control over black destiny began to swing shut again. The country as a whole seemed relieved to be done with the "Negro problem" for a while, even if it meant leaving African-Americans at the mercy of their former white slavers. Fortunately, even though the times got harder, black determination grew as well, with people looking hopefully to a new century for progress.

SECTION FOUR REVIEW ~~~~~~~~~~~~~~~~~~~~~~~~~~~~~~

1. VOCABULARY Write a sentence using the following term: Ku Klux Klan.

2. HISTORY What was the aim of the Ku Klux Klan?

3. POLITICS Which political party sought to establish "white supremacy" in the South?

4. HISTORY What event marked the formal end of Reconstruction?

5. CRITICAL THINKING Put yourself in the shoes of white southerners after the Civil War. Why do you think they felt such opposition to Reconstruction?

CHAPTER SIX REVIEW

VOCABULARY

Write the numbered sentences on a separate sheet of paper. In each sentence fill in the blank with one of these terms: *amnesty*, *Freedmen's Bureau*, *Ku Klux Klan*, *sharecroppers*, *Thirteenth Amendment*.

1. The _____ abolished slavery.

2. President Johnson's granting of _____ to former Confederate leaders angered Congress.

3. Many poor white and black southern farmers became _____, finding themselves trapped in poverty.

4. The _____, the most notorious of the white terrorist organizations, sought to keep African-Americans away from the polls.

5. Relief was provided to the South after the Civil War by the _____.

REVIEWING THE FACTS

1. What plans did President Lincoln have for restoring the southern states to the Union? What were his views on colonization?

2. What constitutional amendments guaranteed rights to African-Americans?

3. Why did Congress step in and take a firm hand in establishing Reconstruction policy?

4. How did the new southern constitutions affect the lives of African-Americans?

5. Who were the first black senators? Who were some of the first black congressmen?

6. What effect did relief organizations have on life in the South?

7. What organizations did African-Americans form to help themselves during Reconstruction?

8. What was the reaction of many white southerners to Reconstruction?

9. Why did Reconstruction come to an end?

CRITICAL THINKING

1. DRAWING CONCLUSIONS In 1862 Charlotte Forten taught her pupils about Toussaint L'Ouverture? What was her reason for

doing this? Do you think she made a good choice? Explain your answer.

2. **INFERRING** What word did Andrew Johnson use to describe his Reconstruction policy? What does that choice of word tell you about his approach to Reconstruction?

3. **MAKING A JUDGMENT** Why do you think Jefferson Davis so deeply regretted the assassination of President Lincoln?

4. **ANALYZING A QUOTATION** A white Reconstruction official in Tennessee reported, "The colored people are far more zealous in the cause of education than the whites. They will starve themselves, and go without clothes, in order to send their children to school." Why do you think education was so important to the freedmen?

UNDERSTANDING PREJUDICE

1. Abraham Lincoln appeared to have had a sincere belief in colonization. How did that view reflect the prejudices of the day?

2. The high point of a meeting between Andrew Johnson and a group of black leaders was when the President agreed to shake his visitors' hands. Why would this have been considered a major step in 1866? What does it tell you about the way most white people viewed blacks?

3. For many years, textbooks portrayed Reconstruction as a dismal failure, with African-Americans described as the ignorant pawns of unscrupulous carpetbaggers and scalawags. Why do you think Reconstruction was once viewed in such a way?

THE SEPARATION OF THE RACES

(1877–1910)

During Reconstruction, the central issue for African-Americans had been how to legitimize their place in American society. For the most part they had done this through political means. With the support of the federal government, black people had helped rewrite state constitutions. In addition, they took part in debates in state and federal legislatures on civil rights. Of most importance was the fact that three constitutional amendments now guaranteed their rights. All these efforts were designed to put African-Americans on a par with their white counterparts—formally and legally.

Reconstruction was a tough test of American democracy. In many ways it was a glorious experiment, with the nation trying to live up to its highest ideals. At the same time, it was a miserable failure. Instead of securing the African-Americans' place in society, the new laws and amendments ended up provoking violent antiblack sentiment among whites.

And so, with a new century fast approaching, many whites began working more frantically than ever to turn the clock back. There *had* to be a way, they argued desperately—in spite of the proven patriotism of black Americans, in spite of the proven capabilities in education and industry of black Americans, in spite of the very laws on which this country was based—to make African-Americans go back in time.

Logic could not do it. So, southern white America turned to violence—sheer, unbridled violence. They worked to make sure, after 1877, that black Americans were denied the basic right, and liberties of a free people and forced to live under a harsh system of segregation. By 1900, most of the gains made during Reconstruction had been lost and the races were separated.

The end of Reconstruction in 1877 dashed the hopes of African-Americans. Thousands fled the South and headed to Kansas and Nebraska to start new lives.

AFRICAN-AMERICANS LOSE GROUND

SECTION ONE

VOCABULARY poll tax integration segregation Jim Crow
Plessy v. Ferguson

MAIN IDEA By 1900 many of the gains made by African-Americans during Reconstruction had been taken away.

OBJECTIVES As you read, answer the following questions:
1. How did southern states prevent blacks from voting?
2. What name was given to the laws that were passed to separate the races?

169

3. What part did the Supreme Court play in the national debate over race relations?

In the mid-1800s, most southerners lynched—hanged without a trial—were white. Most had committed some kind of economic crime, like horse or cattle theft. But after Reconstruction, black lynchings became common. Just before the turn of the century, it was grimly estimated that one African-American was lynched every other day. Why were so many blacks murdered? To prevent them from exercising their rights as American citizens.

Barriers to Voting

With the end of Reconstruction, white legislators enacted new black codes, including unfair voting laws, to confuse and intimidate black people. In 1900 in North Carolina, for instance, whites amended the Reconstruction constitution to include a "grandfather clause." It stated that if a person's grandfather had not been a voter, then that person could not vote either. Well, how many ex-slaves had grandfathers who had been able to vote? Only a handful of freemen could qualify on that score.

Then, white legislators across the South added literacy tests. These tests were unfairly administered, with illiterate whites managing to pass them. In addition, to further discourage poor blacks from voting, states charged a fee to vote called a **poll tax**.

poll tax:
a fee paid by a person in order to vote.

All this meant that within a few decades after the Civil War, many African-Americans were right back where they started—unable to vote. The figures were dramatic. In 1900 there were 181,471 black voters in Alabama. When the state changed its constitution the next year, the number of registered blacks fell to just 3,000. In Louisiana black voter registration fell from 130,334 in 1896 to only 1,342 after its constitution was changed in 1904. Such declines were typical of the entire South. As a result, black public officials found it impossible to win elections.

Where was the federal government in all this? As you have read, Congress and most white Americans had grown tired of the South and its problems. They refused to come down hard on the southern fanatics. Was the highest law of the land indeed supreme? Apparently, only when it was not inconvenient.

Different Approaches

What were African-Americans to do? Debates raged in the black community. Most people favored **integration**. To "integrate" means to bring all the parts of something together to make it whole. This policy sought to place blacks on an equal basis with whites and to allow all people to mingle and develop freely together.

Some blacks—and most whites—opposed integration. They called for **segregation**, the development of the races apart from each other.

As the new century dawned, it was obvious to everyone, blacks and whites alike, that neither concept could work purely on its own. On the one hand, there were many barriers to integration. On the other hand, to keep the American economy going, contact between the races was necessary. A big problem was the notion held by many whites that they needed to be in a superior position, whether or not they deserved it.

integration:
the mixing of the races.

segregation:
the separation of the races.

The Rise of Jim Crow

The need of whites to feel superior to black people and to interact with them as little as possible gave rise to a practice of discrimination that was dubbed **Jim Crow**. Whites began to pass laws that created separate facilities for black people. Blacks were forced to ride on separate railway cars, eat in separate restaurants, attend segregated schools, and live in separate neighborhoods.

The name "Jim Crow" came from a song originally sung by black children at play. After a white entertainer named Thomas Rice popularized the song, however, it became an anthem that made fun of black people. Rice made the words famous all over the world:

Jim Crow:
referring to laws introduced in the South following Reconstruction that segregated schools, railway cars, and all public facilities.

Come listen all you galls and boys,
I's jist from Tuckyhoe
I'm going to sing a little song,
My name's Jim Crow.

171

Weel about and turn about and do jis so,
Eb'ry time I weel about I just Jim Crow.

In the period from 1890 to 1910 Jim Crow laws spread across the South. In 1900 Georgia formally instituted "Jim Crow seats" on its city streetcars. These were certain cars, or sections of cars, reserved only for black people where the service was inferior to that received by whites. In 1901 North Carolina and Virginia adopted the same practice, as did Louisiana in 1902. In 1903 Arkansas, South Carolina, and Tennessee followed suit. Mississippi and Maryland passed such laws in 1904, and Florida in 1905.

Not only were streetcars segregated. The laws required blacks to confine themselves to separate hospitals, schools, rest rooms and drinking fountains—and even separate cemeteries.

Plessy v. Ferguson

Blacks who hoped for federal protection from Jim Crow laws received no help from the Supreme Court. In 1890 liberal white and black attorneys had protested a Louisiana law that prohibited blacks and whites from riding in the same railroad car. One brave black man, Homer Plessy, challenged that law. He marched into a white car and sat down, refusing to move. He was arrested. Plessy's attorneys argued that forcing a black person into a separate car branded him or her as inferior. The state of Louisiana differed, claiming that separate facilities did not demean blacks, as long as they were "equal."

Plessy v. Ferguson:
landmark Supreme Court case in 1896 that legalized segregation.

In the landmark case **Plessy v. Ferguson**, the Supreme Court sided with Louisiana. It agreed that segregation was lawful as long as blacks and whites had equal access to equal facilities. This became known as the "separate but equal" doctrine.

The only justice who disagreed with the *Plessy v. Ferguson* decision was John Marshall Harlan. A former Kentucky slaveowner, Harlan had fought in the Civil War on the Union side. He argued that the U.S. Constitution should be "colorblind":

Our Constitution is colorblind, and neither knows nor tolerates classes among citizens. . . . The thin disguise of 'equal' accommodations...will not mislead anyone.

As Harlan so clearly saw, Jim Crow separatism was a way to reduce blacks to the status of second-class citizens. Never did African-Americans actually enjoy equal facilities as whites. In southern education, for instance, 80 percent of the money spent on education went to white schools.

Prejudice at West Point

In the North, Jim Crow laws were less widespread than in the South. Still, blacks had to deal with all kinds of prejudice. This was true even at West Point, the nation's most prestigious military academy. In 1870 J. W. Smith became the first black cadet. His sponsor, David Clarke, a white educator, was pained by what the young man had to go through:

> Scarcely has a day passed when he has not been assaulted by words, or blows inflicted, to force him to do something for which they might expel him.

Smith, himself, wrote to a friend:

> Your kind letter should have been answered long before this, but really I have been so harassed with examinations and insults and ill treatment of these cadets that I could not write or do anything else scarcely.... These fellows appear to be trying their utmost to run me off.... Not a moment has passed but some one of them has been cursing and abusing me.... What I get to eat, I must snatch for like a dog.

David Clarke went to President Ulysses S. Grant himself, who agreed that Smith should be allowed to stay at West Point. Said Grant, "The battle might as well be fought now as any time."

But finally the malicious cadets got to Smith. Harassed one time too many, Smith struck a white cadet. The academy authorities lost no time in expelling Smith.

"The thin disguise of 'equal' accommodations . . . will not mislead anyone."
—Justice Harlan on the *Plessy* decision

173

Still, Smith's lonely effort was not in vain. On June 15, 1877, Henry O. Flipper of Georgia became the first black cadet to graduate from West Point.

Time and time again, heroic African-Americans, singly and in groups, would continue the fight to break Jim Crow's back.

Highlighting a Hero—George Henry White

By 1900 just one black representative was left in Congress. George Henry White of North Carolina was called the "sole representative for nine million people."

Unintimidated, on January 20, 1900, White introduced the first bill to make lynching a federal crime. And he demanded the enforcement of laws already on the books to protect black people. "The problem of racial injustice must be met," he said. "You will have to meet it. You have got this problem to settle, and the sooner it is settled the better it will be for all concerned."

In spite of the fact that anti-lynching supporters sent petitions from all over the country, Congress never even voted on White's bill.

White coolly questioned his contemporaries, "How long will you sit in your seats and hear and see the principles that underlie the foundation of this government sapped away little by little?"

In spite of the enormous anti-black sentiment washing all around him, White confidently predicted that his people would one day "rise" and elect more African-Americans to Congress. Not until 1928, however, would another black man win election to Congress. He was Oscar DePriest from Chicago.

"You have got this problem to settle, and the sooner it is settled the better it will be for all concerned."
—Congressman George Henry White

SECTION ONE REVIEW ∿∿∿∿∿∿∿∿∿∿∿∿∿∿∿∿

1. VOCABULARY Write a sentence for each of the following words: poll tax, integration, segregation, Jim Crow, *Plessy v. Ferguson*.

2. POLITICS Why did white legislators in the South make voters pass literacy tests and pay poll taxes?

3. **ETHICS** Explain the concept of "separate but equal." Do you think two groups can ever be truly separate but equal? Should they try to be?

4. **CONSTITUTIONAL HERITAGE** Why was *Plessy v. Ferguson* regarded as a landmark Supreme Court case?

5. **CRITICAL THINKING** By 1900 do you think African-Americans should have pursued a policy of integration or segregation? Explain your answer.

BLACK SELF-RELIANCE—WHICH WAY TO TURN?

SECTION TWO

VOCABULARY Niagara Movement NAACP

MAIN IDEA African-Americans searched for a response to the repression they faced. Two very different approaches emerged.

OBJECTIVES As you read, look for answers to the following questions:
1. What hope did the Populist Party offer African-Americans?
2. What advice did Booker T. Washington offer African-Americans?
3. How did W.E.B. Du Bois and others respond to Washington?

By 1900 African-Americans had seen the denial of their political rights. Even worse, they had witnessed the destruction of basic human rights. What could they do to respond?

The Populist Movement—Power to the Poor

One cause for hope was the rise of the farmer-based Populist Party. During the 1880s southern farmers suffered from hard times. The planters, in their zeal to rebuild the South, had planted too much cotton. They grew so much that the prices farmers received for their produce went down. Wealthy farmers could survive. But the effects were devastating for the poor whites and blacks of the region.

175

As a result, poor farmers began to form alliances somewhat like labor unions. The alliances lobbied for state aid for agriculture and more regulation over the railroads that shipped their goods. During the 1880s the Southern Farmers' Alliance was very active in politics. It refused black members, but it did encourage African-Americans to set up their own organization. By 1891 the Colored Farmers' National Alliance and Cooperative Union had more than a million members in twelve states.

With common, practical interests in mind, white and black farmers began moving closer together. It wasn't long before political leaders saw the potential in such an alliance and organized the Populist Party in 1892. One white Populist leader, Tom Watson from Georgia, gained fame for his fiery speeches about how poor whites and blacks were getting shafted by the rich.

Southern Democrats became frantic at the thought of black voters coming back into power, especially if white politicians were not in control. In fact, in North Carolina in 1894 a mixture of Populists and Republicans won a number of victories, briefly gaining control of the state. The year 1895 saw 300 black magistrates appointed in North Carolina, as well as deputy sheriffs, police, and aldermen.

Alarmed southern Democrats pulled out all the stops to prevent the Populists from scoring more gains. They started a campaign of race hatred, aimed at removing African-Americans from politics for once and for all. Then, when the Populist Party agreed to support the Democratic candidate for President in 1896, the revolt in the South against Democratic rule came to an end. The final obstacle to separation of the races was removed.

Whites Join Together

On the verge of true reform on the grassroots level, poor whites had once again been led to believe that they were "better" than black people. This idea became known as "white supremacy."

It was nearly impossible for the majority of poor whites in the South, largely illiterate themselves, to understand their true situation. Had they joined with other poor people, no matter what their color, they might have achieved economic improvement. Instead, they sought largely emotional comfort in siding with their wealthy white counterparts, even though this did little to improve their day-to-day situation.

Poor whites came to believe that by choosing black people as the "scapegoat," their situation would somehow get better. They joined upper-class whites in insisting that African-Americans not be allowed to (1) vote, (2) receive high-quality education, or (3) mingle freely with whites.

Booker T. Washington and Southern Self-Reliance

Booker T. Washington

How were African-Americans, once again desperately searching for resources, going to turn this latest adversity around? One answer came on September 18, 1895, from an energetic young black educator, at the Cotton States Exposition in Atlanta. His name was Booker Taliaferro Washington, principal of the Tuskegee Institute in Alabama and a leading African-American spokesman.

On that fateful day, Washington mesmerized his audience, black and white alike, with his vision of the future. He saw African-Americans working diligently—and humbly—alongside whites, not for the right to socialize with them, but to make money for the good of the South, and ultimately the country as a whole.

"Learn a trade" was the Tuskegee educator's enthusiastic advice. He was convinced that once black people had taught themselves to be efficient workers, they would later be granted their rights as citizens. His philosophy came to be known as "industrial education."

Washington thrust one powerful hand into the air to illustrate how the South's fragile black-white balance could be maintained:

> In all things purely social we can be as separate as the fingers, yet one as the hand in all things essential to mutual progress.

To blacks, his advice on learning a marketable skill and owning one's own home had a practical ring:

> No race can prosper till it learns that there is as much dignity in tilling a field as in writing a poem.

177

"It is at the bottom of life we must begin and not at the top."
—Booker T. Washington

It is at the bottom of life we must begin and not at the top.

He went on to explain the mistakes he believed African-Americans had made during Reconstruction:

Ignorant and inexperienced, it is not strange that in the first years of our new life we began at the top instead of at the bottom; that a seat in Congress or the state legislature was more sought than real estate or industrial skill; that the political convention or stump speaking had more attractions than starting a dairy farm or truck garden.

To the whites in that Atlanta audience, Washington's insistence on blacks "knowing their place" was a dream come true. Here was the answer to dealing with the "Negro problem." At the close of Washington's speech, Georgia's Governor Bullock raced up to the podium and publicly shook Washington's hand. Later, President Grover Cleveland wrote him a congratulatory letter.

But many people, primarily African-American, were outraged. How dare Washington, with a single wave of the hand, wipe out centuries of effort for equality in America?

According to his own writings years later, Washington acknowledged that he knew only too well the tightrope he walked that day. But he felt he had no choice. He was determined to help black people in the South keep from starving. And, given the circumstances of his own birth and upbringing, his perspective was clear.

Washington's Rise to Prominence

Booker T. Washington was born a slave in 1856 in Virginia to a black mother and a white father. He slept on the ground in a shack, eating scraps of food from a rusty pot. As a child, he carried water to the fieldhands. Later, he became one himself.

After the slaves were freed, he moved with his mother and stepfather to Malden, West Virginia, where he was put to work in a salt factory. Young Washington's greatest dream was to learn to read and write like an educated black man whom he had once met. "How I used to envy this man," he later recalled.

Finally, by scrimping, Washington's mother was able to buy him a secondhand spelling book. Then, when a black school finally opened, it was in the next town. Washington, still working a full day in the salt factory, walked to school at night. He tried easing his load by putting the factory clock ahead a little, but he got caught. Soon thereafter, his stepfather sent him to work in a coal mine. In spite of all these hardships, Washington kept focused on his dream:

> I used to try to picture . . . the ambitions of a white boy with absolutely no limit to his aspirations. . . . I used to picture the way I would act under such circumstances; how I would begin at the bottom and keep rising until I reached the highest pinnacle of success.

Then, at his darkest hour, in the pit of that mine, Washington heard about a school, Hampton Institute, that had scholarships for poor black students.

At the age of sixteen, he hitchhiked and walked the 500 miles to Hampton, Virginia. Near starvation, he was so dirty by the time he finally arrived that it took days more to convince a white schoolmistress to give him a chance. Finally, she told him to sweep a room. Washington swept the room four times to make sure it would pass inspection. At last, he was admitted to the school. He had to wash his only pair of socks each night, but he studied as hard as he could.

After graduation, Washington got a job as a teacher, but even that was strenuous and dangerous, as it was during the height of the Klan terror campaign. But Washington persevered, even turning down offers to go into politics or the ministry.

Several years later, he was offered a teaching job at the very place where he had received his start, Hampton Institute. Soon thereafter, he got the chance to take charge of a new school called Tuskegee Institute.

When Washington arrived at Tuskegee, Alabama, he found that the "school" was nothing more than a rundown old plantation and a barn. He even had to borrow $200 from a friend to open the place on July 4, 1881. Undaunted, he and his 30 students rolled up their sleeves, cleared land, cut timber, and, over the next fifteen years, built all the school facilities themselves.

Thus Booker T. Washington labored humbly and diligently, until that fateful day in 1895 when he was asked to speak at the Atlanta Exposition.

Although feted by Presidents and even kings and queens in Europe, Washington remained an educator. In 1915, when he died, Tuskegee Institute had an annual endowment in excess of $2 million, 1,400 students (including undergraduates from Africa and the Caribbean), 2,300 acres of land under student cultivation, and 66 school buildings.

Ironically, just two weeks after his untimely death at 55, an article he had written appeared in the *New Republic* magazine. In it, he publicly stated how he had really felt about segregation laws all those years. He called them "unjust, unnecessary, and inconsistent."

W.E.B. Du Bois's Response

Long before Booker T. Washington denounced Jim Crow, other black leaders spoke out, demanding equality before the law. One intellectual leader who opposed Washington's seeming "second-class citizen approach" was William Edward Burghardt Du Bois.

Du Bois was a brilliant young professor of economics at Atlanta University on the day Washington made his speech at the Exposition. Du Bois feared that if African-Americans gave up their struggle to maintain what few civil rights they did have, as Washington suggested, they would be headed back to slavery.

What good was a house and farm, Du Bois argued, if they could be looted by whites at any time? What good was a family if its mother could be raped or father lynched any day?

The Middle Class Versus the Working Class

Both Booker T. Washington and W.E.B. Du Bois wanted what was best for African-Americans. But they differed on *how* that should happen. Washington represented the black working class. As such, he concentrated on the bare necessities of life. Du Bois, on the other hand, having grown up in better circumstances, represented what came to be known as the black middle class.

"Middle class" means people who were not poor, but not rich either. Whatever their race, middle class people tend to be merchants, owners of small businesses, or professionals providing services like medicine or the law. They have some contact with both the upper and lower classes of society. Usually they aspire to be like the upper classes and frequently are ashamed of their working class brothers and sisters.

W.E.B. Du Bois

Du Bois was different. Although middle class, he had no contempt for the lower class. Indeed, he sincerely believed that the black middle class was the only group with the resources, both material and mental, to pull the working class out of poverty.

He dubbed those young black people with the most potential for leadership the "Talented Tenth." If black people did not encourage their own leaders, he asked pointedly, who would?

> The Negro race, like all races, is going to be saved by its exceptional men. The problem of education, then, among Negroes must first of all deal with the Talented Tenth; it is the problem of developing the Best of this race that they may guide the Mass away from the contamination and death of the Worst, in their own and other races.

The Education of W.E.B. Du Bois

Du Bois' point of view, like Washington's, was shaped in no small part by his upbringing. Du Bois was born in 1868 in Great Barrington, Massachusetts. His great-great-grandfather had been a slave who won his freedom in the Revolutionary War. At an early age, Du Bois showed such signs of brilliance that he won a scholarship to Fisk University. He did so well that, even in such a racist era, he went on to receive a Masters and a Ph.D. from Harvard University, the first black student ever to do so. Later he did post-graduate work at the University of Berlin.

181

Early in his career, Du Bois gained fame as a scholar. His Ph.D. thesis, *The Suppression of the African Slave Trade*, established his reputation in the field of history.

From 1896 to 1910 Du Bois was an economics professor at Atlanta University. In 1900 he published *The Philadelphia Negro*, the first in-depth sociological examination of African-Americans. And in 1903, greatly disappointed by Booker T. Washington and furious at a recent Atlanta race riot, Du Bois penned *The Souls of Black Folk*. In it, he brilliantly pointed out how wasteful it was for whites to keep blacks down, instead of allowing them to be productive members of society:

> Such waste of energy cannot be spared if the South is to catch up with civilization....
>
> Your country? How came it [to be] yours? Before the Pilgrims landed we were here....Actively we have woven ourselves [into] this nation—we have fought their battles, shared their sorrow, mingled our blood with theirs, and generation after generation have pleaded with a headstrong, careless people to despise not justice, mercy, and truth, lest the nation be smitten with a curse. Our song, our toil, our cheer and warning have been given to this nation in blood brotherhood. Are not these gifts worth the giving? Is not this worth the striving? Would America have been America without her Negro People?

"Would America have been America without her Negro People?"
—W.E.B. Du Bois

Du Bois went on to write other important historical and sociological studies, as well as poetry, essays, and novels. In his poignant *Sorrow Songs*, he made a powerful prediction:

> Three centuries' thought has been the raising and unveiling of that bowed human heart, and now behold a century new for the duty and the deed. The problem of the Twentieth Century is the problem of the color-line.

"The problem of the Twentieth Century is the problem of the color-line."
—W.E.B. Du Bois

The Birth of Modern Black Activism

Du Bois, unlike other intellectuals, did not simply sit around and talk about the problems in society. He set out to change them. When Atlanta University began losing grants from white northern philanthropists because of his "radical" writings, he promptly moved North to take action. He was determined that African-Americans have three things: (1) the right to vote, (2) civic equality, and (3) the education of youth according to ability.

On July 11, 1905, Du Bois and 28 other determined young black intellectuals met secretly at Niagara Falls, Canada. The location, and that of later meeting places, was always selected for its rich historical significance to African-Americans. Niagara Falls had been, for many years, one of the main destinations for escaping slaves on the Underground Railroad.

Du Bois and his young intellectuals were determined to create an organization which would aggressively push for full civil rights for all African-Americans. The group incorporated itself as the **Niagara Movement** and, to underscore their determination, met the following year at the site of John Brown's slave revolution, Harpers Ferry.

Niagara Movement: group organized by W.E.B. Du Bois in 1905 to demand equal rights for African-Americans.

The next year, in 1907, the Niagara Movement met in the old abolitionist stronghold of Faneuil Hall in Boston. By 1909, after a shocked nation heard the news of not one, but two race riots in the northern city of Springfield, Ohio, young liberal whites decided to join with their black counterparts to take up the civil rights banner.

The NAACP

On Abraham Lincoln's birthday, February 12, 1909, the National Association for the Advancement of Colored People (**NAACP**) was born. Du Bois and other members of the Niagara Movement joined with celebrated white reformers to found the NAACP. The whites included Jane Addams of Hull House in Chicago; Mary White Ovington, a New York social worker; and Oswald Garrison Villard, grandson of abolitionist leader William Lloyd Garrison.

NAACP: organization formed in 1909 to work for the legal rights of African-Americans.

In May 1910 the NAACP formally came into being. Du Bois, its only black officer at the time, wasted no time in creating a magazine in which the new organization could share its views. The magazine was aptly entitled *The Crisis*. By 1918, *The Crisis* was selling as many as 100,000 copies a month. Du Bois inspired his readers with editorials such as this:

183

"**If we are to die, in God's name, let us perish like men and not like bales of hay.**"
—W.E.B. Du Bois

We have crawled and pleaded for justice and we have been cheerfully spit upon and murdered and burned. We will not endure it forever. If we are to die, in God's name, let us perish like men and not like bales of hay.

White and black attorneys soon joined the NAACP, and under its Legal Redress Committee began waging the battle against injustice—a battle that continues today. They won three landmark cases in the NAACP's first 15 years of existence:

(1) *Guinn v. United States* (1915), in which the Supreme Court declared the "grandfather clauses" in Maryland and Oklahoma to be illegal.

(2) *Buchanan v. Warley* (1917), in which a Louisville, Kentucky, law that had forced black people to live only in certain sections of town, was declared unconstitutional.

(3) *Moore v. Dempsey* (1923), in which a black man convicted of murder in Arkansas was given a new trial.

These cases became precedents for attorneys in other parts of the country to argue the rights of African-Americans.

Highlighting a Hero—Ida Wells-Barnett

One of Du Bois' allies in the struggle for African-American rights was Ida Wells-Barnett. By the time she was nineteen, she had already begun her life-long career as a journalist and human rights crusader. In this white, male-dominated era, Wells boldly launched a series of articles in a Memphis newspaper, detailing lynchings of black people by whites.

In 1892, for example, she exposed the details behind a conspiracy that ended in the lynching of three successful black grocers. Wells was able to document that their white competitors had them bumped off, Mafia-style.

Wells so upset the conservative white male community that she began carrying not one, but two, guns in her handbag for protection. Even at that, she found her press smashed, and she barely escaped from Memphis with her life.

Undaunted, she moved to Chicago and in 1894 published *A Red Record*, documenting lynchings in the South, as well as the gruesome practice of burning innocent black people alive at the stake after covering them with hot tar and feathers:

> If it were known that the cannibals or the savage Indians had burned three human beings alive in the past two years, the whole of Christendom would be roused, to devise ways and means to put a stop to it. Can you remain silent and inactive when such things are done in our own community and country? Is your duty to humanity in the United States less binding?

Ida Wells – Barnett

Like Du Bois, Wells was not satisfied simply to write about injustice. In 1898, she organized a delegation of congressmen and socially conscious women to go to Washington, D.C. They confronted President William McKinley directly, protesting the lynching of a black postmaster.

It's not surprising then, that Ida Baker Wells-Barnett became a founding member of the NAACP and continued championing the human rights of African-Americans until she died in 1931.

Highlighting a Hero—Mary Church Terrell

Mary Church Terrell was another co-founder of the NAACP. Among the first black women to be college-educated in this country, Terrell became a noted educator and the first president of the National Association of Colored Women, founded in 1895. The group's motto was "Lifting As We Climb." It helped establish hospitals, girls' homes, and other charitable institutions for black people in various cities.

Terrell remained dedicated to African-American human and civil rights to the day she died. And to prove it, in 1953, at the age of 89, she led a demonstration into a Washington, D.C., restaurant that had refused service to African-Americans. She was arrested but later vindicated when the group won its case in court. Labelled a "meddler" by angry whites early in her career, Terrell shrugged off their criticism in a 1905 article for the magazine, *The Voice of the Negro*:

> Everybody who has tried to advance the interests of the human race by redressing wrongs or by

"In the United States there is an imperative need of meddlers today...."
—Mary Church Terrell

inaugurating reforms has first been called a meddler....

In the United States there is an imperative need of meddlers today—active, insistent, and fearless meddlers who will spend their time investigating institutions, customs, and laws whose effect upon the citizens of any color or class is depressing or bad....

In the United States there is an imperative need of a host of meddlers who will...go...where corruption of any kind is apparent and transgression of the law is clear.

SECTION TWO REVIEW

1. VOCABULARY Write a sentence for each of the following terms: Niagara Movement, NAACP.

2. POLITICS What caused the downfall of the Populist Party in the South?

3. BIOGRAPHY In his famous Atlanta speech, how did Booker T. Washington use his hand to illustrate his view of the social status of blacks and whites?

4. BIOGRAPHY What, according to W.E.B. Du Bois, was the "Talented Tenth"?

5. CRITICAL THINKING How did the backgrounds of Booker T. Washington and W.E.B. Du Bois shape the views of each on the issue of equal rights?

SECTION THREE   BLACK INNOVATORS

VOCABULARY "Exodus of 1877" Urban League

MAIN IDEA Even in these desparate times, African-Americans made strides in business, technology, and the arts.

OBJECTIVES As you read, look for answers to the following questions:
1. **What notable African-Americans made their mark in the West?**
2. **Who were some leading black inventors?**
3. **What "first" did Dr. Daniel Hale Williams achieve in medicine?**
4. **Who were some of the leading black historians, writers, and poets?**

"The whole South—every single state in the South—had got into the hands of the very men that held us as slaves. . . . We said there was no hope for us and we better go." So reported one black southerner to a committee of Congress investigating why so many African-Americans were leaving the South in the late 1870s. Some were heading north. Others, led by an ex-slave named Benjamin "Pap" Singleton, moved west. In the **Exodus of 1877**," thousands of poor black farmers, their few belongings on their backs, poured into Kansas and Nebraska. They were searching for the freedom and opportunity that was denied them in the South. And they found it. By the 1880s blacks were graduating from high schools and serving in the state legislatures.

**"Exodus of 1877":
migration of blacks to Kansas
and Nebraska to escape harsh
conditions in the South.**

Black Cowhands

Amazing as it may sound to us today, in the Old West large numbers of cowhands were black! There were, literally, 8,000 black cowboys and cowgirls in the Old West! That amounted to nearly one out of every four of this country's 35,000 cowhands around the turn of the century. Because of racial prejudice, most of them remain nameless, but information about a few has survived.

Mary Fields was one. She singlehandedly ran a stagecoach line through the treacherous Montana Territory. Six feet tall and strong as a man, for more than eight years Fields was responsible for getting the mail through the rough Montana wilderness, sometimes having to tote the mail herself when her wagon broke down in bad winter weather. Mary Fields earned a coveted reputation for getting the mail through, regardless of "rain, sleet, or snow."

Leonora Russell was another noted black westerner of the time. In the 1880s, she prospected for gold in Cripple Creek, Colorado. Her uncles, Fred and George Dalton, were part of the infamous band of robbers, the Dalton Gang. Russell eventually moved to Denver where she made her living as an artist.

Deadwood Dick was one of the best-known black cowboys of the 1880s. Born a slave in Tennessee in 1854 with the name Nat Love, he ventured West in 1869. Through sheer perseverance, Love taught himself to ride wild horses and shoot a Colt .45 pistol with deadly accuracy. In Deadwood, Dakota, Love entered a horse roping competition which earned him the reputation as the champion rider in the West. He later wrote:

> I roped, threw, tied, bridled, saddled and mounted my mustang in exactly nine minutes from the crack of the gun. The time of the next-nearest competitor was 12 minutes and 30 seconds. This gave me the record and championship of the West, which held up to the time I quit the business in 1890, and my record has never been beaten. Right there the assembled crowd named me Deadwood Dick and proclaimed me champion of the western cattle country.

The inventor of steer wrestling was Bill Pickett, another African-American cowboy. Born in southern Texas around 1860, Pickett was skilled in roping and in handling cattle for wagon trains. One day, a stubborn longhorn would not get into a railroad stock car. Pickett grabbed the beast by the horns and actually sank his teeth into its tender upper lip! The cowboy even let his hands go, as the animal sank to its knees. Bill Pickett travelled internationally, receiving up to $53,000 per performance to demonstrate this amazing trick.

Matthew "Bones" Hooks was yet another famous black westerner. Born in Dalhart, Texas, in 1867, Hooks earned his reputation as a champion rider at the turn of the century when he rode a bronco that no one thought could be "broken." Not only did Hook stay on the horse, but he rode him "to a standstill." Later, Hooks worked for the Santa Fe Railroad and eventually retired to Amarillo, Texas. In 1932, he established an orphanage for black youngsters called The Dogie Club and started the first Boy Scout troop in Amarillo.

"This gave me the record and championship of the West..."
—Deadwood Dick

Thomas Bass was still another famous cowboy. He was such an expert horse breeder and trainer that wealthy equestrians vied for his services, and even sent him abroad to choose the finest new "horse flesh."

Bass lived in Mexico, Missouri, but he travelled to practically every city of note in the United States and carried off more prizes and ribbons than any other single individual. Bass owned one of the most famous mares of all time, Belle Beach. He rode in President Grover Cleveland's inaugural parade, received visits from Presidents McKinley, Roosevelt, and Taft, and was personally applauded by the Queen of Romania at a St. Louis horse show. Bass also invented a new horse bit which improved a rider's ability to handle his horse.

Famous Black Explorer at the North Pole

While African-Americans were winning fame in the West, the year 1909 saw another black man gain recognition for his exploration of a quite different frontier, the North Pole. Matthew Henson was the first man to reach the "top of the world." He did it on April 6, 1909.

Henson had spent years as chief guide to Commander Robert E. Peary. The two had almost died when, seven times before, they had come tantalizingly close to the North Pole, only to have to turn back from exhaustion and lack of supplies. Finally, in 1909 Henson, nearly exhausted and having lost 35 pounds on the trip, half walked, half crawled the final yards to the North Pole. As he recalled:

We had been travelling eighteen to twenty hours out of every twenty-four. Man, that was killing work! We used to travel by night and sleep in the warmest part of the day. I was ahead most of the time with two of the Eskimos.... The morning of April sixth I calculated how far I had come, and I said to myself, "If I'm not on the Pole, I've crossed it...." Commander Peary was forty-five minutes behind.

In all, Henson devoted 23 years of his life to working with Peary in exploration. Henson learned to speak the

Eskimo language fluently and personally built much of the specialized technical equipment he and fellow crew members used on their dangerous expeditions. In 1945 Congress awarded Henson with a medal for "outstanding service... in the field of science."

The Emergence of Black Labor Unions

Few African-Americans lived lives of adventure as cowhands or explorers. Most lived quiet lives, relying on their own enterprise to get ahead. They formed unions, business organizations, and banks to get what they needed.

It is not hard to imagine the reluctance of white labor unions to accept black members. In spite of efforts to integrate unions, separation remained the order of the day. In 1866 blacks' hopes were momentarily raised when the white National Labor Union announced its plans to break the rules and accept black members. Isaac Myers from Baltimore, the leading black labor leader of the day, was enthusiastic. He assured white workers at the 1869 National Labor Union convention that "White laboring men have nothing to fear from the black laboring men." But old attitudes were hard to change. The union ended up accepting black members only in separate locals.

Myers then organized the National Colored Labor Union in 1869. But by 1872 he was forced to shut down the ambitious effort, after unsuccessfully going up against the white business establishment.

In 1885 another leading union, the Knights of Labor, actually agreed to welcome black workers into their ranks. Some 60,000 black people paid their money and joined the union—one-tenth of the total membership. Thousands of women also joined, some rising to leadership positions. But after a series of unpopular strikes, membership dropped sharply, and by the 1890s the union had folded.

The American Federation of Labor (AFL) then emerged. Although it claimed to welcome black members, few were actually allowed to join. Years later, after the emergence of another large labor union, the Congress of Industrial Organizations, (CIO), black people were able to join a major white labor union.

In the meantime, African-Americans got busy and

> "White laboring men have nothing to fear from the black laboring men."
> —Isaac Myers

formed their own unions, such as the National Association of Afro-American Steam and Gas Engineers and Skilled Workers of Pittsburgh.

National Negro Business Men's League

Booker T. Washington, ever the pragmatist, stepped in and organized the only successful national black business association of that era. At the group's 1900 meeting, he urged the more than 400 delegates who came from 34 states to start as many businesses as possible. Indeed, by 1907 the National Negro Business Men's League had 320 branches.

The Urban League

In 1905 black businessmen and activists formed two organizations in New York City to press for economic advancement for African-Americans. They were the Committee for Improving Industrial Conditions for Negroes and the National League for the Protection of Colored Women. George Edmund Haynes, a farsighted young black Columbia University graduate student, headed yet another committee in New York City to help black workers.

By 1911 the three organizations decided to centralize their efforts. The new organization was called the National League on Urban Conditions Among Negroes. It still exists today as, simply, the **Urban League**. The Urban League has devoted itself to helping African-Americans living in cities make progress in all walks of life. Over the years, it has assisted in everything from helping newly arrived southern blacks adjust to the North, to working with corporations to develop training programs to help people progress beyond entry-level jobs.

Urban League:
organization founded in 1911 to improve the health, housing, job opportunities, and recreational facilities of urban blacks.

Black Businesses

By the turn of the century, in the North as well as in the South, a small percentage of African-Americans had managed to accumulate sizeable holdings in real estate and business. From 1889 to 1905, determined black businessmen opened 28 banks. Only a few survived, but these formed the foundation for the slow but steady development of black business in America.

In 1900 Dr. Aaron McDuffie Moore and John Merrick formed the first successful black insurance company, North Carolina Mutual and Provident Association. Along with a former black grocer, Charles C. Spaulding, they had over $16 million in insurance policies by 1918. The company diversified into other holdings, including a bank and real estate company. Spaulding later recalled how hard he had worked to become a success:

> When I came into the office in the morning, I rolled up my sleeves and swept the place as a janitor. Then I rolled down my sleeves and was an [insurance] agent. And later I put on my coat and became general manager.

In 1905 Alonzo F. Herndon, a well-to-do Atlanta barber, started the Atlanta Life Insurance company. By 1922 its capital stock was worth $100,000.

The driving need for African-Americans to build a stable foundation on enterprises they owned themselves was driven home by John Hope, later president of Morehouse College. At the 1898 Fourth Annual Atlanta University Conference on the Negro in Business, Hope reminded his listeners:

> I have seen too many competent Negroes superseded by whites. . . . We must take in some, if not all, of the wages, turn it into capital, hold it, [and] increase it.

Highlighting a Hero—Madame C. J. Walker

Some African-Americans listened to Hope's advice and became determined to do the impossible in business. Madame C. J. Walker was one of those who beat the odds. She became the first American woman—of any race—to become a millionaire through her own efforts.

Born Sarah McWilliams in 1869 in Delta, Louisiana, to poverty, stricken ex-slave parents, Madame Walker scrubbed floors and took in washing. Hoping to better her lot, she married at the age of fourteen, but was widowed at twenty. With her meager savings, she left the South and headed north to New York. There she observed the sophistication and beauty of black northern women. Inspired, she decided to make her mark in the beauty industry.

By 1905 Madame Walker had invented a special hair softener, a straightening comb, and a variety of facial cosmetics. (Until then, many black women would straighten their hair by using hot flat irons. This method was as ineffective as it was dangerous.) Her cosmetics and hair preparations quickly revolutionized the ways in which black women made themselves attractive. In time, many white women used Madame Walker's products too.

Before she was 40, Madame Walker's business had grown into a million-dollar cosmetic manufacturing company. She had over 2,000 agents selling an ever-expanding line of Walker products. Her fame was such that she made headlines both in her business and social activities. A prominent socialite, she entertained tycoons at her mansion in New York at Irvington on the Hudson. In fact, her home became a major show-piece of prominent African-Americans. Still, she always maintained an interest in those less fortunate. She donated large sums of money to charities and church groups. She even founded an academy for girls in West Africa and bequeathed $100,000 for its support.

Maggie Lena Walker—Banker

Maggie Lena Walker was another black female phenomenon when it came to finances. She too, started with nothing and made her way to the top of her field.

Walker was born in Richmond, Virginia, in 1867, where she was a schoolteacher for several years. She then became associated with the organization she would so ably help develop, the Independent Order of St. Luke. This was a black self-help group in Virginia.

After becoming secretary-treasurer in 1899, she helped the organization turn a profit. She had already worked to set up branches as far away as West Virginia. The institution grew strong enough to establish its own insurance and banking organizations.

Maggie Lena Walker

Mrs. Walker became Chairman of the Board of the bank. It became known as the Consolidated Bank and Trust Company and had a long and successful tenure. Mindful of the needs of less fortunate women, Mrs. Walker also helped establish The Council of Colored Women, as well as serving on the board of the National Urban League. By the time she died in 1934, she had left a career legacy that many young black women could follow.

Black Inventors

In the years after the Civil War blacks patented hundreds of inventions. In fact, according to the United States Patent Office, by 1913 about 1,000 African-Americans had taken out patents! Clearly, African-Americans played a prominent role in the inventive thrust needed to feed the Industrial Revolution.

The Real McCoy

In 1872 Elijah McCoy's invention for automatically lubricating factory machines proved a tremendous boon to industry. McCoy's invention, a special cup that carefully dripped oil into machines while they were still moving, meant that steam boilers and even locomotives could be oiled without interruption, thus saving valuable time. This device came to be known as the first "real McCoy." The son of escaped slaves, McCoy received his education as a mechanical engineer in Scotland. A savvy businessman as well, McCoy took out more than 50 patents with the U.S. Patent Office on the various devices he designed.

Whiz Kid in Shoe Biz

Every one of us owes a debt of gratitude to the efforts of a young black mechanical genius named Jan Ernest Matzeliger. Born in 1852 in Dutch Guiana, Matzeliger was already an apprentice machine shopman by the time he was ten. Still in his teens, he left home in search of opportunity. He became a cobbler's apprentice in Philadelphia, where he learned the art of shoemaking. By 1877, Matzeliger had made his way to Lynn, Massachusetts, the shoe capital of America. There he found work in the M. H. Harvey shoe factory.

At that time, shoes were still made largely by hand. The process of pleating the leather around the toe with tiny tacks—or "lasting," as it was called—was particularly time-consuming. It was of obvious importance, though, because if the upper and lower portions were not well-attached, the shoe would soon come apart.

The plucky Matzeliger decided he would be the one to invent a machine to "last" shoes. His fellow workers hooted with derision. Fortunately, Matzeliger did not pay any attention to them.

Night after night in his cramped little room, he worked with bits of wood, cigar boxes, or packing crates—whatever he could get hold of. He did this after putting in long hours at the factory during the day.

Matzeliger was encouraged, though, when one man offered him $50 for his first crude working model. The young inventor shrewdly turned him down and kept working to perfect his machine.

It would take four more years of painstaking effort before he finally came up with a working model in metal. This time, another man offered him $1,500 for it. Still, Matzeliger refused. He took another six years to build an even better, more simplified device. By 1887, his final creation was so accurate that it made a perfect shoe without tearing even the finest leather.

By this time, no one was laughing. The United Shoe Machinery Company of Boston bought his machine, offering Matzeliger not only a sizable check, but company stock as well. United was able to cut the cost of manufacturing shoes by 50 percent. More people were able to buy better shoes for less money.

To this day, shoe manufacturing equipment still largely conforms to the design of Jan Matzeliger's machine.

Lewis Latimer Gets a Bright Idea

Lewis Latimer, an expert electrical engineer and draftsman, worked closely with Alexander Graham Bell on the develop-

Granville T. Woods

ment of the telephone and with Thomas Edison on the development of the light bulb.

Latimer was born to a poor family in Boston in 1848. After serving in the Navy during the Civil War, he learned his craft by working with a firm of patent lawyers in Boston. He rose to the position of chief draftsman for the firm.

By 1876 Latimer was already making the drawings and helping prepare the patent applications for early Bell telephones.

Even before he started working with Edison, Latimer had come up with a way to make the carbon filaments necessary for incandescent electrical light. At the time, he was working with Connecticut inventor Hiram S. Maxim. Together they put a light bulb into production in the United States and Canada. Latimer shrewdly patented his filament method, as well as several similar other inventions.

Latimer began working with Edison in 1884. He was so brilliant that he was the only black member of the elite research team known as the Edison Pioneers.

Granville T. Woods—"World's Greatest Electrician"

The work of another black inventor greatly improved the safety of the nation's railroads. Granville T. Woods invented an automatic air brake which significantly reduced accidents between railroad trains. He was also part of the team which invented the "third rail," still in use today, which carries the electrical current used to power many modern trains. (Before that, trains ran on coal, and had to be continuously stoked and refueled throughout a journey.) Woods also invented a method for sending telegraph signals between moving trains. This enabled trains to signal each other, greatly reducing the risk of accidental collisions.

Woods invented and sold other devices to the Bell Telephone Company, to Edison Electric, and to Westinghouse. He even went to court against the Edison Company, successfully proving that he had patents to inventions which Edison had claimed. Today Woods is not well known. But in 1888, the *American Catholic Tribune* called him "The greatest electrician in the world."

"Unknown" Inventors

Unlike Latimer or Woods, other inventors never received credit for their innovations. For instance, in 1865 a black chef in Sarasota, Florida, named Hiram S. Thomas introduced none other than potato chips! He called them "Sarasota Chips." But because he did not have the means to protect his invention, it passed out of his control.

Black Contributions in Medicine

Blacks were also making history in other fields. In 1893 Dr. Daniel Hale Williams performed the first successful heart operation in the world. As a result, he became internationally famous. President Grover Cleveland appointed him head of the Freedmen's Hospital in Washington, D.C.

Earlier, Dr. Williams had started the nation's first interracial hospital, Provident Hospital in Chicago. Williams also established the first school for black nurses, since they were not allowed to attend white nursing schools.

Black Historians

The late 1800s saw a flowering of interest in the study of black history. The first black man to write a definitive overview of African-Americans was George Washington Williams. After seven years of constant, careful study, Williams produced a large two-volume work called *History of the Negro Race in America from 1619 to 1880*. The book was published in 1883.

Unaffected by this success, Williams immediately began work on his second book, *A History of the Negro Troops in the War of the Rebellion* (1888).

Williams' early life was a dramatic contrast to his later quiet, scholarly years. At 14, he ran away from his home in Bedford Spring, Pennsylvania, and joined the Army. Before he was twenty, Williams had become a colonel in the Mexican army. Fortunately for black America, he settled down and put his restless energy into research and writing.

Alexander Crummel, a runaway slave, went on to be-

197

come another noteworthy scholar. In 1897, he organized the American Negro Academy whose goal was to develop scholarly studies of African-Americans. Crummel also spent a number of years as a missionary in Liberia.

The Black Press

By 1900 there were three daily black newspapers and 150 weekly newspapers, ranging across 26 states, from Massachusetts to Kansas. This was quite an advance from the first tiny black newspaper, *Freedom's Journal*, co-founded in 1827 by John B. Russworm, the first black man to graduate from an American college.

The new newspapers included the *Albany Iconoclast*, the *Baltimore Crusader*, the *Columbus New Light*, and the Washington *Bee*. Although many of the publications did not last more than a few years, they served a tremendously useful purpose in informing the black reading public as well as paving the way for future newspapers.

The Guardian, first published in Boston in 1901 by activists Monroe Trotter and George Forbes, was the other most influential black newspaper at the turn of the century. Unlike *The Age*, which was considered politically moderate, The Guardian's pages were open to young militants who argued for full and immediate civil and political rights for all African-Americans.

In 1905 *The Chicago Defender* made its debut as a small handbill. But its publisher, Robert S. Abbott, was tenacious and by 1910 he and a creative assistant began, for the first time, to print news for the average black person, rather than just for intellectuals. True to its name, the paper defended the rights of African-American people by publishing accounts of discrimination, as well as calling for social equality. It also helped encourage the great mass migrations of blacks from all over the South to the North, as southern farm workers read copies of *The Defender* with its accounts of life in the "big city." (*The Defender* is still published and enjoys a loyal readership in Chicago today.)

In August 1919, a still more radical newspaper appeared —*The Messenger*. It billed itself as "The Only Radical Negro Magazine in America." Its editors included the militant A. Philip Randolph, who would go on to found the Brotherhood of Sleeping Car Porters, as well as organize the first March on Washington in 1941. *The Messenger* sought to be the voice of the labor movement, which its editors wanted to include downtrodden whites as well as black laborers. In its editorial, "Our Reason for Being," for example, they did not mince words:

> There is a new leadership for Negro workers. It is a leadership of uncompromising manhood. It is not asking for half a loaf but for the whole loaf. It is insistent upon the Negro workers exacting justice, both from the white labor unions and from the capitalists or employers.

Black Writers and Poets

Elizabeth Keckley was not a professional writer, but her spicy account of her years as chief dressmaker and confidante to Abraham Lincoln's wife, Mary Todd Lincoln, aroused a great stir when it appeared in 1868. The book was called *Behind the Scenes; or, Thirty Years as Slave, and Four Years in the White House.* Keckley not only described Mrs. Lincoln's struggles after her husband's assassination, but her own challenges as a young black woman trying to get ahead.

One of the most prolific black short story writers and novelists of the day was Charles Waddell Chesnutt (1858–1932). Born in Cleveland, he taught and worked on a newspaper before becoming a lawyer in 1887. Chesnutt used his experience from travels in North Carolina to write a series of short stories for *The Atlantic Monthly* magazine. He later published three novels, *The House Behind the Cedars* (1900), *The Marrow of Tradition* (1901), and *The Colonel's Dream* (1905). A bloody riot in Wilmington, North Carolina, which drove blacks out of political office, was the backdrop of *The Marrow of Tradition*.

Frances Ellen Watkins Harper (1825–1911) was the best-known black female poet of her day. Along with her fierce dedication to antislavery and human rights activities, she devoted herself after emancipation to the Women's Christian Temperance Union. Her *Poems on Miscellaneous*

199

Subjects, first published in 1854, went through no fewer than twenty editions by 1871.

Paul Dunbar (1872–1906) was the first widely recognized African-American poet. His parents, fugitive slaves who had escaped by way of the Underground Railroad to Dayton, Ohio, loved reading. Young Paul, a prodigy, wrote his first poem when he was just seven. The only black student in his high school, he graduated with honors. Afterwards, however, when his father died, Dunbar was forced to work as an elevator operator.

In 1892 a former teacher managed to have Dunbar appointed main speaker at his high school reunion. Dunbar's cultivated address drew the attention of several white editors. He soon found his early poems published in America and England. His first book of poetry, *Oak and Ivy*, appeared at the end of 1892. The next year, Frederick Douglass gave him a job at the Chicago World's Fair at the Haitian Pavilion.

Dunbar's next big break came when his book, *Majors and Minors*, got a full-page review in *Harper's Weekly* in 1896. He spent the next years writing furiously and lecturing as the darling of the white liberal literary set. He married Alice Ruth Moore, and things seemed to be going well. Still, Dunbar's health was not good. He seems also to have grown bitter over his inability to earn substantial money from his writing. Even acclaim such as being made an honorary colonel by President McKinley only served to make him rankle all the more at his poverty. He drank heavily. Eventually, his wife left him and he drank all the more. Sadly, Dunbar died at the young age of 34.

Dunbar's most famous poems express not only his sorrows but those experienced by all African-Americans. Here is a portion from one of his most famous works.

Sympathy

I know why the caged bird sings, ah me,
When his wing is bruised and his bosom sore,—
When he beats his bars and would be free;
It is not a carol of joy or glee,
But a prayer that he sends from his heart's deep
  core,
But a plea, that upward to Heaven he flings—
I know why the caged bird sings!

"I know why the caged bird sings!"
—Paul Dunbar

Black Music

Sissieretta Jones (1868–1933), an avid student at the New England Conservatory of Music in Boston, got her first big break in 1887, when she gave a benefit concert before an audience of 5,000. By the next year, she had begun performing on the musical stage in Boston.

By 1892 the captivating young Sissieretta had become the star of a top black New York musical entitled the "Madison Square Garden Jubilee." After three years of phenomenal success, Jones's manager entered into serious negotiations with New York's Metropolitan Opera House which wanted to take the bold step of using the black diva in the operas "Aida" and "L'Africaine." The project never came to be, but the young black superstar did perform at a reception for President Harrison at the White House.

For three more decades, as a top concert soloist, and later as the leader of her own musical comedy revue, Sissieretta Jones mesmerized the American and European music public.

SECTION THREE REVIEW

1. VOCABULARY Write a sentence for the following terms: "Exodus of 1877," Urban League.

2. BIOGRAPHY For what is Madame C.J. Walker remembered?

3. SCIENCE AND TECHNOLOGY Why do Americans owe a debt of gratitude to Jan Matzeliger? To Granville T. Woods?

4. LITERATURE Paul Dunbar wrote of African-Americans being "caged birds." What did he mean?

5. CRITICAL THINKING What lesson is there in these pages about overcoming seemingly unbeatable odds?

CHAPTER 7 REVIEW

VOCABULARY

Write the numbered sentences on a separate sheet of paper. In each sentence fill in the blank with one of these terms: *"Exodus of 1877," Jim Crow, NAACP, Plessy v. Ferguson, poll tax*.

1. Many African-Americans fled the South at the end of Reconstruction. Some took part in the _____, traveling to Kansas and Nebraska.

2. _____ laws required the separation of the races in schools, railway cars, and all public facilities.

3. In order to vote, southerners were required to pay a _____.

4. _____ was the landmark Supreme Court case that legalized segregation.

5. The _____ was formed in 1909 to work for the legal rights of African-Americans.

REVIEWING THE FACTS

1. How did southern states prevent blacks from voting?
2. What name was given to the laws that were passed to separate the races?
3. What part did the Supreme Court play in the national debate over race relations?
4. What hope did the Populist Party offer African-Americans?
5. What advice did Booker T. Washington offer African-Americans?
6. How did W.E.B. Du Bois and others respond to Washington?
7. What notable African-Americans made their mark in the West?
8. Who were some leading black inventors?
9. What "first" did Dr. Daniel Hale Williams achieve in medicine?
10. Who were some of the leading black historians, writers, and poets?

CRITICAL THINKING

1. **DRAWING CONCLUSIONS** How does this chapter illustrate the power and importance of the ballot box?
2. **MAKING A JUDGMENT** Whose views—those of Booker T.

Washington or W.E.B. Du Bois—do you think speak more directly to the situation of African-Americans today? Explain your answer.

3. ANALYZING Paul Dunbar died young and discouraged, a seeming "failure." And yet we recall his work today and honor his literary achievements. How do you explain this contradiction?

UNDERSTANDING PREJUDICE

1. Jim Crow came from a song that was ultimately used to make fun of African-Americans. Are there songs today that you believe are demeaning to groups in American society? To women? How do such songs illustrate the negative power of music?

2. Supreme Court decisions often reflect the passions and prejudices of the time. How was this the case in the *Plessy* decision? Find out what decisions the Court has made in recent years regarding civil rights. Do you think a different climate prevails from that of 100 years ago? Explain your answer.

3. Why were the achievements of individuals such as Madame Walker and Ida Wells-Barnett so striking? What additional prejudices did they have to overcome?

4. In many traditional societies men and women lead rigidly segregated lives. What benefits are there to such practices? What disadvantages?

A NEW CENTURY AND NEW OPPORTUNITIES

(1898–1940)

> Great ideals are the glory of man alone. No other creature can have them. Only man can get a vision and an inspiration that will lift him above the level of himself and send him forth against all opposition or any discouragement to do and to dare and to accomplish wonderful and great things for the world and for humanity. The path is not easy, the climbing is rugged and hard, but the glory at the end is worthwhile.
>
> Matthew Henson, black explorer

A new century was soon to dawn. African-Americans had survived attacks and atrocities, sometimes on sheer guts and gusto. Often with nothing but their bare hands, they had carved out educational, administrative, and agricultural niches that had allowed them to grow in American society. African-Americans had proven that they could not be conquered. They could not be killed.

But there were many more milestones to be reached. After all these years, amazingly, many whites were still trying to push blacks back. Indeed, the conquest of people of color across the globe reached its height in the late 1800s. Even the United States took part, gobbling up territory in the Pacific and the Caribbean.

SECTION ONE   **THE INTERNATIONAL SCENE**

VOCABULARY manifest destiny imperialism

African-Americans who had fought for democracy abroad in World War I, like these troops, returned home to a segregated society.

MAIN IDEA The late 1800s were a time of cruel exploitation. Americans conquered the West, while Europeans took over much of Africa.

OBJECTIVES As you read, look for answers to the following questions:
1. Why did European countries start conquering other peoples and setting up colonies in the late 1800s?
2. How did South Africa fall into European hands?
3. How did the Berlin Conference aid Europeans in dividing up Africa? What measures did Africans take to resist?

America's interest in overseas territories was something new. For much of its history, this nation's development was largely internal, due to the fact that the country was so vast. So-called American "settlers" headed west in their covered wagons to take any lands they could get their hands

205

manifest destiny:
a doctrine of the 1800s stating that the United States was meant to expand across the continent to the Pacific Ocean.

on. The process was even given a name—**manifest destiny**. This meant that white America had decided that its "destiny" was to rule the North American continent from the Atlantic to the Pacific. It would "develop" the land, even if that meant killing or uprooting the Native American peoples who lived on it.

But by about 1880 the nation reached from "sea to shining sea." Thus, it started to look outward.

Not surprisingly, Europeans were doing the same thing —but on a much larger scale. Remember, most European countries like Great Britain, Belgium, and Portugal are small and would fit within the boundaries of one large state in the United States. So, they didn't have room for their populations to expand internally like the United States.

The Europeans moved into all parts of the world. All too often this expansion resulted in the destruction of an area's native people.

imperialism:
establishing political or economic control over other countries.

The European governments profited from all this, not only by relieving their overcrowded cities, but also by receiving a percentage of the profits from the settlers' ventures. This exploitation system was called **imperialism**. It refers to countries that literally took over a conquered country and, regardless of distance, made it a *direct* part of the so-called "mother country." Imperialism was cruel in that it completely disrupted the normal development of the conquered nation, forcing it to use its people, resources, and land not for its own advancement, but for the profit of someone else.

The Conquest of South Africa

Of particular interest is the conquest of South Africa. Actually, this began some centuries earlier when, in 1652, Dutch "settlers" reached the Cape of Good Hope in South Africa. This was just 26 years after the Dutch had come to America and settled present-day New York.

And, much like in America, these poor whites, anxious to own something of their own, did not balk at wholesale massacres of the Bushmen and the enslavement of the Hottentots to do it. There was some intermarrying and mixing of the races to be sure. South African mulattoes—or coloreds, as they were called—were, like their American counterparts, often placed above their brothers and sisters in society because of the lighter color of their skin.

By the early 1800s Great Britain had taken control of southern Africa. The Dutch settlers deeply resented the British. Why? For one thing, in 1834 the British government ended slavery in all its possessions, thus freeing the Dutch settlers' many slaves. (This did not mean, however, that black people became equal citizens in society.)

Many Dutch settlers looked for ways to escape British rule. Between 1835 and 1845 about 15,000 Dutch farmers, traveling by wagon train, headed north to the land of the Zulus. All the way, they complained about the "shameful and unjust . . . freedom of our slaves." Of course, they forced their former slaves to go with them on this move north, known as the Great Trek.

Before long, the trekkers made contact with the powerful Zulu nation. In Zululand, the whites began a war against the noble king Dingaan (din-GAHN). By the end of 1838 the trekkers defeated the Zulu at the Battle of Blood River (so-named because the river ran red with Zulu blood).

Far from the British, most of the Dutch settled on an inland plateau, creating the Orange Free State and the Transvaal Republic. They would not remain at peace for long. The discovery in the 1860s and 1880s of valuable minerals on the land of the Afrikaners, as the descendants of the Dutch settlers now called themselves, attracted large numbers of English-speaking miners. Determined to break away from British influence, the Afrikaner republics went to war with Great Britain in 1899. The bloody Boer War, as it is known, ended in defeat for the Afrikaners in 1902. The British then combined the British and Afrikaner colonies into the Union of South Africa.

From the start, South Africa was built on racial inequality. Only white men could vote. Whites ran the mines and the factories. They also owned most of the land. English- and Afrikaner-speaking settlers still had their differences. But they were united in keeping Africans under white control.

Rhodes Controls Rhodesia

Meanwhile, an Englishman named Cecil Rhodes was leading a forcible takeover of the region north of the Transvaal.

Rhodes, who had made a fortune in the diamond and gold fields of South Africa, sponsored a column of white settlers into the fertile highlands later named the Rhodesias. This area was already occupied by the Ndebele (en-day-BAY-lay) who had moved there to escape the Great Trek 50 years earlier. The Ndebele almost defeated the greedy invaders in 1896–1897, but armed with machine guns Rhodes' forces kept control.

Even though he had promised not to, Rhodes shoved the African people off their traditional homelands, in the same way whites had done to American Indians. Rhodesia groaned under the yoke of white rule until 1964 when the northern part of Rhodesia became Zambia. Not until 1980 did southern Rhodesia become the independent nation of Zimbabwe.

Europeans Carve Up Africa

Independence for African colonies was not on the agenda in the late 1800s, however. The European race to exploit Africa had reached such vicious proportions that the rulers of the various nations, like Queen Victoria of England, Kaiser Wilhelm of Germany, and King Leopold of Belgium, called a summit conference in Berlin in 1884 to resolve the situation.

Of course, these ruthless rulers never discussed the rights of the sovereign people who lived in these regions. Instead, they pulled out a map and began dividing the entire African continent among themselves! The Congo went to Belgium. Southwest Africa, Togoland, the Cameroon, and Tanganyika became German colonies. Most of southern and eastern Africa went to Great Britain, while France received much of West and North Africa. Spain, Italy, and Portugal were also allowed to stake out claims.

The Berlin Conference of 1884–1885 made it easier for European powers to take over Africa without fighting among themselves. In Ethiopia in East Africa, however, a great freedom fighter, Emperor Menelik II, was able to keep Europeans out of his country. In 1896 an Italian army invaded Menelik's kingdom. At Adowa they met an Ethiopian army carrying modern European arms. The Italians suffered a stunning defeat. The other European countries agreed to recognize the country's independence making Ethiopia, along with Liberia, the only part of Africa not under European control.

Even though Africa had fallen to European conquest, resistance to foreign rule never ended. It only changed form, as open warfare turned into guerrilla skirmishes and scattered rebellions. Most countries would regain their independence by the 1960s.

The First Pan-African Congress

Enraged at the greed of Europe, the brilliant W.E.B. Du Bois boldly wrote to the European rulers at the Berlin summit conference, and personally denounced their actions before the world. And in 1900, he backed up his words with action by convening the first Pan-African Congress. It was held in London. Thirty-two representatives from Africa, the United States, and the Caribbean attended. At that meeting, the delegates protested the treatment of black people everywhere, but particularly in southern Africa.

Liberal whites were growing concerned with the problem of international racism and colonialism. In 1911 a number of sociologists and anthropologists met in London at the International Congress of Races to address these issues. Du Bois spoke at that gathering as well.

SECTION ONE REVIEW ~~~~~~~~~~~~~~~~~~~~~~~

1. VOCABULARY Write a sentence for each of the following terms: manifest destiny, imperialism.

2. ECONOMICS For what reasons do countries choose to start colonies?

3. HISTORY Why did Dutch settlers in South Africa resent British rule? What did the two groups have in common, however?

4. BIOGRAPHY Why is Emperor Menelik II remembered as a great African freedom fighter?

5. CRITICAL THINKING Compare the treatment of the people of Africa in the late 1800s with that of American Indians at the same time.

SECTION TWO

THE BLACK MILITARY

VOCABULARY Spanish-American War World War I
Great Migration

MAIN IDEA Black troops distinguished themselves in the Spanish-American War and in World War I, but saw little improvement in their treatment at home.

OBJECTIVES As you read, look for answers to the following questions:
1. What role did black troops play in combat in the years after Reconstruction?
2. How did most African-Americans show their willingness to participate in this nation's military efforts?
3. Why did large numbers of black southerners move north after 1900?

By 1900 the United States had conquered the Great Plains and defeated the Spanish in the Spanish-American War. These were, however, minor skirmishes compared to the world wars that lay ahead. In all these conflicts, the nation depended on the skills and bravery of African-American military men. Time and again, African-Americans looked upon success in the military as a means of winning esteem from white American society. Time and again, the American government called upon African-Americans to fight. But sadly, as soon as the conflicts were over, it was business as usual as far as race relations were concerned. Still, staunchly, proudly, black military men continued to fight for their country.

Black Troops in the Years After Reconstruction

After the Civil War, black troops were used largely as peace-keeping forces in the South, as the federal government sought to rebuild the country. But after Reconstruction ended, the federal government hit upon a new plan for its black troops. The idea was astonishing in its irony.

Why not use one group of oppressed people to kill the other? And sure enough, that's just what they did. The government stationed its four remaining black regiments, the 9th and 10th Cavalry and the 24th and 25th Infantry, in the West. Their mission? To keep the trails "safe" for the "settlers" moving West. The enemy? The blacks' brothers and sisters, the Native Americans.

The black soldiers, perhaps with misplaced loyalty, proceeded to carry out their mission all too well. Between 1866 and 1890, the black troops fought over 100 recorded battles with Indian warriors. The government was amazed at their success. After all, they had been given the worst equipment and broken down horses. So, the government hastened to award fourteen of these tough men with the nation's highest military decoration, the Congressional Medal of Honor.

Sergeant Emanual Stance of Company F, 9th Cavalry, was the first African-American to receive the Medal of Honor during the Indian Wars. Stance and a few of his men had been searching for two white children kidnapped during an Indian raid. Suddenly, they found themselves, fighting off a huge number of Indians. The battle lasted for two days.

Stance and his fellow black soldiers did their duty. They stood and fought, thus earning such important recognition.

The Spanish-American War

In the **Spanish-American War** of 1898, African-American soldiers again distinguished themselves. A prominent black historian, Kelly Miller, commented at the time on the problem of black people finding themselves "dominated at home [so that] they themselves imposed on people fighting for liberation in Cuba (and later the Philippines)."

The war started in Cuba, a Spanish colony in which American businesses had heavy investments. For years, Spain's rulers had cruelly put down Cuban revolutionaries who had sought independence for the island. In 1898, the sinking of the American battleship *Maine*, in which 22 black sailors were among the 260 men who lost their lives,

Spanish-American War: the 1898 war between Spain and the United States, won by the United States.

211

brought a harsh response from the United States. Assuming that Spain was responsible for the explosion aboard the *Maine*, Congress quickly passed a declaration of war.

With the American army numbering a mere 28,000 soldiers, the government found itself having to call upon its four black Army regiments. Many other African-American men around the country tried to enlist but were discouraged from doing so, as some whites continued to fear for their safety if blacks were armed.

The Spanish-American War lasted just ten weeks. Nevertheless, the 10th Cavalry was honored for its efforts at the Battle of Las Guasimas, while the 10th and the 25th were honored for their fighting prowess at El Caney. But it was the fighting 24th Infantry who provided the crucial backup for Teddy Roosevelt and his Rough Riders to survive at the decisive Battle of San Juan Hill. All in all, six brave black soldiers, ranking from private to sergeant major, received Medals of Honor in the Spanish-American War.

One of them was Private George H. Wanton. On June 30, 1898, along with other fighting units, the 10th Cavalry attacked rebel strongholds in Tayabacoa, Cuba. Private George H. Wanton watched many of his fellow fighting men fall. Finally, after several attempts failed to save the wounded men, Private Wanton volunteered for the job. Under heavy enemy fire, he brought many wounded soldiers to safety.

On July 1, 1898, in nearby Santiago, Cuba, Sergeant Major Edward L. Baker bravely dodged hails of bullets to rescue a wounded comrade from drowning. Both men were among the six black Medal of Honor recipients.

Despite continuing prejudice and discrimination, black soldiers worked hard and fought well, so much so that they won the admiration of many of their white counterparts. Said one white southerner, "Of all the men I saw fighting, there were none to beat the 10th Cavalry and the colored infantry, and I don't mind saying so."

"Of all the men I saw fighting, there were none to beat the 10th Cavalry and the colored infantry, and I don't mind saying so."
—White southerner on blacks at Battle of San Juan Hill

Black Nurses During the Spanish-American War

Black women also took part in the war effort. In July 1898, the Surgeon General requested that a corps of black women be recruited in Washington, D.C., to nurse patients suffering from typhoid fever. It was generally believed that, because they originally came from Africa, black people were immune to such fevers.

This, of course, was not true. Nevertheless, 32 brave black women volunteered to leave their homes and nurse desperately ill troops who had been sent to Camp Thomas in Georgia.

These women performed so heroically that enthusiastic legislators introduced a bill in Congress to create a permanent Army nurse corps. This legislation went into effect in 1901, making women an official part of the Army. In 1908 Congress set up a Navy Nurse Corps.

World War I

A much more deadly conflict, **World War I**, began in 1914 when Austria declared war on Serbia following the assassination of an Austrian archduke. Within days, the war in Europe grew more intense. A system of treaties and alliances dragged almost every country on the continent into the fighting. On one side were the Allied Powers of Great Britain, France, Russia, and Italy. Opposing them were the Central Powers of Germany, Austria-Hungary, and the Ottoman Empire.

For three years the United States remained neutral. Then, in 1917, with France and England threatened, America felt it had no choice but to join the war. African-Americans were among the first to volunteer for duty.

But make no mistake. World War I was not all it was made out to be for African-Americans. On the surface, there were jaunty slogans about freshfaced American "doughboys" going abroad to "save" their European allies. And there was talk of this being the "war to end all wars." But throughout the war years, black soldiers were forced to fight two battles. One was against the European enemy. The other was against their longtime foe, American racism.

Most of the 370,000 African-Americans in uniform were confined to service behind the lines, in menial noncombat duties. Maintaining their spirit of patriotism, these black soldiers of the "Services of Supply" units worked so hard, day and night, that their fellow soldiers soon dubbed them,

World War I:
a global conflict, between 1914 and 1918, in which the Allied Powers defeated the Central Powers.

213

simply, "SOS." Only 20,000 African-Americans soldiers saw combat action. Those who did fought bravely in all the major battles.

Debate over Black Recruitment

As soon as the United States entered the war, some whites actually tried to prevent blacks from recruiting for service overseas. Many shuddered privately in fear at the thought of arming hundreds of thousands of African-Americans whom they had mistreated so severely. Would America start out fighting one war with its European enemies, only to discover it had another one in its own backyard? The risk seemed too great. President Woodrow Wilson underscored this attitude by declaring that the war was a "white man's war."

On the other hand, some white southern racists saw the war as a way of sacrificing black soldiers to spare white lives. In the words of one southern newspaper:

> It seems a pity to waste good white men in battle with such a foe. The cost of sacrifice would be nearly equalized were the job assigned to Negro troops. An army of a million could probably be easily recruited from the Negroes of this country without drawing from its industrial strength or commercial life. We will be sacrificing white blood and drawing our skilled labor when unskilled labor was available.

African-Americans themselves were split over the war issue. Some wondered why, if black people were not allowed full rights at home, they should be expected to die overseas to defend them.

W.E.B. Du Bois disagreed. He urged African-Americans to press for military service. He wrote: "Close ranks! ... Let us, while this war lasts, forget our special grievances and close our ranks shoulder to shoulder with our own white fellow citizens." Robert S. Abbott, publisher of *The Chicago Defender*, echoed that sentiment in his paper: "I say with absolute certainty ... we are Americans always!"

Most African-Americans heeded these words and rushed

"Close ranks! ... Let us, while this war lasts, forget our special grievances and close our ranks shoulder to shoulder with our own white fellow citizens."
—W.E.B. Du Bois

patriotically to enlist. Black leaders such as California attorney Oscar Hudson received official permission to travel throughout his home state to promote black army volunteers. He organized enough men for six black army companies. Then, in May 1917, Congress passed a Selective Service Act, calling to service young men of all races.

Black Army Officers

The recruitment issue thus decided, controversy then raged over the training of black officers to command these troops. Black leaders argued that the government should not deny "the right of our best [Negro] men to lead troops of their race in battle." The government balked, claiming it was "illegal" for black officers to be trained in camps with white officers.

To make its point, the Army tried to force its highest-ranking black officer into retirement. His name was Colonel Charles Young. A brilliant officer, Young was also one of the few black graduates of West Point. Imagine his humiliation when he was forced out of the military because, the government claimed, he had high blood pressure.

In a dramatic bid to clear his name, this exceptional soldier jumped on a horse—with full field gear on his back—and rode from his home in Ohio all the way to Washington, D.C. Embarrassed by Young's presence, as well as by protests from black citizens across the country, the Army reinstated him. But desperate not to have Young lead black troops, the government reassigned him to Haiti as a military attache, where he remained throughout the war.

Finally, with the controversy regarding black officers mounting, the War Department compromised by setting up a separate black officers' training camp at Fort Des Moines, Iowa. It sent 1,000 "college-trained and college-worthy" young African-American men there.

The Story of the 369th Infantry

It was in this hostile atmosphere that the all-black 369th Infantry Division was shipped overseas.

These raw recruits and officers barely had a chance to recover from their European voyage before they were sent directly to the front lines, where the fighting was heaviest. In fact, they didn't know it at the time, but they were the among the first American troops to go to the front.

These brave young men were incorporated into the French 161st Division. They fought against the Germans in the heaviest lines of fire for an incredible 113 days straight!

And, still with barely any rest, these same black soldiers spearheaded the last great attack which ended World War I in an Allied victory. On September 25, 1918, the 369th began a tortuous, deadly journey, directly through enemy lines, across France's Vosges Mountains, all the way to the Rhine River. Most of the time, these hardy heroes had no artillery cover at all.

On September 27, these soldiers were ordered to take out a German machine gun station near the town of Sechault. To get to it, they had to cross nearly a mile of open land, in clear sight of the gunners. Crawling on their bellies, one by one, the men fell. It seemed like certain death for all of them.

Suddenly, the remains of another badly hit battalion joined them. The enemy stopped firing for seconds. In that scant time, Major Arthur Little ordered one of the black companies to seize the German position. With nothing but raw courage and fixed bayonets, the men rushed the trench where the Germans were holed up, falling on them ferociously.

Over and over again, the men of the 369th repeated such desperate maneuvers, as they drove the Germans back —mile by bloody mile—until November 11, 1918, the day fighting ended.

Their feat was so heroic that the French awarded the unit and 170 of its officers the Croix de Guerre, France's highest honor for bravery in military action. Their pride was tempered, however, by the knowledge that only 725 of their original 3,000 black comrades were still alive or on their feet at war's end.

Highlighting Heroes—Henry Johnson and Needham Roberts

The two most highly decorated black fighting men in World War I were Privates Henry Johnson and Needham Roberts. Both were part of the brave 369th Infantry Division. These two men were on duty in the most dangerous portion of the war zone, the area separating the American and German lines and called "No Man's Land." They had the important mission of manning a critical observation post.

Suddenly, they were set upon by a surprise German raid. Both men fought like tigers. Vastly outnumbered and wounded, Johnson and Roberts managed to use their rifles and hand grenades. When those ran out, they fought the enemy hand-to-hand. The two courageous black soldiers managed to kill four Germans and wound another 32! Both Johnson and Roberts won the Croix de Guerre.

War hero Henry Johnson

Black War Hero in the French Foreign Legion

Eugene Jacques Bullard was the only African-American to become a fighter pilot during World War I. And the only reason he had that opportunity was because Bullard fought in the famed French Foreign Legion.

Although born in America, Bullard had tired of racial discrimination and had left this country. Young, bright, and strong, he had become a top prize fighter and had toured all over Europe and the Middle East by the time war broke out.

Bullard first joined the Foreign Legion as an infantryman, but after being wounded he volunteered to join the brand new Aviator Corps. (At that time, flying was new, since it had just been in 1903 that the Wright Brothers had made the first successful flight.)

The nickname of Bullard's flying unit was "Swallows of Death." They lived up to it by flying in combat against German fighter planes. Bullard is credited with downing two German planes, and his French comrades dubbed him "The Black Swallow." Bullard's plane carried the hand-painted motto which indicated his feeling that, as a black man, he was the equal of any other—"All Blood Runs Red."

Bullard survived the war, and in the 1940s he married and returned to the United States.

Black Nurses During World War I

Shortly before the outbreak of World War I, a group of stalwart black women organized the National Association of Colored Nurses. They were determined that African-American nurses gain proper recognition and be accepted as professionals.

The U.S. Army did not call upon the services of black nurses until September 1918, right before the end of the war. And the only reason it did so was because of the outbreak of a deadly worldwide flu epidemic, which eventually would kill 22 million people. The Army, in desperation, sent 18 black nurses to hospitals in Ohio and Illinois. Because of the critical shortage of medical personnel, these black nurses tended both black and white patients. They soon earned high praise from the hospital administrators with whom they worked.

Migration North During World War I

The early 1900s, and particularly the World War I years, brought about a major opportunity for African-Americans. Just as in the Civil War, whites were forced to go to black people for help. World War I (1914–1918) created shortages in the northern work force, as millions of young men went off to war. The war also halted the flow of white immigrants from Europe. So, many northern businesses sent agents to the South with enticing offers of factory jobs and opportunities to get off the farm.

Great Migration:
the movement of large numbers of African-Americans out of the South, starting in the early 1900s.

Southern black people had viewed the North as a kind of "heaven" ever since the days of the Underground Railroad. As a result, they packed up their belongings and moved to the big northern cities in numbers so great that this movement became known as the **Great Migration**. Historians estimate that from 1915 to 1920, as many as 500,000 black southerners took a chance on the American Dream and moved north. Before this, in 1910, only 10.6 percent of all black workers were employed in industrial or manufacturing areas. By 1920, that number had skyrocketed to 31.2 percent.

Westward Ho!

The Great Migration brought large numbers of African-Americans to the West as well as the North. Ever since the

218

Gold Rush days, black people had been heading west, seeking new opportunities. By 1910, California's black population was already more than 21,000, with the majority in the Los Angeles area.

In San Francisco and northern California, the turn of the century saw many black people as owners of small businesses, such as cafes, boarding houses, and variety stores. In fact, for many years in San Francisco, the only shoe manufacturing company was owned by the energetic and prosperous black business team of Mifflin W. Gibbs and Peter Lester. San Francisco even boasted a black shipping line, all of whose stockholders were black. It was called The Navigation Company of Colored Men. There was also at least one black whaling master, William T. Shorey, who owned a fleet of fine schooners.

Major Setbacks

On the West Coast, as in the North, many African-Americans faced major setbacks not long after establishing themselves in their newly adopted homes.

In both areas the problem was the same—finding and keeping jobs. Before and after World War I, the continuous influx of immigrants onto the shores on both coasts meant more competition for jobs. In northern California, the competition came largely from Asian immigrants; in southern California from Hispanics. In the North, Irish and other European immigrants battled blacks (often literally) for factory jobs. In 1916, in East St. Louis, Illinois, factory owners brought in thousands of black workers when the white workers went out on strike. Rabid, the white workers took out their fury on the hapless outsiders, gunning down at least 100 and burning the dwellings of 6,000 more.

In the South, meanwhile, whites began to punish anyone urging black people to assert their independence and move North. In Birmingham, Alabama, and Jacksonville, Florida, government officials started demanding exorbitant "license fees" from the black men who were being paid as migration agents for northern businesses. These fees sometimes were as high as $1,000. In at least one southern town, the black agent's treatment was much more direct. It was death.

White hysteria grew so high, that it actually became a crime to read *The Chicago Defender* or the NAACP's *The Crisis* in Georgia, Mississippi, and South Carolina.

SECTION TWO REVIEW

1. VOCABULARY Write a sentence for each of the following terms: Spanish-American War, World War I, Great Migration.

2. HISTORY What role did black troops play in the Indian Wars?

3. HISTORY What obstacles did black troops face in participating both in the Spanish-American War and in World War I?

4. ECONOMICS How did World War I bring new job opportunities for African-American workers?

5. CRITICAL THINKING To what degree did immigration result in social tensions in the 1900-1920 period? Do you think immigration should have been halted? Explain your answer.

SECTION THREE   PIONEERS IN THE FIGHT FOR EQUALITY

VOCABULARY UNIA Great Depression collective bargaining black Cabinet

MAIN IDEA Two black leaders—Marcus Garvey and A. Philip Randolph—offered different approaches for advancing the cause of black Americans.

OBJECTIVES As you read, look for answers to the following questions:
1. How did Marcus Garvey offer hope to African-Americans?
2. What was A. Philip Randolph's approach to improving life for African-Americans?

It became painfully obvious in the years after World War I that, in spite of black America's patriotic efforts, whites were still not prepared to grant African-Americans their constitutional rights. In fact, the early 1920s witnessed a revival of the Ku Klux Klan. White Americans put on more sheets than ever, inciting violence throughout the country.

What to do? Two black leaders emerged with different ideas for meeting the same goal.

Marcus Garvey

The more flamboyant of these leaders was Marcus Garvey. As a child on the Caribbean island of Jamaica, young Marcus read about his hero, Napoleon Bonaparte, and dreamed of a better life for himself and his family. Garvey's father was a laborer on road construction, but he made enough money to send his son to school until he was 16. Then, young Garvey became an apprentice in a printing plant. It was here that he showed early signs of the charisma that would make him the leader of the largest international black organization the world had ever seen.

By the time he was 22, Garvey had become plant foreman and soon led all the printers in Kingston, Jamaica, to strike for better pay. They got it. Inspired by this success, Garvey began organizing all the black workers on the island. He was, himself, a striking ebony-skinned man who understood firsthand the prejudice of whites and light-skinned mulattoes.

The Universal Negro Improvement Association

The year 1917 found Garvey in the United States. He had come with the intention of soliciting funds to set up self-help schools in Jamaica modelled after Booker T. Washington's Tuskegee Institute. But Garvey soon found his way to that new mecca for African-Americans, New York City's Harlem.

The exciting atmosphere of Harlem stimulated him, and he decided to stay in America. Soon, he was speaking up and down the East Coast. By March 1917, enthralled followers found themselves signing up to join his newly created Universal Negro Improvement Association (**UNIA**). His UNIA, he said, would unite black people all over the world to go back to Africa to found a "strong Negro nation."

UNIA:
organization, founded by Marcus Garvey, the goal of which was the return of all black people to Africa.

221

"Up, you mighty race!" he called to his followers, his deep voice booming out of his short, rotund frame:

> We have died for 500 years for an alien race. The time has come for the Negro to die for himself.... Race is greater than law! Wake up, Ethiopia! Wake up, Africa! Let us work toward the one glorious end of a free, redeemed and mighty nation. Up, you mighty race! You can accomplish what you will.

"Up, you mighty race! You can accomplish what you will."
—Marcus Garvey

"Back to Africa!" he urged his readers in his weekly newspaper, *The Negro World*. And with that, Garvey boldly launched the most unprecedented black business undertaking in the history of this nation.

Why unprecedented? Because it was financed *completely* by average working black people. Deeply and desperately believing in the need to control their own destiny, they humbly put dollar bills into envelopes and mailed them to the one man who assured them they could do it. Millions of these crumpled, sweat-stained bills flowed into UNIA coffers, soaked with the aspirations of the two million people who sent them. The UNIA was said to have received some $10 million between 1919 and 1921!

Until then, as we have seen, a few black business leaders had managed to put together their own companies. But never before had the black community in America, as a nation, united in one grand economic enterprise.

Opposition to Garvey

Could this bold plan work? Opinions flew, thick and fast. Some older, more conservative black leaders quivered visibly, fearing Garvey would provoke an open split between blacks and whites in America.

W.E.B. Du Bois, himself an expert in Pan-Africanism, urged black people not to invest in the conquest of Africa. "Do not take desperate chances in flighty dreams," he urged.

Black labor leader A. Philip Randolph agreed with Du Bois. Randolph, working within the organized union system, was appalled at Garvey's wild promises and nontraditional manner. And he was grieved that black people should be giving their hard-earned money to a man he believed to be dishonest.

The black church's reaction to Garvey was summed up by Episcopal minister Dr. Robert Bagnall: "Garvey [is] egotistic, tyrannical, intolerant, cunning, avaricious, without regard for truth."

Garvey Keeps Up the Pressure

Garvey paused only long enough to dash off fiery rebuttals to his detractors in his weekly newspaper. Sneering publicly, he told his followers, "Uncle Tom Negroes must give way to the new Negro, who is seeking his place in the sun."

Marcus Garvey

Then he was off again, creating new enterprises to support his "Back to Africa" plan. First, he set up his own steamship line, The Black Star Line. And he sent UNIA representatives to negotiate with Liberian leaders for land to start a colony there.

Meanwhile, to keep the momentum going, Garvey held his first annual International Congress on August 1, 1919, in New York City. Twenty-five thousand delegates streamed into Madison Square Garden from the United States, as well as from South America and Africa.

Garvey held huge parades down Lenox Avenue in Harlem, leading UNIA members dressed in lavish uniforms bedecked with gold tassels and braid, complete with honorary titles such as "Duke of Uganda" and "The Most Noble Order of the Nile." Women marched as part of the Universal Black Cross Nurses.

For these black working people, it was a dream come true. Chests swelling with pride, people seemed to be thinking, "I am somebody!" Is it any wonder that they looked up to Marcus Garvey as almost a god? Who else gave them any hope?

By 1920 Garvey addressed the religious issue as well, founding the African Orthodox Church. In his church, Jesus and Mary were depicted as black. As for political issues, he established the "Court of Ethiopia," with himself as Provisional President-General of Africa.

Garvey's Downfall

But by 1923, it became increasingly apparent that Garvey suffered from a lack of professional personnel to implement his dreams. One by one, his plans unravelled.

For instance, UNIA officers bought three ships at tremendously inflated prices for the Black Star Line. One vessel, *The Yarmouth*, cost $165,000, but immediately broke down as it set sail for Cuba. It finally managed to limp into Miami with sails made of bedsheets. Garvey was forced to get rid of the floating hulk for $1,600.

Garvey continued to forge ahead, still stubbornly believing he could succeed without real business expertise. He started other businesses such as a hotel, restaurant, laundry, and grocery store. In theory, they could have worked. But Garvey could not bring himself to let anyone else handle his affairs. He watched them all fold.

Through it all, Garvey's followers offered him their love. They still needed someone to tell them that their black skin was as good or better than white or light brown, and that they could establish an African society that would rival any in America.

Then, in his impatience to create an all-black nation, Garvey went so far as to advocate black separatism by publicly endorsing the goals of Ku Klux Klan. It was just too much. Garvey's enemies called for his downfall. By May 1923, they had turned over evidence to the government of mail fraud in the UNIA's solicitation of funds, forcing him into court.

More cocky than ever, Garvey dismissed his very able lawyer after just one day's trial and proceeded to defend himself. Unfortunately, he had no real knowledge of the law. So, in spite of some of the finest speeches he had ever made, Garvey talked himself into five years in prison and a $1,000 fine.

In 1927 President Calvin Coolidge commuted Garvey's sentence, but on the condition that he go back to Jamaica. As resilient as ever, Garvey, upon his return to Jamaica, won a seat on the Kingston City Council and started another newspaper, *The Black Man*. After more legal troubles and time in jail, Garvey headed to England. There he boldly petitioned the League of Nations, an early version of the United Nations, for land in Africa. He died in London in 1940.

In spite of his business and financial failures, Garvey's amazing success in inspiring average black folk was to remain unsurpassed until the arrival on the American scene of Martin Luther King, Jr.

The Impact of the Great Depression

Marcus Garvey's UNIA was gone, and with it the hopes of millions of black working people. To make matters worse, in 1929 the nation's economy started a dizzying downward spiral. Rich and poor alike were slammed to the bottom of the economic heap, as the stock market crashed and the nation entered the **Great Depression**. White collar executives found themselves running elevators or pushing brooms. And throngs of black men and women found themselves out of work entirely.

Great Depression:
the period of severe economic
hardship lasting from 1929 to
World War II.

By the time America limped into the 1930s, a black person with a job was considered lucky. And certain jobs, in spite of the economic nosedive, had slightly better pay and perks. One such industry was that of railroad car porters and maids.

The Plight of Railway Workers

Mass airplane travel was still decades away. If you had to go somewhere, you took a train. And since it took a week to go across the country, if you could afford it you rented a sleeping car. Trains, then, were traveling mini-hotels. And the black porters and maids provided all the services that went with them. The only problem was that, unlike the conductors and other personnel who were white, these black workers had much longer hours for much less pay. They had to travel 10,000 miles per month. And after working faithfully for 45 years, the highest salary they could expect was $59 a month, plus tips. There was no such thing as a union for them.

Still and all, in the black community railroad porters and maids were only a cut below teachers and civil service employees in prestige. They mingled with the wealthiest whites, wore uniforms, and got to travel. The porters and maids seemed caught. How could they demand the kind of money their white counterparts got, without risking the loss of their jobs? They had been debating these issues for years, even before the Depression had started.

The Pullman Company was the major corporation that supplied the train lines with their service personnel. In 1918 the government decided to allow Pullman workers to set up unions, which whites did, negotiating for shorter hours and more pay. But Pullman flatly refused to recognize a porters' union.

The Rise of A. Philip Randolph

In desperation, a few of the more courageous porters met in 1925 with a young, radical, black labor organizer. His name was Asa Philip Randolph. Since Randolph was not a porter and could not be fired by Pullman, the porters asked him to head their newly formed union, the Brotherhood of Sleeping Car Porters.

Randolph thought long and hard about taking the job. Born in Florida in 1889 to a poor family, young Randolph had worked as a railroad laborer to help pay his way through high school. He went to New York in 1906 to attend college, but had trouble paying his way. At every job, it seemed, he tried to organize his fellow workers for better conditions and was promptly fired!

He finally graduated from New York City College and, along with a wealthy young black friend, Chandler Owen, started a black newspaper called *The Messenger*. The young men used their paper to call for a "revolution" of the masses as the "only sure guarantee of social justice."

And, when World War I came, Randolph declared himself a pacifist and refused to go to war. He was jailed for his stand.

Knowing of his courage and thinking that this might be the only man who could stand up to the Pullman Company and save them, the porters approached Randolph.

Randolph accepted the job. With barely any pay, the young David decided to take on the Goliath of industry, vowing to win, no matter how long it might take. It would, in fact, take twelve long years before victory was even within sight.

At this time there was very little government regulation of industry. So, the Pullman Company ignored Randolph's Brotherhood and went right on threatening to fire any porters who fought for union rights. Indeed, it fired hundreds of black men, replacing them with Filipino and Mexican workers. And Pullman publicly denounced Randolph as a "Communist."

The Porters' Strike

Randolph and his fledgling group bore this stoically. Finally, in 1928 Randolph took the desperate measure of calling for a strike. He hoped to call national attention to the porters' plight and get the federal government to intervene. In 1926 Congress had passed the Railway Labor Act, and since then its Mediation Board had intervened in several railroad negotiations.

Randolph realized he was asking the Brotherhood members to risk everything. Would they? Could they?

Again, the Pullman Company struck terror in the porters' hearts by firing black workers and hiring more Filipinos. Even William Green, president of the large, white, American Federation of Labor, privately advised Randolph to "postpone" any ideas of a strike.

Most of the Brotherhood members, anxious about their families and their own lives, pulled out. *The Messenger* ceased publication, and the Brotherhood office all but shut down.

Just when it seemed that all was lost, the NAACP persuaded a wealthy white philanthropic group, the Garland Fund, to donate $10,000 to the Brotherhood.

Meanwhile, Randolph started a new newspaper, *The Black Worker*, and continued to hammer his message home. The AFL still would not allow the Brotherhood to join its ranks. So, standing alone, Randolph went on with the black members he had. Finally, in 1934 Congress passed the Railway Labor Act. This new law guaranteed **collective bargaining**. The Brotherhood now had nearly 8,000 members and $500,000 in its treasury. Finally, it forced the Pullman Company to acknowledge it as the exclusive bargaining agent for the porters and maids.

But it was 1937 before the company finally signed an agreement. Victorious, the porters and maids received $2 million dollars in wage increases. Their working hours were cut by one-third, and the distance they had to travel went down to 7,000 miles per month.

collective bargaining: the process of negotiation between an employer and a labor union to settle disputes.

Plans for a March on Washington

Most men, having won such a victory, would have been content. But not Randolph. In 1941, he spearheaded the most ambitious black protest movement since the slave revolts of the South.

In the late 1930s, as danger of another world war came closer to America, blacks protested discrimination in the war and defense industries. Of the 30,000 defense workers in New York City, for example, only 142 were black. Randolph decided to organize a mass march of protest in Washington, D.C. Such a march on the nation's capital had only been tried twice before, in 1894 and in 1932, but never by African-Americans.

When word of the march spread, white government officials, including New York mayor Fiorello LaGuardia and President Franklin D. Roosevelt, met with Randolph to urge him to change his mind. But the great labor leader was adamant:

> Verily, the biggest problem confronting Negroes today is economic, that is, getting work and wages to buy food, clothing and shelter. Thus the March on Washington Movement sets forth as the cardinal and primary cornerstone of its program: economic action.

Fearing a race riot, President Franklin Roosevelt issued Executive Order 8802, just one week before "M-Day." It said, "There shall be no discrimination in the employment of workers in defense industries and in Government because of race, creed, color, or national origin. . . ."

The presidential decree also set up the nation's first Committee on Fair Employment Practices. This group was charged with investigating violations of the executive order. Triumphantly, Randolph called off the march. Another victory was at hand. For the first time since the Emancipation Proclamation of 1863, a President had issued an order protecting the rights of African-Americans.

A. Philip Randolph had put the pressure on President Roosevelt, and it had worked. African-Americans had learned how to organize and win. And they wanted never to go back again.

Mary McLeod Bethune

Actually, Roosevelt's Democratic administration was the most sympathetic to African-Americans since the days of

Reconstruction. Black voters rewarded FDR with their support, shifting from the Republican Party to the Democrats (a shift in allegiance which continues to this day).

Among Roosevelt's supporters was a remarkable black woman, Mary McLeod Bethune. In 1904 Mrs. Bethune founded the Daytona Normal and Industrial Institute for Negro Girls. This institution subsequently merged with the Cookman Institute to become Bethune-Cookman College. Later, she became a close friend of Eleanor Roosevelt, wife of the President.

Mrs. Roosevelt saw to it that Mrs. Bethune had access to important educational circles. Later, when President Roosevelt began the unprecedented habit of meeting with black leaders to hear their views on civil rights, he included Mrs. Bethune in that important circle.

In fact, Roosevelt went on to name her as an official Presidential Adviser. During the early days of his administration, she was one of the organizers of the National Youth Administration. This federal agency distributed some $40 million and set up programs for many underprivileged young Americans of all races.

From 1936 to 1944, Mrs. Bethune's federal government title was Director of the Division of Negro Affairs. Her fearless championing of the rights of black students, especially in the South, helped lead to such things as recognition of Negro History Week. Roosevelt named more blacks like Mrs. Bethune to federal positions than any President before him. By 1939, those appointed were being called Roosevelt's **black Cabinet**.

black Cabinet:
the name given to those African-Americans whom President Franklin Roosevelt placed in significant federal positions.

A Historic Concert

The story of Marian Anderson is another example of why African-Americans supported the Roosevelt administration. One of the greatest concert singers the world has ever seen, in 1939 Anderson gave the most famous concert of her career. It was not in a concert hall at all, but on the steps of the Lincoln Memorial in Washington, D.C. Anderson had been scheduled to perform at the famous Constitution Hall, but at the last minute the "blueblood" Daughters of the American Revolution had refused her permission to do so. Eleanor Roosevelt was so upset by the racial snub that she resigned from the DAR in protest. Meanwhile, the Secretary

229

of the Interior invited her to sing outdoors, at the Lincoln Memorial. And she did so. A host of notables, including the First Lady, several Supreme Court justices, and congressmen, attended the famous concert, which drew a huge crowd of 75,000 people.

SECTION THREE REVIEW

1. **VOCABULARY** Write a sentence for each of the following terms: UNIA, Great Depression, collective bargaining, black Cabinet.

2. **BIOGRAPHY** How did Marcus Garvey try to unite black people all over the world?

3. **ECONOMICS** How did the Great Depression affect African-Americans?

4. **BIOGRAPHY** What methods did A. Philip Randolph use to advance his goals?

5. **CRITICAL THINKING** How realistic was it, in the 1920s, to expect a "Back to Africa" plan to succeed? Explain your answer.

SECTION FOUR   A CULTURAL FLOWERING

VOCABULARY Harlem Renaissance

MAIN IDEA The 1920s saw African-Americans make their mark in a variety of cultural endeavors.

OBJECTIVES As you read, look for answers to the following questions:
1. Who were some of the leading artists of the Harlem Renaissance?
2. What African-Americans gained fame on the musical stage?
3. How were African-Americans generally portrayed in the movies?

African-Americans were also making breakthroughs on the cultural front. By the early 1920s, so many leading black writers and artists had moved to Harlem that this period of creativity became known as the **Harlem Renaissance**. For the first time, black artists could celebrate black life and find a market for their work. But there was plenty of activity in other regions too. On the West Coast it centered around the phenomenon of motion pictures. And more adventurous still, some creative African-Americans made their way to Europe and the Soviet Union.

Harlem Renaissance: a black literary and artistic movement of the 1920s.

Harlem's Hopefuls

During the Roaring Twenties, Harlem became *the* place for liberal white intellectuals to meet their black counterparts and talk about "a better life." All the time, flirtatious flappers danced the night away, doing the "Charleston." Through it all, a core of black intellectuals, though hemmed in their small, cramped apartments, were confident that they could usher in a truly new age. Their black pride pulsing, they wrote passionately of everything from life on the streets to life on the old plantations.

Highlighting a Hero—Langston Hughes

Perhaps the best-known artist of the Harlem Renaissance was a poet, essayist, and playwright named Langston Hughes. This talented writer described the plight of the average black person with honest, unpretentious clarity. Born in Joplin, Missouri, Hughes spent his early years with his grandmother in Kansas, before going to high school in Cleveland, where he lived with his mother. His early talent had already emerged by the time he graduated as class poet. He spent a year with his father, who was living and working in Mexico City, and then studied at Columbia University in New York.

After a disagreement with his father, Hughes had to leave college and go to work. Perhaps because he had already traveled so widely as a child, he sought out work that required travel as well, spending two years on a freighter that went as far as Africa. He worked in Paris for a short

231

time as a doorman before returning home. In New York once again, he met one of the popular white liberal intellectuals of the day, Carl Van Vechten, who introduced him to the Harlem literary set.

In 1925, Hughes won first prize in *Opportunity Magazine's* writing contest for his "Weary Blues." From then on, he wrote steadily—novels, plays, and books of poetry. Hughes also published anthologies of other black writers to let the public know about their work. One of these is *Poems from Black Africa.* One of Hughes's most famous poems, "Harlem," illustrates the frustration of so many African-Americans:

"What happens to a dream deferred?"
—Langston Hughes

> What happens to a dream deferred?
> Does it dry up
> like a raisin in the sun?
> Or fester like a sore—
> And then run?
> Does it stink like rotten meat?
> Or crust and sugar over—
> like syrup sweet?
> Maybe it just sags
> like a heavy load,
> *Or does it explode?*

Highlighting a Hero—Claude McKay

Claude McKay was considered the spokesman for the more militant of the young black Harlem writers. Born in Jamaica, McKay came to the United States in 1913 to study agriculture at Tuskegee Institute. But his need to express himself through poetry drew him first to New York, then to London. He published in literary magazines in both cities.

Like Hughes, many of McKay's poems reflected the life of black working folk, as opposed to the elite. In fact, McKay often wrote in the Jamaican dialect known as *patois.*

His most noted book of poetry was called *Harlem Shadows* (1922) and his landmark poem was the stirring plea, "If We Must Die":

> If we must die
> Let it not be like hogs

232

Hunted and penned in an inglorious spot
While round us bark the mad and hungry dogs
Making their mock at our accursed lot....

Though far outnumbered
Let us show us brave
And for their thousand blows
Deal one death blow.

This was the same poem that British Prime Minister Winston Churchill would quote before Congress during World War II, when he came to plea for support to defeat Hitler.

Highlighting a Hero—Zora Neale Hurston

Zora Neale Hurston, another memorable figure of the Harlem Renaissance, came from the tiny, all-black town of Eatonville, Florida. She made her way to New York, working as a maid for a Gilbert & Sullivan production, before going on to become one of the few black women of her time to graduate from Columbia University. Earlier, at Howard University, she had studied under Alain Locke, educator and chief essayist of the New Negro cultural movement. Through him, she met Langston Hughes and other writers who urged her to begin publishing her work.

Hurston was more fascinated with rural black life than with the urban scene, so she returned home to Florida many times, to listen to neighbors swap folk stories and spin yarns. These became the background material for her first novel, *Jonah's Gourd Vine* (1934), and for many of her later works.

Other Noted Harlem Renaissance Writers

A black writer known for his quiet, lyric style was Countee Cullen. Cullen's love poem, "If You Should Go," reflects a gentle spirit:

Go quietly; a dream
When done, should leave no trace

That it has lived, except a gleam
Across the dreamer's face.

James Weldon Johnson became well-known as both a writer and editor. In 1927 he published *God's Trombones*, a collection of "folk sermons in verse." In 1928 he came out with a controversial novel, *Autobiography of an Ex-Coloured Man*, about racial mingling. And, through his work as executive secretary of the NAACP, he is most widely remembered for the lyrics to "Lift Every Voice And Sing," the song often called the "Negro National Anthem."

Roland Hayes and the World of Music

By the turn of the century, the musical world had become an outlet of sorts for African-Americans. The first black man to find success on the legitimate concert stage was Roland Hayes.

Born in Georgia, Hayes attended Fisk University, where he began to develop his voice as a member of the Jubilee Singers. In 1917, when no whites anywhere would help him get work on the legitimate concert stage, Hayes gathered up his courage, took his $400 in savings, and rented Boston's Symphony Hall himself! He tried to get the governor's wife to become a patroness, but she, along with other whites, threw up a "storm of protest" at his audacity.

Nevertheless, the courageous young Hayes went on, and his melodious tenor voice did the impossible. White and black concertgoers raved over his performance.

In 1920 Hayes decided to go a step further. He took his entire savings of $1,100 and headed for London. In spite of his earlier success, he had to finance his own concerts. He kept at it for a year, later recalling that "I practically lost my mind. I was hungry, my spirits were low, the weather was stormy and cold, and I came down with pneumonia."

At this, his lowest point, King George V and Queen Mary invited him to give a concert at Buckingham Palace. This command performance brought offers flooding in, including a concert at Carnegie Hall. He later sang for royalty throughout Europe.

Hayes's success paved the way for other black concert stars such as Paul Robeson and Marian Anderson.

234

Black Performers in the Limelight

African-Americans like Hayes were rare on the legitimate stage, however. Most became "hoofers" or "crooners" in minstrel shows, which later became known as vaudeville.

In this era before movies and television, these stage shows were actually the creation of white performers. As far back as the 1840s, white entertainers like Thomas D. Rice and Daniel Decatur Emmett found they could get laughs by clumsily imitating the sprightly movements of nimble black dancers. To add to the raw humor, they smeared burnt cork on their faces and painted on big lips. These men were just one step away from circus clowns, who did virtually the same thing, only painting their faces white and putting on big noses. And both bore striking resemblances to the bumbling court jesters of old.

In the early minstrel shows, there were several standard "types." They were all played by whites. One was known as Jim Crow, a kind of rough, black "country bumpkin." His Irish counterpart was Mike Fink, also supposed to be long on brawn but short on brains. The other extreme was Jim Dandy, impeccable in ruffled shirt and top hat, a blackfaced counterpart to the white character, Yankee Doodle Dandy.

By Civil War's end, when African-Americans were finally allowed on stage, all they could do was play variations on these already established themes.

In 1865 Charles Hicks, a black performer, organized the first black minstrel show. Audiences loved the act, but Hicks faced such abuse from white theater owners that he was forced to turn over management of the troop to a white entrepreneur, Charles Callender. Under Callender's direction, the group went so far as to paint their own faces black! But it worked. They were hugely successful.

In 1898 black producer Bob Cole introduced "A Trip to Coontown," the first show to be written, produced, and managed by African-Americans. Unlike its predecessors, the play had a story with a plot, rather than just a series of jokes and dances. Also in 1898, the black talent of Paul Dunbar, Will Marion Cook, and James Weldon Johnson combined to produced "Clorindy—The Origin of the Cakewalk." In this show, the music known as "ragtime" got to show its stuff.

By 1921 New Yorkers were flocking to a theater on 63rd

Street to see "Shuffle Along." Noble Sissle and Eubie Blake wrote the lively music. One of their songs, "I'm Just Wild About Harry!," is fondly remembered today.

"Shuffle Along" ushered in the Jazz Age. "Talk about pep!" one reviewer enthused. Searching for more, white partygoers ventured farther and farther into Harlem. In 1924, they flocked in such numbers to see "Runnin' Wild" that its new dance, "The Charleston," became an immediate hit.

Many talented African-American performers got their start in the black New York musicals of the 1920s. Josephine Baker, who was to go on to international fame in Paris, was in the chorus line of "Shuffle Along." Florence Mills's brief but sensational career took off in 1926 with "Blackbirds." And Bill "Bojangles" Robinson also became a star in that same play. Fats Waller's famous song, "Ain't Misbehavin'," was introduced in "Hot Chocolates" in 1929.

Highlighting a Hero—Scott Joplin

Scott Joplin gained fame for the musical form he called "Ragtime," a lively, syncopated toe-tapping rhythm.

Joplin was born in 1868 in Texarkana, Texas. He inherited his love of music from his father and mother, then went on to perfect his technique at the George R. Smith College for Negroes in Sedalia, Missouri. By 1899, he had composed "The Maple Leaf Rag."

By 1900 Joplin was in St. Louis, Missouri, as director of an opera company, and was composing his first early "ragtime opera." Four years later Joplin ventured to New York, where he wrote his most ambitious ragtime opera, "Treemonisha."

Like many other artists, Joplin's genius went largely unrecognized until after his death. His beloved "Treemonisha" would not be fully performed until 1972, and his upbeat ragtime tunes would not receive national acclaim until years later, when they were used in the motion picture, "The Sting."

"Empress of the Blues"—Bessie Smith

The greatest jazz singer of all time, Bessie Smith was born into abject poverty in Selma, Alabama. She began singing her own "downhome" version of the blues in small cafes when she was discovered and made a star by Columbia Records.

By 1923, Smith's "Down-Hearted Blues" had sold over 2 million copies, and the next few years saw Smith recording with top artists like Louis Armstrong and earning an incredible $2,000 a week.

Tragically, Smith's funds were mismanaged, and she died from injuries in an auto accident after being refused admittance to a white southern hospital. Her legacy lives on in her incredible music, which was incorporated into the overall American music scene.

Bessie Smith

Highlighting a Hero—Duke Ellington

Edward "Duke" Ellington was one of the top creative geniuses of the Jazz Age, as the 1920s were often called. In 1923 Ellington made his way to New York and formed his first band, Ellington's Kentucky Club Orchestra, named after the club in which they performed. Throughout the next decades, the dapper "Duke," as adoring fans dubbed him, appeared elegantly in top hat and tails, previewing one musical innovation after another. In 1943, for instance, he interwove jazz into the traditional concert format in his smash hit, "Black, Brown, and Beige."

Ellington took every opportunity to include as many other talented performers in his concerts as he could, showcasing jazz artists like Johnny Hodges, as well as such gifted singers as Ella Fitzgerald.

"Black" Plays Produced by Whites

The success of African-American performers led to the discovery of black themes by white artists. In 1926 Paul Green, a white dramatist, won a Pulitzer Prize for "Abraham's Bosom," one of the first tragedies dealing with black characters. Its success led to the dramatic play about black people's "tragic" circumstances, "Porgy." Later, the play was made into the musical "Porgy and Bess," by George and Ira Gershwin. The fiery dramatist, Eugene O'Neill, took black tragedy one step further, with his "All God's Chillun Got Wings." When the play opened in 1924, it rocketed a young unknown, Paul Robeson, into immediate stardom. And controversy.

Highlighting a Hero—Paul Robeson

Paul Robeson was born in New Jersey on April 9, 1898. His father, William Drew Robeson, was a runaway slave who had become a Presbyterian minister. From him, young Robeson and his two brothers inherited an extraordinary drive to succeed. His older brothers became a doctor and a minister.

At Rutgers, young Paul Robeson had to overcome color prejudice At first, hostile football team members actually broke his ribs. In the end, however, he was named to that university's prestigious All-American team. He graduated Phi Beta Kappa and was chosen to give the commencement address. In 1923 he graduated at the top of his law school class from Columbia.

Destiny was to lead him in another direction. Under the encouragement of his equally well-educated black wife, Eslanda, Paul Robeson began to spend much of his spare time with the black literary crowd, which also included such liberal white writers and artists as Carl Van Vechten and Eugene O'Neill.

Little did Robeson know, when he took part in an amateur theatrical production at the Harlem YWCA in 1924, that he was being observed by these young writers.

"Some magic emanated from the man," writer Kenneth MacGowan excitedly observed. The next thing Robeson knew, Eugene O'Neill was asking him to take the lead in "All God's Chillun Got Wings." Robeson took the part. The daring play immediately became the center of furious controversy, because its theme was interracial marriage.

Perhaps partly in reaction to being swept into such a furor, the next year Robeson shifted from drama to singing. Gifted with a superb bass voice, he performed his first concert of spirituals at the Greenwich Village Theater in 1925.

From then on, Robeson's combined acting and concerts took him all over the world as *the* black performer. In London he appeared to rave reviews in *"The Emperor Jones."* Later he sang "Ol' Man River" in the musical Showboat, where he was immediately offered $5,000 to perform in vaudeville. That same year, when he sang at New York's Carnegie Hall, audiences had to be turned away.

The Robesons escaped the worst of the Depression by living in Europe. In 1934, the couple visited the Soviet Union for the first time. Paul Robeson was so used to universal approval for his artistic work, that, naively perhaps, he did not expect criticism for his growing interest in socialism.

Apparently, he did not think about the larger implications of his public statements about the Soviet system's "brotherhood of man." By the 1940s, more and more, he was connected in the public's mind with the brutal Soviet regime. In 1943, for instance, when he performed *Othello* in New York, a group he had helped start, The Council of African Affairs, was put on the government's list of "Communist" organizations. In 1946 Robeson himself was hauled before California's Joint Committee on Un-American Activities. The committee accused him of belonging to no fewer than 34 "Communist-front" groups.

Robeson, as open as ever, testified, "I think the best country in the world to test the principles of Marxism might be the America of today." That America, black and white, turned its back on Robeson, now that he was no longer content to soothe them with his slave songs. They had no more use for the performer they had created. During the virulently anti-Communist "McCarthy era," during which time Senator McCarthy and others accused scores of Americans of being sympathetic to communism, Robeson and his wife settled in England. In ill health, he returned to America in 1963 where he lived until his death thirteen years later.

Paul Robeson

African-Americans in the Movies

At the turn of the century, a squeaky, creaky new invention was taking shape that would revolutionize American culture forever—motion pictures. The first appearance of black people in movies came in 1902, in a French film called "Off to Bloomingdale Asylum." In the United States, blacks first appeared in 1905 in "The Wooing and Wedding of a Coon." Both movies were obviously derogatory, with black characters singing and dancing as in the minstrel shows.

239

And so the pattern was set. Fortunately, a brave and talented young Pullman porter decided to stake all he had on creating films that had positive black characters.

His name was Oscar Michaeux (mee-SHOW). He went on to write, direct, and produce at least ten films with his own film company, first in Chicago and later in New York. His first two films were "The Homesteader" (1919) and "The Brute" (1920).

Michaeux's films were overshadowed, however, by one of the most popular movies of the day. In 1915, a young white filmmaker named D. W. Griffith got the idea of doing an "epic" about blacks and whites during Reconstruction. He called it "Birth of a Nation." In it, black politicians were corrupt and evil. Incredibily, the Ku Klux Klan was seen as the savior of the defeated South! Although the film provided work for many budding black actors and actresses, it provoked a hail of criticism from African-Americans across the country, and was, in fact, banned in some cities. Still, it was immensely popular among white audiences.

One of the young black actresses in "Birth of a Nation" was the glamorous Madam Sul-Te-Wan. Actually, she was born plain little Nellie Conley, in Louisville in 1874. But she had big dreams. As a girl, when she delivered laundry to the white actresses at the Buckingham Theater, she would watch them perform from backstage.

When she and her mother moved to Cincinnati, Conley got her first theatrical work as a dancer. In time, Conley changed her name to the dramatic Madam Sul-Te-Wan, and organized her own touring group.

At one point on the West Coast, Madam Sul-Te-Wan tried out for work as an extra in Griffith's film. Struck by her beauty, the director hired her at the princely salary of $5 a week and wrote new scenes just for her. He filmed her as a wealthy black young society matron, quite a contrast from the roles for all the other black people in the film. Unfortunately, as it turned out, Griffith cut these scenes from the movie before it was released, feeling more comfortable with the other "darkie" roles.

Madam Sul-Te-Wan went on to appear in other films, including "Porgy and Bess" in 1959 and "Carmen Jones" in 1962.

By the 1930s, sound had come to movies. In 1933 Paul Robeson appeared in "The Emperor Jones," the first time a black actor was given a starring role in a film. In 1939, Hattie McDaniel won an Oscar for Best Supporting Actress as Mammy in "Gone With the Wind." Still, positive roles for African-Americans in films were the great exception.

Lena Horne—Movie Star

With the outbreak of World War II, MGM executives began looking for a black star. With straight hair and near-white features, they found her in Lena Horne. She was to make eleven movies as the country's leading black "pin-up girl." As was common in the fantasy musicals in that day, when Lena Horne appeared on screen, orchestra music would appear out of nowhere, and she would sing her sultry songs.

Horne did not come by her movie career lightly. She was born into a comfortable Brooklyn home in 1917 where her grandfather liked to listen to classical music. But her parents separated just after she was born, and since her mother wanted to develop her own career as an actress, young Lena had to live with one relative after another in the South.

By sixteen, Lena had made her way back to New York and was dancing in the chorus line at the famous Harlem hot spot, The Cotton Club. After she began singing in the posh Cafe Society in 1940, she briefly married a nice, middle-class black man from Pittsburgh, Louis Jones. After they were divorced, she moved to the West Coast for a fresh start.

Once in Hollywood, Horne realized she would never be given the roles of her contemporaries like Joan Crawford and Bette Davis. So she strove to develop a style all her own, unlike what she called the audience's "own preconceived notion of a Negro woman." She recalled:

The image I chose to give them was of a woman who they could not reach.... I am too proud to let them think they can have any personal contact with me. They get the singer, but they are not going to get the woman.

In 1947, in keeping with her maverick style, Horne married white composer Lennie Hayton. This created a

241

storm of controversy in Hollywood. Later, in the 1950s, the storm became a typhoon as strong-minded Horne refused to back away from her association with friends like Paul Robeson, only to find herself branded a "Communist sympathizer." The studios shunned her, even giving a role she coveted, that of a young mulatto woman in the remake of "Show Boat" to white actress Ava Gardner.

But Lena Horne's steely determination eventually won the day. After years of being passed over, she made a triumphant comeback in the 1960s, continuing into the 1970s and 1980s, mesmerizing a whole new generation with her cool style and warm voice.

Joe Louis—The "Brown Bomber"

Jack Johnson was the first black man to win international recognition as a sports figure when he became boxing's world heavyweight champion in 1908. What Jack Johnson did for African-Americans in the years before World War I, famed boxer Joe Louis did just before World War II.

Joe Louis was born in 1914 in Alabama. His family followed the Great Migration north, so that the young fighter grew up in Detroit. He began amateur boxing there and quickly distinguished himself in the ring.

After turning professional, Louis faced the current heavyweight champ, Jim Braddock, in 1937. Louis stopped him in the eighth round and strapped on the championship belt that he would not take off until his retirement in 1948.

Black novelist Richard Wright, wrote movingly about what Joe Louis meant to African-Americans:

> Four centuries of oppression, of frustrated hopes, of black bitterness, felt even in the bones of the bewildered young, were rising to the surface. Yes, unconsciously they had imputed to the brawny image of Joe Louis all the balked dreams of revenge, all the secretly visualized moments of retaliation, and he had won! Good Gawd Almighty! ... It could be done! Didn't Joe do it? You see, Joe was the consciously-felt symbol. Joe was the concentrated essence of black triumph over white.

SECTION FOUR REVIEW ∧∧∧∧∧∧∧∧∧∧∧∧∧∧∧∧∧∧∧∧∧∧∧∧∧

1. VOCABULARY Write a sentence for the following term: Harlem Renaissance.

2. BIOGRAPHY Who is probably the best-known artist of the Harlem Renaissance?

3. BIOGRAPHY What breakthrough did Roland Hayes make?

4. CRITICAL THINKING Why do you think African-Americans were often relegated to minstrel roles on the stage and in the movies?

5. CRITICAL THINKING Compare the poems by Langston Hughes and Claude McKay in this section. What similarities are there in the poems' themes? What differences?

CHAPTER EIGHT REVIEW

VOCABULARY

Write the numbered sentences on a separate sheet of paper. In each sentence fill in the blank with one of these terms: *Great Depression*, *Great Migration*, *Harlem Renaissance*, *imperialism*, *UNIA*.

1. Marcus Garvey's _____ offered hope to millions of African-Americans.
2. The _____ was a time of cultural flowering for the black community in the United States.
3. European _____ led to the conquest of most of Africa in the late 1800s.
4. The stock market crash of 1929 led to the economic downturn known as the _____ .
5. Hundreds of thousands of southern blacks left their homes and moved north during the _____ .

REVIEWING THE FACTS

1. Why did European countries start conquering other peoples and setting up colonies in the late 1800s?
2. How did South Africa fall into European hands?
3. How did the Berlin Conference aid Europeans in dividing up Africa? What measures did Africans take to resist?
4. What role did black troops play in combat in the years after Reconstruction?
5. How did most African-Americans show their willingness to participate in this nation's military efforts?
6. Why did large numbers of black southerners move north after 1900?
7. How did Marcus Garvey offer hope to African-Americans?
8. What was A. Philip Randolph's approach to improving life for African-Americans?
9. Who were some of the leading artists of the Harlem Renaissance?
10. What African-Americans gained fame on the musical stage?
11. How were African-Americans generally portrayed in the movies?

CRITICAL THINKING

1. **EVALUATING** Do you think African-Americans were right to participate in this nation's military efforts? Explain your answer.

2. **ANALYZING A QUOTATION** Marcus Garvey said, "Race is greater than law!" What did he mean? Do you agree with him? Why or why not?

3. **MAKING A JUDGMENT** Does any individual in the public eye today play a role comparable to that of Joe Louis in the 1930s and 1940s? Who? Why?

UNDERSTANDING PREJUDICE

1. Consider the fact that African-Americans participated in the subjugation of the Plains Indians during the late 1800s. Can you cite other instances where oppressed peoples have been at each others' throats? Why is it to the advantage of the oppressor to encourage such situations?

2. Consider Eugene Bullard's motto, "All Blood Runs Red." How could such a motto help put an end to all prejudice?

3. Paul Robeson's political views led to the destruction of his career. To what degree do you think racial prejudice might have played a part in this affair?

4. George Washington Carver (1864–1943) was one of this country's greatest scientists and a great humanitarian as well. Do research and find out more about his life. Then write a short essay about him, showing how Carver's life was a testament to his determination to overcome difficulties.

FROM GLOBAL CONFLICT TO THE CIVIL RIGHTS MOVEMENT

(1940–1970)

When you talk of 'black power', you talk of bringing this country to its knees. When you talk of 'black power', you talk of building a movement that will smash everything Western civilization has created. When you talk of 'black power', you talk of the black man doing whatever is necessary to get what he needs. We are fighting for our lives.

Stokely Carmichael

What momentous years—the war years through the 1960s! This era saw a world war that put a stop not only to Adolf Hitler's plans to take over the world, but to laws enforcing segregation at home. It saw Presidents cooperate openly with black leaders on civil rights legislation. And it saw the highest court in the land uphold the law on behalf of African-Americans. It ended with exciting calls for black power.

SECTION ONE   ## BLACK SOLDIERS AT WAR

VOCABULARY World War II Korean War

MAIN IDEA African-Americans participated in two more wars—World War II and the Korean War. By the Korean War they were fighting side by side with Americans of all races in integrated units.

By the early 1960s, as the civil rights movement became a mass movement, thousands of people took part in nonviolent protests against racial injustice.

OBJECTIVES As you read, look for answers to the following questions:
1. What were Adolf Hitler's racial views? How did those views lead to World War II?
2. What disadvantages did African-Americans face during World War II?
3. What action did President Truman take in 1948 concerning black troops?

Imagine going to bed one night, and waking up the next day to find out that your country was at war. That's exactly what happened on December 7, 1941. Without warning, Japanese fighter planes dropped their deadly payloads on the United States fleet anchored in Hawaii's Pearl Harbor. The United States was at war.

Hitler's Racism

Though war for the United States started in the Pacific, world attention had long been focused on Europe. For several years, German dictator Adolf Hitler had terrorized Europe, proclaiming that Germans belonged to a "master race" and that they had the right to take over neighboring countries. Blaming Jews for all the world's problems and considering people of color to be "subhumans," Hitler and his racism poisoned world affairs in the 1930s.

Those views became well known to the American public during the 1936 Olympic Games, held in the German capital of Berlin. At those games a talented African-American athlete named Jesse Owens won four gold medals in track and field. This tremendous feat, made under Hitler's watchful eye, surpassed what any Olympic athlete had done up to that time. Hitler was so infuriated that a black man should show up his supposedly "superior" people, that he actually refused to shake Owens' hand when he presented him with his medals! The incident made headlines the world over.

African-Americans and World War II

In the years immediately after the Olympics, Hitler seized land from neighboring Czechoslovakia. Then he annexed German-speaking Austria. But when he sent his troops into Poland in 1939, Great Britain and France entered the fray. **World War II** was on. At first, the United States stayed out of the conflict. All that changed when Germany's ally, Japan, attacked Pearl Harbor in 1941.

From the home front to the fighting front, African-Americans contributed to the eventual victory over Germany and Japan. More than a million black men and women served in the armed forces. The military remained segregated, however, and most blacks were stuck with the grunt work, as "messmen." One black recruit complained, "We can take no pride in our armed forces. We can become no more than flunkies in the army and kitchen boys in the navy."

World War II:
a global conflict fought between 1939 and 1945 during which the United States and its allies defeated Germany, Italy, and Japan.

"We can take no pride in our armed forces. We can become no more than flunkies in the army and kitchen boys in the navy."
—Black recruit during World War II

But as the war went on, African-Americans made slow gains. In all, 22 black combat units fought in Europe. Among them, the 969th Field Artillery won a Distinguished Unit Citation for outstanding courage. Near the end of the war in Europe, at the decisive Battle of the Bulge, blacks and whites fought side by side to drive back a fierce German attack. General George S. Patton told his troops, "I don't care what color you are, so long as you go up there and kill [Germans]." But segregation returned to all units after the German surrender in 1945.

Black Generals

Despite the racism that had existed for so long in the armed forces, a small, determined group of black soldiers managed to rise through the ranks.

During World War II, 7,000 blacks were trained with whites as officers. One, Benjamin O. Davis, Sr., became the first African-American general in the army in 1940.

Benjamin Davis was most definitely a career military man. Born in 1877, he was only 21 when he fought in the Spanish-American War as a First Lieutenant. Davis spent several years in the American army in the Philippines, and then taught at Tuskegee Institute and Wilberforce University. In 1942 he became Adviser on Negro Problems in Europe, and in 1944 was named Special Assistant to the Commanding General in France.

During his tours of service, General Davis rendered invaluable service, earning the Distinguished Service Medal, the Bronze Star, and the French Croix de Guerre. After 50 years of service, he retired in 1948, with honors from President Harry Truman.

Interestingly, General Davis's son became the second black general in the regular armed forces. A graduate of West Point, the younger Davis received his pilot training at the Tuskegee Army Air Base in 1942. After duty in World War II, General Davis, Jr., commanded an air force division in the Korean War.

General Davis, Jr., was a Deputy Chief of Staff at the Pentagon, and also served as a Commander in Chief in the Middle East, Southeast Asia, and Africa before retiring in 1970.

Black Women at War

During World War II, in July 1943, the U.S. Congress created the Women's Army Corps. At first, the African-American women who joined were only allowed such duties as hospital service for black soldiers. As the war continued, however, their tasks were expanded to such positions as lab technicians and librarians.

In 1944 the Army opened its hospital doors to African-American nurses. By the end of the year, they were treating white soldiers for the first time. On March 8, 1945, Phyllis Mae Dailey became the first black woman in the Navy Nurse Corps. In later wars, black women served successfully in the Nurse Corps as well.

In 1945, 800 black women formed the 688th Central Postal Battalion in Europe. This battalion was given the important mission of establishing a central postal directory in Europe. The unit received praise for its performance, which included arranging for the delivery of 3 million pieces of backlogged mail!

Highlighting a Hero—Dorie Miller

While fighting went on against Germany in Europe, the United States faced Japan in the Pacific. From the day of the attack on Pearl Harbor, African-Americans distinguished themselves.

In fact, on that fateful day a young black mess attendant named Dorie Miller scored a notable victory. Miller's captain was hit in the initial Japanese attack on the American fleet. Seeing this, Miller threw down the laundry he had been collecting, ran up on deck, pulled the wounded captain to safety, and then began firing at the enemy with an anti-aircraft gun he had never before used! He shot down four enemy planes before his ship was evacuated. For his extraordinary courage he was awarded the Navy Cross.

The Korean War

Japan's eventual defeat did not bring peace to Asia for long. In 1945 the nation of Korea was divided into two parts. On

Dorie Miller

June 25, 1950, Soviet-backed North Korean troops launched an attack on South Korea. To help the beleaguered south, the United Nations sent in an international force, most of them American troops.

During the **Korean War** (1950–1953) at least two black infantrymen received the Congressional Medal of Honor, and many other black military personnel received commendations. One, General Roscoe Robinson, Jr., was a Rifle Company Commander. He received the Bronze Star for his fearless leadership in various crucial infantry assignments. In 1982 he would go on to be named the first black four-star general in the army.

The Korean War was the first modern conflict in which blacks and whites fought in integrated units. In 1948 President Truman had issued an executive order banning racial segregation in the armed forces. It was an acknowledgment, long overdue, of the contributions African-Americans had made to the defense of their nation. The war itself, however, ended with Korea still divided. Unlike World War II, the conflict in Korea had seemed only a distant concern for most Americans. That is why it is sometimes called "the forgotten war."

Korean War: conflict (1950–1953) in which American troops helped prevent the take-over of South Korea by North Korea.

SECTION ONE REVIEW

1. VOCABULARY Write a sentence for each of the following terms: World War II, Korean War.

2. HISTORY What events in Europe led to the outbreak of World War II? How and when was the United States drawn into the conflict?

3. BIOGRAPHY Who was named as the first African-American general?

4. CRITICAL THINKING How do you think black troops felt upon their arrival home in 1945 after having helped defeat Hitler's forces?

5. CRITICAL THINKING Why do you think President Truman banned racial segregation in the armed forces?

251

SECTION TWO   THE MODERN CIVIL RIGHTS MOVEMENT

VOCABULARY *Brown v. Board of Education* **Montgomery bus boycott civil disobedience sit-in freedom ride March on Washington Vietnam War**

MAIN IDEA The struggle against racial injustice gained momentum in the years after World War II.

OBJECTIVES As you read, answer the following questions:
1. How did a Supreme Court decision in 1954 affect the struggle for equal rights?
2. What lesson did civil rights demonstrators learn during the Montgomery bus boycott?
3. What was the outcome of the demand for voting rights?

The end of World War II marked the beginning of a major civil rights push by African-Americans. It was led by a new generation of leaders who were educated, articulate, and determined to build on the hard-won progress of their predecessors. Returning home, they found racial discrimination —something they had been fighting overseas—and were determined to end it.

Thurgood Marshall, Black Legal Champion

One of the most influential men in the new black leadership of the 1940s and 1950s was a hard-driving lawyer named Thurgood Marshall. (He was actually baptised "Thoroughgood Marshall" when he was born in Baltimore, in 1908, but he later legally shortened his first name to Thurgood.)

Young Marshall's family was middle class: his mother was a schoolteacher while his father, William, was a headwaiter at a local country club. William Marshall was a man of insatiable curiosity who loved to discuss and debate ideas. His sons, especially young Thurgood, picked this up. The verbal advantage would serve the young man well.

After law school, young Marshall went to work for the NAACP. His very first case as NAACP special counsel, in

1938, actually went to the Supreme Court. A student named Lloyd Gaines was suing to be admitted to the University of Missouri Law School. At that time, southern states commonly got around admitting black students by paying for them to go to college in other states. The University of Missouri wanted to send Gaines to the University of Maryland.

But this time was different. Gaines said "no." Thurgood Marshall represented him in court, arguing that Gaines was entitled to "equal protection of the laws," as guaranteed by the Fourteenth Amendment.

The Supreme Court agreed, declaring that 'equality of education must be provided within the borders of the state." This landmark decision opened the way for African-Americans in other states to demand equal pay for black teachers, as well as more funds and facilities for their schools.

By 1943 Marshall was at it again. This time, he traveled to Texas to argue that African-Americans should have the right to sit on juries with whites. Marshall did this after a jeering bailiff had literally kicked a prominent black attorney down the Dallas courthouse steps.

Not only did Marshall convince the governor, but he got him to order the Texas Rangers to defend the right of blacks to jury service. Later in the year, the Supreme Court upheld Marshall's effort.

The more cases Marshall won, the angrier the southern legislatures became. They screamed that they must protect themselves against the swelling "black tide" that would "destroy the South's precious way of life."

Thurgood Marshall and School Desegregation

Marshall and his NAACP associates rolled up their sleeves and worked even harder. Between 1945 and 1950, Marshall traveled 50,000 miles and argued scores of cases in southern courts. Two of these successful cases became the precedents for the Supreme Court's history-making 1954 school desegregation decision, which changed the face of America forever.

The first case was *Sweatt v. Painter*, in which white Texans refused to admit a qualified black student to the state's law school. Texas legislators even hastily created a "black law school" to get around his admittance, arguing that the school was "separate but equal." The Supreme

253

Court disagreed, ordering that Sweatt be admitted to the established law school.

The second case was *McLaurin v. Oklahoma State Regents*. McLaurin, a black student, had been admitted to the University of Oklahoma, but was forced to live and study on a completely segregated basis. The Supreme Court upheld Marshall, who said that such isolation "destroyed the equality of educational benefits."

The *Brown* Decision

Brown v. Board of Education: the Supreme Court decision of 1954 declaring racial segregation in public schools to be unconstitutional.

In 1954, thanks to Marshall and the NAACP's long years of hard work, the Supreme Court issued probably the most noteworthy decision of the century. In **Brown v. Board of Education**, the Court declared that the doctrine of "separate but equal" in the nation's schools was unconstitutional.

The case got its name from a nine-year-old girl in Topeka, Kansas, named Linda Brown. Linda attended an all-black elementary school across town. Her lawyers argued that she should be allowed to go to a white school closer to home. Not only was her school inferior to the white school, they said, but racially segregated schools could *never* be equal. Why? Because they degraded black youngsters by teaching them that white society considered them inferior, not good enough to mix with white children.

The Supreme Court agreed. The heart of its decision was the famous sentence, "Separate educational facilities are inherently unequal." The "separate-but-equal" doctrine, once upheld in the *Plessy* decision (Chapter 7), had been knocked down.

Thurgood Marshall's Appointment to the Supreme Court

Marshall's trailblazing days were by no means over. In 1961 federal authorities appointed him as a judge for the Second U.S. Circuit. Four years later, he was named Solicitor General of the United States—the top attorney of the entire nation. In this position, Marshall was the "chief legal spokesman" in the cases that the U.S. government brought before the Supreme Court. Then, in 1967 Thurgood Marshall truly made history when he became the first African-American member of the U.S. Supreme Court itself.

Martin Luther King, Jr., and the Montgomery Bus Boycott

Marshall's victory in the *Brown* case was an inspiration for a young black minister who would champion the cause of civil rights, first in the South and then throughout the nation. That minister was the Reverend Martin Luther King, Jr.

Like Marshall, Reverend King's early life was quietly middle class. After graduating from Morehouse College in Atlanta, where he was born, young King received his Ph.D. from Boston University. By 1954, he had moved to Montgomery, Alabama, where he became pastor of the Dexter Avenue Baptist Church. Little did he know what awaited him in that quiet southern city.

Despite the Supreme Court's positive stands, segregation was still the order of the day in cities like Montgomery. But one day, a quiet black woman, Rosa Parks, chose to break the law. On December 1, 1955, she sat in a seat at the front of a Montgomery bus. Such seats were normally reserved for whites. But when a white passenger got on, she simply refused to get up and give him her seat.

How could she do such a thing? The white driver and white passengers were in an uproar! They had Mrs. Parks arrested for her "crime" of insubordination. Her arrest sparked the **Montgomery bus boycott** of 1955–1956—one of the great rebellions of the modern civil rights movement.

Parks's arrest outraged the black community. Since 75 percent of the Montgomery bus riders were black, they decided the time had come to boycott the entire bus system. And so it was, as is often the case, that an individual act of courage led to massive change.

Dr. King's job was to make sure that all of Montgomery's 50,000 black citizens knew about the boycott, and he agreed to head up the Montgomery boycott committee. The Reverend Ralph Abernathy had the task of negotiating with the white officials.

This was not the first black boycott of Jim Crow facili-

Martin Luther King, Jr.

Montgomery bus boycott: the 1955-1956 boycott of the bus system of Montgomery, Alabama, by black citizens protesting segregated seating.

ties in history. But it was one of the most effective, for two reasons.

First, Montgomery's black community was united. The boycott went on for more than a year, and despite the hardships it brought, nearly every black person stuck to it.

Second, the boycott's impact was enormous because of a new phenomenon that aided the movement greatly. The phenomenon was called television. Never before had people been able to sit in their own living rooms and watch live news stories. Young people, black and white alike, whose consciences were stirred, began to flock to the South, causing the mild rumble of quiet protest to become an earthquake that would threaten to shake the nation to its very foundation.

With the help of the NAACP, the Montgomery boycott committee went on to win its case. Late in 1956 the Supreme Court ruled that segregation on buses was illegal. The battle had been won in spite of the jailing of Dr. King and 100 other black leaders and the bombing of Dr. King's home.

Nonviolent Protest

A great lesson that observers of the bus boycott learned was Dr. King's nonviolent approach, called **civil disobedience**.

civil disobedience: the refusal to obey unjust laws, usually by nonviolent means.

Dr. King knew that using nonviolence was a lot to ask of black people who had watched their mothers and sisters, fathers and brothers being raped and lynched. But he was convinced that nonviolence was the only way to overcome the South's deeply ingrained prejudices. Inspired by the Christian values of love and peace, as well as the nonviolent methods—including boycotts and peaceful demonstrations —that Mohandas Gandhi had used to bring about India's independence from Great Britain in 1947, King told white America:

> We will match your capacity to inflict suffering with our capacity to endure suffering. We will meet your physical force with soul force. We will not hate you, but we cannot...obey your unjust laws.... We will soon wear you down by our capacity to suffer. And in winning our freedom we will so ap-

peal to your heart and conscience that we will win you in the process.

Reverend King's nonviolent protests were so successful that they led to a wave of activism throughout the South. The original Montgomery boycott committee eventually developed into a larger organization called the Southern Christian Leadership Conference (SCLC). King was elected president. As he later wrote, he accepted his responsibilities because he felt he had to:

> One night...I couldn't sleep....In this state of exhaustion, when my courage had all but gone, I decided to take my problem to God. With my head in my hands, I bowed over the kitchen table and prayed aloud.... 'I am here taking a stand for what I believe is right. But now, I am afraid. The people are looking to me for leadership, and if I stand before them without strength and courage, they too will falter. I am at the end of my powers. I have nothing left. I've come to the point where I can't face it alone.'
>
> At that moment I experienced the presence of the Divine as I had never experienced Him before. It seemed as though I could hear the quiet assurance of an inner voice saying: 'Stand up for righteousness, stand up for truth; and God will be at your side forever.' Almost at once my fears began to go. My uncertainty disappeared. I was ready to face anything.

In 1959 Dr. King moved to Atlanta where he became co-pastor with his father of the Ebenezer Baptist Church.

Sit-Ins and Freedom Rides

The black protest movement gained so much momentum that by 1963, there were an estimated 10,000 racial demonstrations for racial justice! Rosa Parks's original "sit-in" on that Montgomery bus had grown to a nationwide movement.

Many high school and college students, ready for change,

"In winning our freedom we will so appeal to your heart and conscience that we will win you in the process."
—Martin Luther King, Jr.

sit-in:
a method of nonviolent protest whereby people sit down in a public place and refuse to move.

freedom ride:
a bus trip by protesters in the South to call attention to discrimination in transportation.

defied authorities throughout the South, staging **sit-ins** at restaurants, lunch counters, movies, recreational facilities —demanding the same service as whites. They also organized **freedom rides**, bus trips by whites and blacks to test whether the laws for desegregation of interstate bus lines were actually working.

There were so many protests that in 1960 the youthful protestors formed the Student Non-Violent Coordinating Committee (SNCC).

Dr. King and the SCLC also continued their efforts, continuing to make headlines. Two of the biggest news stories came in 1960 and in 1963. In 1960 Dr. King was arrested without bail during an Atlanta sit-in. Presidential candidate John F. Kennedy, fearing for King's safety, intervened to have him freed. And in April 1963 Police Chief Eugene "Bull" Connor ordered the jailing of nearly 3,000 black people during nonviolent protests against segregation in Birmingham, Alabama. Trying to halt the campaign, vicious white segregationists bombed the black Sixteenth Avenue Baptist Church, killing four young girls.

King was one of those arrested in Birmingham. While in jail, he wrote:

> The nations of Asia and Africa are moving with jetlike speed toward the goal of political independence, and we still creep at horse-and-buggy pace toward the gaining of a cup of coffee at a lunch counter. I guess it is easy for those who have never felt the stinging darts of segregation to say 'wait.'
>
> But...when you are humiliated day in and day out by nagging signs reading 'white' and 'colored'...living constantly at tiptoe stance... plagued with inner fears and outer resentments; when you are forever fighting a degenerating sense of 'nobodyness'—then you will understand why it is difficult to wait....
>
> The question is not whether we will be extremist but what kind of extremist will we be.

Civil rights demonstrators "sit in" at a segregated lunch counter

The March on Washington

By the summer of 1963, Dr. King, A. Philip Randolph, and New York civil rights activist Bayard Rustin decided that it was time to organize a march on Washington, D.C. President Kennedy had proposed a strong civil rights bill. King and the others hoped that a massive rally in the nation's capital would put pressure on Congress to pass it.

And so, on August 28, 1963, "freedom buses" and "freedom trains" brought marchers from across the country to Washington, D.C. There, in the hot summer sun, with the Lincoln Memorial as a backdrop, Dr. King made one of the most famous speeches in American history. He spoke simply of his vision for a united nation, free of the tyranny of racism:

> I have a dream! I have a dream that one day this nation will rise up and live out the true meaning of its creed: 'We hold these truths to be self-evident; that all men are created equal.'

"I have a dream!"
—Martin Luther King, Jr.

Some 250,000—at least 60,000 of them white—took part in the **March on Washington**. At the time, it was the largest political rally in American history.

March on Washington: massive civil rights rally in Washington, D.C., in August 1963.

"Freedom Summer"

In the weeks and months after the memorable march, there was hope that King's dream might come true. In 1964, after President Kennedy's assassination, Congress passed the civil rights bill. The Civil Rights Act of 1964 outlawed racial, religious, and sexual discrimination in public places and by employers. It also gave the federal government more power to enforce all civil rights laws.

Still, violence continued. During the so-called "Freedom Summer" of 1964, 37 black churches were burned or bombed in Mississippi alone, and 1,000 people were arrested for taking part in demonstrations. In addition, the bodies of three young civil rights workers were found in an earthen dam in the backwoods of Philadelphia, Mississippi. They were a black—James E. Chaney—and two whites—Andrew Goodman and Michael Schwerner. Federal officials arrested 21 suspects, but no one was ever convicted of the crime.

Meanwhile, as a result of the March on Washington, Martin Luther King, Jr., had gained enormous acclaim. In

259

1964 he received the most prestigious international award, the Nobel Peace Prize, the youngest man ever to do so. This distinction underscored the importance of Dr. King's efforts and spurred him to widen the scope of his interests.

The Drive for Voting Rights

In spite of the Civil Rights Act of 1964, few black southerners could vote. Without the vote, they could not expect much progress. Dr. King attacked the issue head on.

In 1965 he led a massive voter registration campaign in Alabama. Along with John Lewis, head of SNCC, he organized a march of 25,000 demonstrators from Selma to Alabama's capital, Montgomery, demanding the right to register to vote. At the edge of Selma, state troopers, many on horseback, attacked the marchers, firing tear gas at them and beating them with clubs. Television cameras captured the horrifying episode, sending these bloody images to a shocked nation.

The television coverage so moved liberal whites and northern blacks that thousands of them rushed to Alabama to take part in the protest. Some lost their lives. A white Unitarian minister, the Reverend James J. Reeb, was beaten to death. A white homemaker from Detroit, Viola Liuzzo, was shot by a carload of Klansmen while driving marchers to Selma.

The violence stirred President Lyndon Johnson and Congress to action. The Voting Rights Act of 1965 sent federal officials to the South to monitor elections and to make sure discriminatory practices in voting were halted. It also outlawed literacy tests and other means of keeping black voters from the polls. In the next four years, the number of black southern voters tripled.

Civil rights march, early 1960s

Vietnam War:
a war from the 1950s until 1973 in which the United States unsuccessfully tried to prevent a Communist take-over of South Vietnam.

The War in Vietnam

As time went on, Dr. King undertook a new cause, stopping the war in Southeast Asia. In 1965 the United States had decided to send large numbers of troops to South Vietnam to keep Communist North Vietnam from taking it over. Not since the Civil War had an issue so divided the United States as the **Vietnam War.**

On April 15, 1967, King addressed 200,000 antiwar protestors in New York. He spoke to another huge crowd in Washington, D.C., in February 1968. Dr. King told them that he believed poor people in Vietnam and in the United States had a common enemy—wealthy business interests in America. And, he said, similar tactics were being used against both to keep them down. Labeling the United States "the greatest purveyor of violence in the world today," Dr. King accused the American power structure of a "cruel manipulation of the poor."

What would have happened if Dr. King had united hundreds of thousands of antiwar protestors and antipoverty protestors? He might have forced a profound change in the very way this country is run.

Two Assassinations

But we will never know. On April 4, 1968, during a visit to Memphis in support of striking sanitation workers, Dr. King was shot and killed as he stepped out of his motel room. He was only 39 years old.

Another assassination was soon to follow. Robert Kennedy, as Attorney General under his brother, President John Kennedy, had taken a stand for civil rights during critical periods. These included the 1961 freedom rides, when he sent 600 federal marshals to Montgomery, Alabama. In 1963 Robert Kennedy pushed for enforcement of the 14th and 15th Amendments to the Constitution, following the assassination of Mississippi NAACP leader Medgar Evers. And in 1966, as a senator, he helped create black self-help organizations, such as New York's Bedford-Stuyvesant Renewal Program, one of the first "urban renewal" programs in the country.

While campaigning for the presidency of the United States in 1968, Robert Kennedy was shot in a Los Angeles hotel. The deaths of Robert Kennedy and Martin Luther King, Jr., seemed to indicate that the country was sinking into chaos.

Highlighting a Hero—Coretta Scott King

Coretta Scott King, widow of Martin Luther King, Jr., is a heroic woman in her own right. Coretta Scott was born in

Perry County, Alabama, where she and her brother and sister attended a one-room schoolhouse crowded with 100 other children. There were two teachers for all of them. Despite this, she went on to graduate from high school and college and, later, to study voice at the famed New England Conservatory of Music in Boston.

It was in Boston that she met the serious young minister who would so change her life. Young Coretta had dreamed of becoming an important concert performer like Marian Anderson. But she decided to marry Martin Luther King, Jr., and return to the South to help him with his life's work.

Mrs. King became a model of strength and determination to African-Americans everywhere as she survived the many disasters that crashed upon her and her husband, as they struggled to create a civil rights movement. In spite of having four small children to care for, she often had to travel to help raise money for the SCLC. She stood courageously by when a fanatic stabbed her husband, when he was arrested so many times, and, finally, when he was murdered.

After her husband's death, Coretta Scott King continued her efforts by working with the SCLC. She went on to create the King Center for Social Change in Atlanta, which continues Dr. King's human rights activities.

Steps Toward Equal Rights

Between the 1940s and the 1960s, the intense civil rights pressure that was brought to bear on the federal government resulted in four important executive orders, three civil rights acts, a constitutional amendment, and a voting rights act. All helped to implement change. They are as follows:

Executive Order 8802
President Roosevelt signed this order in 1941. It eliminated discrimination in defense facilities during World War II.

Executive Order 9981
This order, signed by President Truman in 1948, eliminated segregation in the armed forces.

Executive Order 10730
President Eisenhower signed this order in 1957, forcing Arkansas Governor Orville Faubus to obey the law and eliminate segregation in Little Rock's high schools.

Executive Order 11053
This order was signed by President John F. Kennedy in 1962. It called for the integration of the University of Mississippi and the use of federal troops, if necessary, to enforce it. As a result, James Meredith, a black air force veteran, was allowed to enroll in and graduate from "Ole Miss."

Civil Rights Act of 1957
This act created a Presidential Commission on Civil Rights to investigate and protect the right of African-Americans to vote. It had weak powers of enforcement, however, and proved to be ineffective.

Civil Rights Act of 1964
Extremely comprehensive, this act prohibited racial, religious, and sexual discrimination in public places and by employers. It also gave the federal government more power to enforce all civil rights laws.

Amendment 24
This amendment prohibited using the poll tax to deny voting rights in federal elections.

Voting Rights Act of 1965
This act did away with literacy tests and other discriminatory devices.

Civil Rights Act of 1968
This act banned racial discrimination in housing. Congress passed it just six days after Dr. King's assassination.

SECTION TWO REVIEW ᐱᐱᐱᐱᐱᐱᐱᐱᐱᐱᐱᐱᐱᐱᐱᐱᐱᐱᐱᐱᐱ

1. VOCABULARY Write a sentence for each of the following terms: *Brown v. Board of Education*, Montgomery bus boycott,

263

civil disobedience, sit-in, freedom ride, March on Washington, Vietnam War.

2. BIOGRAPHY What role did Thurgood Marshall play in the civil rights movement?

3. ETHICS What influenced Martin Luther King, Jr., to urge nonviolence to secure the rights of African-Americans?

4. HISTORY What was Dr. King's position on the Vietnam War?

5. CRITICAL THINKING Why was the drive for voting rights of such key importance to civil rights leaders?

SECTION THREE   GROWING MILITANCY

VOCABULARY ghetto Black Panther Party

MAIN IDEA By the late 1960s the civil rights movement had grown more militant.

OBJECTIVES As you read, look for answers to the following questions:
1. Why did the civil rights movement grow more militant?
2. Why did so many urban riots break out in the 1960s?
3. What was the aim of the Black Panther Party?

By the late 1960s a growing gulf had arisen between the younger civil rights leaders and their older counterparts. Some young leaders charged that the older leaders were "selling out" to the white power structure and becoming "Uncle Tom's." One even referred to Martin Luther King, Jr., as a "chicken-eating preacher" who had reached a secret agreement with the "white establishment." Why had the African-American protest movement become more militant?

First, black people were disappointed at the slow gains the civil rights movement was making. Many public facilities and schools, for example, were still segregated. And southern states continued to uphold discriminatory local laws. For example, seventeen states still had laws forbidding interracial marriage, with punishments of up to five years in prison and a $1,000 fine.

The second reason for increased black militancy was that the gains of the civil rights movement had not improved life in the urban black **ghettos** of the North and West. Unemployment and job discrimination continued to plague the black community. Black laborers were still on the margins of power in the workplace, and there seemed no escape from poverty. Nonviolent protest did not seem likely to change things for the better.

ghetto:
an inner-city neighborhood from which, for reasons of economics and prejudice, members of a particular group are unable to leave.

The Watts Rebellion

The conditions building in the ghettos exploded into violence in 1965. The worst race riot since World War II erupted in the Watts neighborhood of Los Angeles in August of that year. Black people took to the streets for six full days after the arrest of 21-year old Marquette Frye for alleged reckless driving. Such arrests were common. But, due to the heightened racial tension, many black people now openly accused the police of being an occupying force whose aim was to keep them down, rather than protect them.

And so the protestors took their anger out, first on the police, and then on those nonblack shopkeepers they felt were exploiting their community. Many black businesses were looted and burned in the process as well.

During the Watts Rebellion, $30 million in property was destroyed and at least 34 people died. In the years since then, the federal government has poured millions of dollars for improvement projects into the Watts area, but the basic character of the area has changed little.

Burn, Baby, Burn!

Following Watts, riots continued to break out in the ghettos. There were more than 140 major urban riots between 1964 and 1968, causing enormous damage and loss of life.

In Chicago, on July 14, 1966, a hot summer night, police went to the West Side to turn off fire hydrants that black children had opened. The appearance of the police touched off a riot that lasted three days. Some 5,000 black protestors threw Molotov cocktails into police cars. Others burned and looted stores. Four thousand National Guardsmen had to be called out to quell the hostilities.

In Atlanta, two months later, a riot broke out when police shot a black man suspected of stealing a car. Protestors opened fire on two white policemen. They even pulled Atlanta's mayor from the roof of a car when he tried to intervene.

The 1967 Detroit riot started after police were blamed for harming patrons arrested at a black club. More than 14,000 police and National Guardsmen were called out. By the time the fighting ended, some 14,000 fires had been set to local businesses and property, with $43 million in damage and 43 people dead.

Worse was yet to come. In April 1968, after news of Dr. King's assassination spread, so did a wave of urban rebellions, the likes of which America had never seen. The violence, involving 125 cities, lasted a week. Hardest hit were Baltimore, Chicago, and Washington, D.C. The government called in some 70,000 National Guard troops to restore order. Forty-six people died in the process, and at least 3,500 were injured.

Stokely Carmichael and the Rise of "Black Power"

In 1966, during the urban riots, a young militant black leader named Stokely Carmichael was arrested. Newly appointed as chairman of the SNCC, Carmichael voiced the frustration of many younger members of the civil rights movement who had lost faith in nonviolence. Upon his release from jail he said, "We've been saying freedom for six years. What we're going to start saying now is black power."

The slogan caught on, and demands for black power swept the nation.

Stokely Carmichael was born in 1941 on the Caribbean island of Trinidad. When he was eleven, his parents brought him to the United States. He grew up in a middle class, predominantly white neighborhood in New York City and graduated from Howard University in 1964, having majored in philosophy.

During Carmichael's college years, he interrupted his studies with frequent trips to the South, where he became one of the young leaders of the freedom rides. By 1966 his

"We've been saying freedom for six years. What we're going to start saying now is black power."
—Stokely Carmichael

brash confidence and quick mind had earned him the top spot in the SNCC.

Carmichael and the other more radical SNCC members began studying proposals by an even more radical group called the Revolutionary Armed Movement (RAM) whose leader, Robert Williams, was in self-imposed exile in Cuba. Williams' message was direct: black people should consider themselves urban guerrillas, and should arm themselves with surplus army weapons, as well as homemade Molotov cocktails.

More and more SNCC members took up the call. H. "Rap" Brown, who succeeded Stockely Carmichael as SNCC head, urged blacks to "wage guerrilla warfare on the honkie white man." He said, "If America doesn't come around, burn America down."

Later, Carmichael would moderate his views, as he and other young black leaders began to emphasize the common problems of poor people, whatever their color. He wrote:

> Black people do not want to 'take over' this country. They don't want to 'get whitcy'; they just want to get him off their backs, as the saying goes.... The white man is irrelevant to blacks, except as an oppressive force. Blacks want to be in his place, yes, but not in order to terrorize and lynch and starve him. They want to be in his place because that is where a decent life can be had.

In 1968 Carmichael married famed South African singer Miriam Makeba. They moved to Guinea, in West Africa, at the invitation of the country's president, Sekou Touré. Carmichael studied politics with former Ghanaian president Kwame Nkrumah, who was also living in exile in Guinea. Unfortunately, the Makeba-Carmichael marriage did not last. Carmichael, who changed his name to Kwame Ture, went on to marry a Guinean woman and remain in West Africa.

The Black Panthers

In 1966, to advance the cause of black separatism, SNCC decided to create a new party, a "people's party." They named it the **Black Panther Party**.

Black Panther Party: political party which sought to take control of the inner cities for black people.

267

Originally, this party's aim was to put forward black candidates in the 1965 Lowndes County, Alabama, elections. From the Howard University SNCC contingent, activist Courtland Cox came up with the early drawings for the symbol of this new party. It was a black panther.

The Black Panther Party did not take hold in Alabama in 1965. But in 1966, it was reborn in a new form in Oakland, California. Local young black activists Huey Newton, Bobby Seale, and Bobby Hutton were its founders. Its new purpose was to take control of the inner cities for black people.

Modeling themselves after the tough United States Special Forces (the Green Berets) who were serving in Vietnam, the Black Panthers wore black berets and black gloves. And with the same kind of macho pride, they trained in military tactics.

At first, the Black Panthers took to the streets to protect the black community when the police wouldn't. As Huey Newton put it, "We've never advocated violence; violence is inflicted upon us. But we do believe in self-defense for ourselves and for black people." Soon they enlarged their scope to include attacks on white businesses and government offices.

Huey Newton

Huey P. Newton, probably the best-known Panther leader, was born on February 17, 1942, in Monroe, Louisiana. His father, Walter, a sharecropper and a Baptist minister, had only narrowly escaped being lynched for standing up to local whites, and so the family moved to Oakland when Huey Newton was just one year old.

As Huey Newton himself told it, he was "illiterate" when he graduated from Oakland Technical High School. Then, stumbling upon a copy of Plato's *Republic* one day, Newton finally found something interesting enough to read. He read it five times, continued reading and finally learned to read well. He went on to graduate from Merritt College. On campus, Newton helped form one of the country's first black student organizations, the Afro-American Society.

While at Merritt College, Newton was introduced to the two men who would have the most profound impact on his life. One was Bobby Seale, with whom he would later co-found the Black Panthers. The other was Black Muslim leader Malcolm X (Chapter 10). Newton later explained, "It was [Malcolm's] insistence that blacks ought to defend themselves with arms when attacked by police [that] became one of the original points in the program of the Black Panthers."

Newton cast the Black Panthers into the limelight, when on May 2, 1967, at the California State Capitol Building in Sacramento, he proclaimed his Executive Mandate No. 1:

Symbol of the Black Panther Party

> Black people have begged, prayed, petitioned and demonstrated, among other things, to get the racist power structure of America to right the wrongs which have historically been perpetrated against black people. All of these efforts have been answered by more repression, deceit and hypocrisy....
>
> The Black Panther for Self-Defense believes that the time has come for black people to arm themselves against this terror before it is too late.... We believe that the black communities of America must rise up as one man to halt the progression of a trend that leads inevitably to their total destruction.

Just five months later, Huey Newton was part of a shoot-out with police in Oakland. One policeman was wounded, another killed. Newton was convicted of voluntary manslaughter and spent three years in prison before his case made it to the California Supreme Court, which dismissed the charges.

He was to continue on his rocky path, in and out of prison. According to Newton, the intense pressure of his "front line" confrontations led him to begin using drugs, but he fought them, entering numerous drug rehabilitation programs.

Newton studied law at San Francisco Law School, and in 1980 received his Ph.D in social philosophy from the University of California, Santa Cruz. Then, on August 22, 1989, Huey Newton, just 47, was found shot to death on an Oakland street frequented by drug dealers. It was very near the same street where he and his Black Panthers

269

had served free breakfasts to poor schoolchildren twenty years before.

Black Power and Black Pride

The black power movement did not mean that all African-Americans had become extremists. For many, black power meant gaining respect through political or economic power. More blacks were elected to office, cooperatives were formed in black neighborhoods, and black-owned businesses were on the rise. Many groups sought community control of local institutions such as the schools. They insisted that textbooks begin teaching African and African-American history, topics almost completely ignored until the 1960s. Black power, argued many, was no more than the process by which other ethnic groups in American life had improved their position.

The goal of developing self-pride and dignity was important to militants and moderates alike. The phrase "black is beautiful" became popular. Until this time, blacks had felt it necessary to straighten their hair. Now they began to let their hair grow out naturally into "afros." African clothing started to be worn too. Black power became, in short, a celebration of black identity.

"Black is beautiful."
—Slogan of late 1960s

SECTION THREE REVIEW 〰〰〰〰〰〰〰〰〰〰〰

1. VOCABULARY Write a sentence for each of the following terms: ghetto, Black Panther Party.

2. HISTORY Why did the civil rights movement become more militant in the 1960s?

3. BIOGRAPHY What role did Stokely Carmichael play in the struggle for racial justice?

4. CRITICAL THINKING To what degree do you think the urban riots of the 1960s were effective? Ineffective?

5. CRITICAL THINKING Explain what the expression "black power" means to you.

AFRICAN-AMERICAN CULTURE DEVELOPS

SECTION FOUR

MAIN IDEA The postwar years saw the emergence of African-American culture on the national scene.

OBJECTIVES As you read, answer the following questions:
1. Who were some of the outstanding African-American artists of the post-World War II years?
2. What gains did African-Americans make in the entertainment industry?
3. Why is Jackie Robinson's achievement of such importance?

In the years after World War II, African-Americans played a larger role in the nation's cultural activities. Many talented artists carried on the traditions of the Harlem Renaissance. Sports teams also boasted outstanding black players.

African-American Novelists Gain Acclaim

Probably the most talented of the black writers of the 1930s and 1940s was Richard Wright. Early on, Wright recognized his responsibility as a serious artist. In 1937 he wrote:

> The Negro writer who seeks to function within his race as a purposeful agent has a serious responsibility.... He is being called upon to do no less than create values by which his race is to struggle, live and die.

Wright, a man of action, took up the challenge himself, and in 1940 wrote *Native Son*, a telling indictment of American society. The story of a young black man indicted for murder in Chicago, *Native Son* became a best seller. So did the equally passionate *Black Boy*, published in 1944.

During the Depression Wright joined the Communist Party and went into exile in Africa and France. Later, however, he abandoned communism when he found that the price of membership was the loss of artistic freedom.

271

Richard Wright was not the only best-selling black author of the day. Ralph Ellison's *The Invisible Man*, a powerful attack on racism, won the National Book Award in 1952.

But it is probably James Baldwin, who burst upon the literary scene in the 1950s, who is best remembered for his novels that deal with the dilemma of the black person coping in America. Born in Harlem, Balwin began life preaching in his father's storefront churches as a young boy. But he gave up the pulpit for writing, when, after high school, he received two writing scholarships.

In 1953 Baldwin completed his first novel, *Go Tell It On the Mountain*, while living in Paris. He went on to write other novels such as *Another Country, Giovanni's Room*, and *Notes of a Native Son*. His long essay, *The Fire Next Time*, written in 1963 on the anniversary of the Emancipation Proclamation, gained wide acclaim for its passionate statement of African-American anger set in an historical context. In it, Baldwin implied that if white America did not end racism, it would bring about its own destruction. Always, Baldwin returned to the central theme that he described in his book of essays, *No Name in the Street:*

> To be an Afro-American, or an American black, is to be in the situation, intolerably exaggerated, of all those who have ever found themselves part of a civilization which they could in no way honorably defend...and who yet...[hoped] to make the kingdom new, to make it honorable and worthy of life.

Gwendolyn Brooks—Black Poet

Gwendolyn Brooks's stirring, lyrical poetry so moved readers, black and white, that she became the first black woman to receive a Pulitzer Prize. She won the prestigious award in 1950 for *Annie Allen*, a long narrative poem about a woman growing up in Chicago.

Brooks was born in Topeka, Kansas, in 1917, and grew up in Chicago. By 1945 she had published her first book of poetry, *A Street in Bronzeville*, and become one of *Mademoiselle* magazine's "Outstanding Women of the Year." She also received two Guggenheim fellowships which allowed her to keep writing. In 1968 she was named Poet Laureate of Illinois, succeeding Carl Sandburg.

Gwendolyn Brooks is an outstanding example of a woman who shared her heart with her public and has been much loved for it. The following poem talks about the wisdom of a young child in a poor family:

It's Christmas Day. I did not get
The presents that I hoped for. Yet,
It is not nice to frown or fret.

To frown or fret would not be fair.
My Dad must never know I care
It's hard enough for him to bear.

Lorraine Hansberry—Black Playwright

Lorraine Hansberry wrote the first serious black play to be a hit on Broadway. "A Raisin in the Sun" dealt with a black family trying to buy a house in an all-white neighborhood. When the play appeared in 1959, it was the most controversial drama of its time, winning the New York Drama Critics Award. Actor Sidney Poitier later starred in the equally successful film version.

Black Culture Explodes in the 1960s

In the 1960s, black culture surged onto the American scene amid the raised fists of Black Panthers and cries of "Black Power!" Black nationalism emerged as a lifestyle. African-inspired wardrobes and hairdos became popular. Meanwhile, dynamic writers and thinkers worked hard to describe the African-American experience. The list of artists is so long, it is impossible to mention them all.

Chief essayist and playwright of this new generation was LeRoi Jones. Jones, who later changed his name to Imamu Amiri Baraka, was born in 1934 in Newark, New Jersey. His father worked for the Post Office, and his mother was a social worker. After spending time in the air force, Baraka published his first book in 1961, *Preface to a Twenty-Volume Suicide Note.*

It was with his 1964 play, "The Dutchman," that Baraka won wide acclaim, because of its brutally honest portrayal of racial problems in America. Other works by Baraka, such as "The System of Dante's Hell" (1966) and "Home" (1966), were widely quoted by young African-Americans searching for a new identity. Here is some of what Baraka had to say:

"Political power . . . is the power to create. . . ."
—Imkamu Amiri Baraka

Political power is . . . the power to create . . . to be free to go where ever you can go (mentally, physically as well). Black creation—creation powered by the black ethos brings very special results.

Think of yourself, black creator, freed of European restraint. . . . Think what would be the results of the unfettered blood inventor-creator with the resources of a nation behind him. To imagine—to think—to construct—to energize!

See everything fresh and "without form"—then make forms that will express us truthfully and totally and by this certainly free us eventually.

The 1960s saw many young black poets, writers, and thinkers emerge to articulate the positive spirit of the day. Don L. Lee (Haki Madhubuti) was a leader of the Chicago school of poets. He went on to back up his words with actions, founding a school for black children in Chicago.

Ed Bullins and Richard Wesley were leading playwrights in New York. They established the New Lafayette Theater in Harlem, writing and producing plays such as "Clara's Old Man" and "In the Wine Time." Bullins had previously been one of the founders of Black Arts/West in the radical Fillmore District in San Francisco.

Several works of nonfiction were very successful. Among them were *Soul on Ice*, the work of Black Panther minister of education Eldridge Cleaver; Claude Brown's *Manchild in the Promised Land*; *The Autobiography of Malcolm X*; and *Coming of Age in Mississippi* by Anne Moody.

Through her poetry Nikki Giovanni was the angry but determined voice of many black women. Giovanni's poems covered the gamut of issues for African-American women.

Finally, Paule Marshall, through her two novels *Brown Girl, Brownstones* and *The Chosen Place, The Timeless People*, has dealt with the experiences of black people who are born in the Caribbean and then emigrate to the United States.

African-Americans Entertainers

Traditionally, one of the few ways African-Americans have been able to achieve recognition in the wider society has been through the relatively non-threatening path of entertainment. The years after World War II saw the emergence of a host of African-American entertainers who broke color barriers and became internationally recognized stars.

The list of innovative African-American entertainers from the 1940s through the 1960s is a long one. It includes Nat "King" Cole, whose honey-colored voice won him his own nationally syndicated television program in 1957. Actress-singer Pearl Bailey became the first black female star on television in the 1950s. Audiences loved her homey style. She went on to star on Broadway in "Hello, Dolly," and serve as a delegate to the United Nations.

Dick Gregory gained fame, both as a comedian and, after 1965, for undertaking a series of fasts in support of the civil rights movement.

Actor James Earl Jones won Broadway's cherished Tony award for the best male performance in 1968 for his portrayal of boxing champion Jack Johnson in the play "The Great White Hope." Actress Eartha Kitt's up and down career almost came to an end when, in 1968, she attended a White House luncheon where she publicly criticized President Lyndon Johnson's Vietnam War policies.

In 1965 actor Sidney Poitier became the first black man to win an Oscar for his role in "Lilies In The Field."

Dancer/choreographer Katherine Dunham was the first person to put ethnic Caribbean and African dances on the concert stage. Dancers Arthur Mitchell, who founded The Dance Theater of Harlem, and Alvin Ailey, who established The Alvin Ailey American Dance Theater, both demonstrated the talent of African-Americans on the classical dance stage.

Controversial nightclub singer Nina Simone put her career on the line many times to popularize songs that dealt with the African-American struggle. One of her best-known songs was a Billie Holliday ballad, "Strange Fruit," which depicted the lynching of a black man in the South.

Opera diva Leontyne Price became one of the most celebrated singers in the world. She sang with the Metropolitan Opera in New York, and had starring roles in such productions as "Aida" and "Antony and Cleopatra."

275

Jackie Robinson Breaks the Color Line in Baseball

Only within the last 50 years have African-Americans been allowed to compete freely in various professional sports. Baseball, for example, became a battleground in the struggle for equality after World War II.

Although African-Americans had played on major league teams before 1900, this practice was halted at the turn of the century. Talented players, such as Satchel Paige, were forced to play in the "Negro leagues."

By 1940 Paul Robeson and other black civil rights leaders had sat down with baseball owners and discussed getting a black man into the majors. The breakthrough would not come until after the war, when Brooklyn Dodgers' owner Branch Rickey decided to sign Jackie Robinson.

Robinson, born in 1919 in Georgia, had been raised in Pasadena, California. He left college in his junior year to play professional football for the Los Angeles Bulldogs. Robinson's dream at the time was to become a top coach. After serving in the army in World War II, reaching the rank of lieutenant, he switched to baseball with the hope of finding a good coaching post.

But fate was to intervene when he was offered a playing job. In 1945 the Dodgers signed Robinson to its farm club, the Montreal Royals, where he awaited his chance to go to New York.

That chance came in 1947. After agreeing with Branch Rickey not to fight back against those who shouted insults at him on the diamond, Robinson began playing for the Dodgers. The strategy worked. In his first year Robinson not only broke the color barrier, but he won the National League's "Rookie of the Year" award. A respected star, he amassed an excellent record of hitting, fielding, and stealing bases, and was voted the National League's Most Valuable Player in 1949. Robinson retired in 1956, and in 1962 was named to the Baseball Hall of Fame. By then more and more blacks had entered professional sports.

Muhammed Ali—A New Kind of Sports Star

Jackie Robinson gained fame by letting his actions speak louder than his words. A new sports star burst on the scene in the 1960s, and his words were as loud as his actions. He was Muhammed Ali, and at the height of his career he was the most famous person in the world.

Ali was born Cassius Clay in Louisville, Kentucky. In 1960 he came to international attention when he won a gold medal in light heavyweight boxing at the Rome Olympics. In 1964 he turned "pro" and won the heavyweight boxing championship, knocking out Sonny Liston. At the same time, he changed his name and joined the Nation of Islam (Chapter 10).

Ali successfully defended his title through 1966. He dazzled fans with his charming wit and off-the-cuff poems. In describing his fighting approach, he told reporters, "I fly like a butterfly and sting like a bee." But in that year, after being drafted by the army, he refused, as a conscientious objector, to fight in Vietnam. For this stand he became a hero to members of the antiwar movement as well as to many African-Americans. The World Boxing Association, however, took away his title—an action later overturned in court. Ali came back to win the championship in 1974 and 1978, ensuring his place in sports history.

"I fly like a butterfly and sting like a bee."
—Muhammed Ali

SECTION FOUR REVIEW

1. LITERATURE What are Richard Wright's two best-known works?

2. BIOGRAPHY Who was the first black woman to win a Pulitzer Prize?

3. ENTERTAINMENT Who were some of the outstanding black entertainers of the 1950s and 1960s?

4. SPORTS For what reason is Jackie Robinson remembered?

5. CRITICAL THINKING Why do you think that members of minority groups sometimes have an easier time gaining acceptance as entertainers or sports stars than in everyday life?

CHAPTER NINE REVIEW

VOCABULARY

Write the numbered sentences on a separate sheet of paper. In each sentence fill in the blank with one of these terms: *civil disobedience, Korean War, March on Washington, Montgomery bus boycott, World War II.*

1. Martin Luther King, Jr., urged civil rights protestors to follow a policy of nonviolent _____.

2. The _____ marked the beginning of the modern civil rights movement.

3. The _____ was the first modern war in which blacks and whites fought in integrated units.

4. Adolf Hitler's racist theories led to _____, the most destructive global conflict of all time.

5. The 1963 _____ marked a high point of optimism for civil rights advocates in the United States.

REVIEWING THE FACTS

1. What were Adolf Hitler's racial views? How did those views lead to World War II?

2. What disadvantages did African-Americans face during World War II?

3. What action did President Truman take in 1948 concerning black troops?

4. How did a Supreme Court decision in 1954 affect the struggle for equal rights?

5. What lesson did civil rights demonstrators learn during the Montgomery bus boycott?

6. What was the outcome of the demand for voting rights?

7. Why did the civil rights movement grow more militant?

8. Why did so many urban riots break out in the 1960s?

9. What was the aim of the Black Panther Party?

10. Who were some of the outstanding African-American artists of the post-World War II years?

11. What gains did African-Americans make in the entertainment industry?

12. Why is Jackie Robinson's achievement of such importance?

CRITICAL THINKING

1. **MAKING JUDGMENTS** Explain the significance of the Brown decision.
2. **EVALUATING** What factors helped the Montgomery bus boycott succeed? Which of those factors do you think was the most important? Why?
3. **ANALYZING** What role did religion play in the civil rights movement?
4. **COMPARE AND CONTRAST** How did Stokely Carmichael and other young black leaders disagree with Dr. King's approach in the fight for civil rights? In what areas do you think they would have agreed?

UNDERSTANDING PREJUDICE

1. Following the Japanese attack on Pearl Harbor in 1941, authorities in the United States rounded up some 120,000 Japanese-American citizens and forced them into internment camps—concentration camps—far from their homes. (Canada did the same things to its citizens of Japanese extraction.) Why do you think this was done? What justification do you think authorities used? How does the decision show racist thinking?

2. President during the 1950s, when the civil rights movement was getting under way, Dwight Eisenhower once said, "You cannot change people's hearts merely by [changing] laws." What did he mean? Do you agree with his statement?

3. Many white Americans—particularly in the South—resisted desegregation with violence. Why do you think this was so?

4. Dr. King believed firmly that "injustice anywhere is a threat to justice everywhere." What does this statement mean? Describe how you think King would apply it to different groups in the United States today. (Consider, for example, Russian Jews, Arab-Americans, Haitian-Americans, Puerto Ricans.)

AFRICAN-AMERICANS TODAY

By the 1990s, many African-Americans felt that they were losing ground. For instance, in 1989 the Supreme Court curtailed the effectiveness of affirmative action laws, measures that sought to give preference to women or minority members who apply for jobs or for admission to schools. And in 1990 the Department of Education tried to cut back the number of scholarships that colleges receiving federal funds could give.

To respond to these and other disturbing trends, many African-American activists turned their energies to politics to effect change. Others moved in the opposite direction, working for separation of the races. But all took heart from promising trends in South Africa.

SECTION ONE   POLITICS AND PROTEST ON THE CONTEMPORARY SCENE

VOCABULARY Rainbow Coalition

MAIN IDEA Many black leaders are playing a leading role in America's political life today.

OBJECTIVES As you read, look for answers to the following questions:
1. Who are some of the leading black politicians today?
2. What important point did Jesse Jackson make in his efforts to win election as President?

The political arena in recent years has seen many African-Americans win election to offices at all levels of government.

The fight for freedom continues in South Africa as it does in the United States. Here, following his release from prison, Nelson Mandela (left) receives a hero's welcome at the White House.

Nowhere has success been greater than at the local level, where black mayors now head many of the nation's largest cities.

Black Elected Officials

Los Angeles mayor Tom Bradley won election in 1989 to an unprecedented fifth term in office. First elected in 1973, Bradley had been the city's Chief of Police before taking office.

New York's first African-American mayor is David Dinkins. Formerly the borough president of Manhattan and a New York State assemblyman, Dinkins had a private law practice before entering politics.

Washington, D.C.'s, first female mayor is Sharon Pratt

Dixon. A former utility company executive, she won election to the office held by Marion S. Barry, Jr., who was convicted of drug and perjury charges in 1990.

During the last two decades, increasing numbers of African-Americans have also run for Congress. In 1991 Congress had 26 African-American representatives. New York congressman Ed Towns chaired the Congressional Black Caucus. Among its members is Christopher Shays of Connecticut, the first Republican congressman since Oscar DePriest left office in 1934. The nation also had its first elected black governor, Douglas Wilder of Virginia.

Jesse Jackson's Early Years

Surely the best-known black politician in America today is Jesse Jackson. Jackson's evolution from "country preacher" to national politician is an example of how many concerned African-Americans have chosen the "within-the-system" approach to force change.

Jesse Louis Jackson was born on October 8, 1941, in Greenville, South Carolina. Throughout his life, Jesse Jackson has taken adversities and turned them into battle armor. His first battle was with the other children in his own neighborhood, who made fun of him for his illegitimate birth. His mother, Helen Burns, married Charles Henry Jackson, who formally adopted him in 1957, but not before young Jesse had to learn to fight with his voice, as well as his fists.

Jackson's second battle came when he confronted the racism of his hometown. Despite the comfortable living his parents provided as a post office clerk and a hairdresser, he still had to confront the fact that African-Americans were supposed to "stay in their place." As a small child, Jackson and his schoolmates had to walk six miles to the black elementary school, passing "Whites Only" signs and a modern white high school along the way.

In the evenings, he would sit at his grandmother's knee, where he would draw strength for the next day's battle. "If you fall, boy, you don't have to wallow," she would say. "Ain't nobody going to think you're somebody, unless you think so yourself."

Jesse, at eight, was the first African-American boy to

Reverend Jesse Jackson

"Ain't nobody going to think you're somebody, unless you think so yourself."
—Jesse Jackson's grandmother

sell small items at the local "Whites Only" football stadium. By nine, he made his first regular public speeches at the National Sunday School Convention. At twelve, he was caddying at the Greenville Country Club. And during his teenage years, while cleaning part-time at a local bakery, he and a friend tried to organize the workers to demand better conditions and more pay.

Jackson's political skills emerged early as well. A teacher recalled, "Whatever office was available, Jesse would be there signing his name." By the ninth grade, he was president of his class, the honor society, and the student council. Jackson also became a high school football champion. He drove himself to do well in his studies too. His teacher noted, "He was the only football player who ever asked for his assignment if he was going to miss class."

> "He was the only football player who ever asked for his assignment if he was going to miss class."
> —Teacher of Jesse Jackson

For college, Jackson decided to go to the University of Illinois. After he faced ugly discrimination against black students, however, he soon transferred back to the South. At the Agricultural and Technical College of North Carolina, Jackson quickly became an honors student, president of the student body, and quarterback of the football team.

Civil Rights Protestor

By 1963 Jackson was deeply involved in the civil rights arena, leading sit-in's in Greensboro, North Carolina. For ten months, students entered theaters and restaurants which would not allow black patrons. Jackson told his youthful followers, "I know I am going to jail. I'm going without fear." Indeed, he was arrested and served a short time.

Within months, downtown Greensboro had become integrated, and Jackson's fame spread. He soon made up his mind to join forces with Martin Luther King, Jr. His chance came during the 1965 Selma March. According to Andrew Young, then one of Dr. King's top aides, instead of waiting for instructions like all the other student marchers, Jackson stepped out of the crowd and began "directing marchers" himself, as if he were already an SCLC official. Later, he is said to have "popped up" out of the throng, giving an impromptu speech, even though he was not on the program.

During this period, Jackson made friends with the Reverend Ralph Abernathy, Dr. King's key assistant. It was

Abernathy who is said to have persuaded a reluctant King to let the young man have a job with the Chicago SCLC office.

By then Jackson had married his college sweetheart, Jacqueline, who picketed with him in his early activist days. The couple would have four children in all: Santita, Jesse, Jr., Jonathan Luther, and Yusef DuBois.

Jackson was in his element in Chicago. Working tirelessly, he seemed to be everywhere, so much so, that by the time Dr. King visited the city for an open housing campaign, he appointed Jackson head of SCLC's newly formed "Operation Breadbasket." Dr. King had created the project to force white businesses to hire more African-Americans and pay more attention to their consumer needs.

Then, on that fateful, tragic date of April 4, 1968, Jackson was summoned to the Lorraine Motel in Memphis, along with Dr. King's other key aides. Dr. King had decided to put together a massive protest march by sanitation workers there. But on that evening, fate intervened. On the motel balcony, the civil rights leader was brutally gunned down.

Seizing the moment, Jackson launched himself into history. Working furiously, he developed "Operation Breadbasket" into a force to be reckoned with, doing everything from holding weekly information forums to staging economic boycotts of major supermarket chains. The end result was that Jesse Jackson emerged as Dr. King's civil rights successor on the national scene.

Jackson Makes Political History

In 1971 Jackson announced that he would form a third national political party. The Liberation Party, as it was envisioned, would be made up of blacks and whites, and would nominate an African-American for President in 1972.

At the time, few people took Jackson seriously. But he took the American Dream seriously. And so, with characteristic determination, he began what would become a sixteen-year struggle that would end in 1988, with his amazing second-place finish at the Democratic nominating convention for President.

Even though the Liberation Party did not come into

being, the principles behind it gave birth to Jackson's so-called **Rainbow Coalition**. This organization allowed Jackson to gain high political visibility. He began jetting back and forth across the country—and the world—lending a hand in everything from Harold Washington's election as mayor of Chicago, to helping free political prisoners in Cuba.

Jackson's insistence on turning up everywhere, whether invited or not, and his constant flow of statements about his deeds, angered many people, black and white alike, who argued he was simply on an "ego trip." Nonetheless, in 1983 Jesse Jackson announced his candidacy for President of the United States. Jackson's Rainbow Coalition was on the move.

By the time the Democratic Convention of 1984 was over, the party's choice was Walter Mondale. But, his loss notwithstanding, Jesse Jackson had made an important point: that an African-American could make a serious run for the nation's highest office.

Keeping his sights set high, despite intense pressure to back off, Jackson geared up to go through the exhausting election ordeal again in 1988. Despite his loss to Massachusetts governor Michael Dukakis, Jackson had made progress in broadening his Rainbow Coalition to include farmers, blue-collar workers, and environmentalists. He finished first in eight state primaries and second in many others.

Jackson has sometimes been branded an "opportunist" for his continual efforts to move up the rungs of America's political ladder. Others say that his views are far too liberal to be accepted by most Americans. But, he insists, his efforts are for the poor: "Someone must defend them." Then he exhorts his followers to find a "common ground," with common sense, as his grandmother used to do:

> Grandmama could not afford a blanket.... Instead, she took pieces of old cloth...and sewed them... into...a thing of beauty, power and culture....Be as wise as my grandmama....When we form a great quilt of unity and common ground, we'll have the power to bring about health care and housing and jobs and education and hope to our nation.... We, the people, can win!

Jackson captured a new position in 1990, that of "shadow lobbyist to the United States Senate" for the District of

Rainbow Coalition: Jesse Jackson's coalition of political backers of all races.

"We, the people, can win!"
—Jesse Jackson

General Colin Powell

Columbia. Because the District is not a state, it is not eligible to have its own senators. Although Jackson cannot vote on any senatorial issues in this new position, he is able to promote the District's interests, including its quest for statehood.

A Rising Black Leader—Colin Powell

Meanwhile, some critics predict that Jackson's day in the limelight has passed. They say that new, more moderate black leaders will rise to the top. Among those mentioned for high office is Governor Douglas Wilder of Virginia. Another possibility is General Colin Powell, currently the nation's senior professional military officer. Four-star general Powell is the first black Chairman of the Joint Chiefs of Staff, overseeing all American military operations.

Powell, born in Harlem of Jamaican parents, made his way to the top by sheer hard work. Graduating at the top of his ROTC (Reserve Officer Training Corps) class at City College in New York, he went on to serve two tours of duty in Vietnam. Altogether he won eleven medals in Vietnam, including the Legion of Merit in 1972.

On his return to the United States, Powell earned a masters in business administration from George Washington University. He then accepted his first political position—that of White House fellow, a coveted internship in which middle managers are groomed for larger responsibilities. His competence and quiet efficiency were soon noticed, and in the next years he served in a number of military and political positions, rising quickly through the ranks. Powell became the youngest Chairman of the Joint Chiefs in 1989, just a few months after President Reagan presented him with his fourth star.

Since then, he has had to contend with military action all over the world. Under presidential direction, Powell oversaw the deployment of American troops to the Philippines to aid President Corazon Aquino in 1989. He also directed the invasion of Panama in 1989, which ended with the capture of General Manuel Noriega. In early 1990 he sent troops to Liberia, in West Africa, to rescue Americans trapped in a civil war.

Surely Powell's greatest challenge was to oversee the

successful American effort in 1991 to liberate Kuwait from Iraq. In so doing, he became a familiar and trusted leader for the American public.

SECTION ONE REVIEW 〰〰〰〰〰〰〰〰〰〰〰〰〰

1. VOCABULARY Write a sentence using the following term: Rainbow Coalition.

2. POLITICS What were the results of Jesse Jackson's efforts to win election as President?

3. BIOGRAPHY What were some of the criticisms of Jesse Jackson?

4. HISTORY How did Colin Powell make history?

5. CRITICAL THINKING In recent decades the overwhelming majority of black political leaders have been Democrats. What advantages does that create? What disadvantages?

THE NATION OF ISLAM

SECTION TWO

VOCABULARY Black Muslim Mohammed Koran

MAIN IDEA In the search for equal justice, some African-Americans have called for the creation of a separate black nation in the United States.

OBJECTIVES As you read, look for answers to the following questions:
1. What are the Black Muslims' three main ideas?
2. Who shaped the Nation of Islam into a modern force?
3. Who were two of the leading Black Muslim ministers of modern times?

Jesse Jackson and Colin Powell represent one approach for African-Americans. Another is held by the **Black Muslims**, or the Nation of Islam. They are currently closest to Marcus

Black Muslim:
a religious group that calls for separation of the races.

287

Garvey's dreams of a separate black nation "doing for itself" in America.

Beliefs of the Nation of Islam

Black Muslim belief includes three main ideas:

(1) African-Americans will never gain participation in this country's system.

(2) Instead of complaining, African-Americans should separate from their white counterparts and develop their own "nation within a nation" inside United States boundaries.

(3) By strengthening and honoring the black family, and by creating independent educational, religious, and business structures, the creation of such a nation is truly possible.

These beliefs date back to 1930 when Allah (God) was said to have appeared in the person of Fard Muhammad, a Detroit salesman. Claiming to be of Arabic origin, Muhammad described the world from an Islamic point of view. One of his followers, a slim, dynamic young man named Elijah Poole, was especially captivated by the doctrine of black spiritual self-awareness and pride. Soon he became Muhammad's right-hand man, even accepting the new name of Elijah Muhammad. Eventually, after Fard Muhammad's departure, he inherited leadership of the entire movement and was responsible for shaping it into a modern force.

The Impact of Elijah Muhammad

Elijah Poole was born in Georgia. His father and grandfather were both Baptist ministers, but he was destined to strike out in a new direction. In fact, so staunch was his determination to save black people from the "wilderness of North America" through the Black Muslim faith, that he even went to prison for it. Elijah Muhammad was behind bars from 1942 to 1946 because he would not support America's efforts in World War II.

Elijah Muhammad, like millions of people in the Middle East and Africa, was a Muslim. Muslims follow the teachings of **Muhammad** (570?–632 A.D.), who wrote Allah's re-

Muhammad: prophet and founder of Islam.

288

velations in a holy book called the **Quran** (koh-RAHN). Muslims around the world study the Quran and consider it absolute, in much the same way that Christians revere the Bible.

But Elijah Muhammad included other aspects in the Black Muslim religion in America. According to him (as told by Master Fard Muhammad), all black people are descendants of an ancient lost tribe named Shabazz. As Master Muhammad explained, this tribe was the brainchild of a man named Shabazz who lived near the holy city of Mecca some 50,000 years ago. Dr. Shabazz, according to this theory, decided he would create a race of people who would "conquer the jungle." But such an act was a "rebellion against God." So he and his people were put out of the "holy precinct" and away from "civilized" people. During that period, these black people "lost the root of God." And they "began the process of disintegration" into smaller tribes and lost unity.

Eventually enslaved, these people were forced to come to America. That is why, to this day, Black Muslims either use the letter "X" or take an Arabic name, to replace their American last name—their "slave name."

And it is why the Nation of Islam considers itself a "nation within a nation." In this sense, the Nation of Islam in America has something in common with traditional Muslims in the Middle East, who say they have been struggling to maintain their way of life against the encroachments of "outsiders" for hundreds of years.

In the United States, the fight has not been on desert sands, but on deserted corners in cities like Detroit. And, rather than using swords or guns in this holy war, the Nation of Islam's weapons have been largely economic. Followers have developed temples, schools and businesses, as well as their own newspaper, now known as *The Final Call*.

Elijah Muhammad's strength was his belief that by adhering to the Black Muslim philosophy, African-Americans, no matter what their social status, could pull out of their racial dilemma. By the 1950s, the Black Muslims had gained as many as 50,000 followers. It was during this time that one of the religion's most dynamic figures joined its ranks. He would be known as Malcolm X.

Quran:
the sacred text of Islam, believed to contain the revelations made by Allah to Muhammad.

289

Malcolm X—Ahead of His Time

Malcolm X was named Malcolm Little when he was born in Omaha, Nebraska, on May 19, 1925. One of eight children, Malcolm (like Elijah Muhammad) was the son of a Baptist minister. His mother was raised in Grenada, in the Caribbean.

By the time Malcolm was a young man, his early church influence had given way to a life of crime. In fact, in 1946, at the age of 21, he began serving a prison sentence for burglary in Massachusetts.

While in prison, Malcolm converted to the Islamic faith. A year after his release in 1952, he became an Assistant Minister in the Nation of Islam's Temple No. 1 in Detroit. Two years later he was named minister of the prestigious temple in Harlem. There he married Betty Shabazz, a strong-willed black woman who shared his ideals.

By the early 1960s Malcolm X was the standard bearer for an entire generation of black militants. His speeches fired the imagination of countless young black activists who were frustrated by the approach of Martin Luther King, Jr. (who Malcolm once scornfully described as "a little black mouse sitting on top of a big white elephant.") Malcolm's message about "house Negroes and field Negroes," for example, had a powerful effect:

> So, you have two types of Negro. . . . You have the house Negro and the field Negro. . . .
>
> And this is the thing that the white people in America have got to come to realize. That there are two types of black people in this country. One who identifies with you so much so he will let you brutalize him and still beg you for a chance to sit next to you. And then there's one who's not interested in sitting next to you. . . . He wants something of his own. . . . The masses of black people in this country are no more interested in token integration than they would be if you offered them a chance to sit inside a furnace somewhere.
>
> The Honorable Elijah Muhammad teaches us that the only completely satisfactory solution is when the black man has his own and the white man has his own. . . .

This new type of black man, he doesn't want integration; he wants separation. Not segregation, separation. . . . Separation is when you have your own.

They don't call Chinatown a segregated community, yet it's all Chinese. But the Chinese control it. . . . They choose to live by themselves. . . . This makes them equal because they have what you have. . . . Integration in America is hypocrisy in the rawest form.

Malcolm X and Elijah Muhammad had much in common. They both despised the white power structure in America for what it had done to black people. But Malcolm, younger and more fiery, did not shy away from leaving his temple to travel around the country, publicly denouncing the "white devil."

A Split in the Ranks

As it turned out, Malcolm also did not hesitate to denounce Elijah Muhammad. In 1963, deeply disillusioned and having doubts about the Black Muslim movement, he accused Mr. Muhammad, by then in his seventies, of having fathered babies with nine teenaged girls:

Yes, he's immoral. You can't take nine teenaged women and seduce them and give them babies and . . . then tell me you're moral. . . . And I'm not speculating, because he told me this himself.

Elijah Muhammad ordered Malcolm X to make no more public statements. The reason given at the time was that following President Kennedy's assassination in 1963, Malcolm had made an inflammatory statement, saying that "the chickens [had] come home to roost."

The strain between the two powerful men became unbearable, and finally, early in 1964, Elijah Muhammad expelled Malcolm X from the Black Muslim movement. A month later, Malcolm X announced the formation of his new group, the Muslim Mosque, Inc.

Malcolm X renounced the Black Muslims and became a

"This new type of black man, he doesn't want integration; he wants separation. Not segregation, separation."
—Malcolm X

Malcolm X

member of the traditional Sunni Islam faith. Then he went to Mecca and Africa on a pilgrimage that would change his life.

On his trip, he visited scores of countries in the Moslem world. Upon his return, he told followers, he had "broadened [his] scope." He began talking more of the "brotherhood of man" united under one God:

So we're not against people because they're white. But we're against those who practice racism. . . . We're for peace.

We adopted the real, orthodox religion of Islam, which is a religion of brotherhood.

The Assassination of Malcolm X

And so, on he went. As vocal as ever, Malcolm X worked hard to unite African-Americans, Africans, and Middle Eastern people in his fight against racist oppression. He also continued to denounce his former leader, Elijah Muhammad.

On February 21, 1965, Malcolm X was assassinated during a rally at the Audubon Ballroom in New York City. Three men, two of them allegedly Muslims, were sentenced to life in prison for the crime. Many suspicions have been raised, however, about the possible role of the federal government in Malcolm's death.

Betty Shabazz Carries On

Following the assassination, Betty Shabazz, Malcolm's widow, picked up the pieces of her life and raised her children. She later served as Director of Communications and Public Relations for the Medgar Evers College of the City University of New York. Betty Shabazz remembers:

Malcolm was . . . all-giving, all-helping, and it didn't look like anybody was helping him. . . . And I was thinking that maybe I was the person to help him. He is the one person during my lifetime that I am delighted to have known. . . . He loved his parents.

He loved his people, and later he loved me with the same passion.

They attempted to promote him as a violent person, a hater of whites. . . . Yes, he disliked the behavior of some whites. One needs only to examine history and analyze the present condition of the African diaspora to justify his conceptual framework.

We can say, "Peace on Earth," we can sing about it, preach about it, or pray about it, but if we [cannot] make it happen inside of us, then it will not be!

Minister Louis Farrakhan

The ouster of Malcolm X as minister of the Nation of Islam's New York Temple left quite a void. But it was soon filled by a young minister named Louis X, then head of the Boston temple. Shortly after moving to New York, Minister Louis received a new last name, "Farrakhan," from Elijah Muhammad. ("Khan" of "Farrakhan" means "ruler" in Arabic.)

Actually, just after Elijah Muhammad's death, his son Wallace Dean assumed the successorship of the religion. But Louis Farrakhan soon emerged as the only man dynamic enough to keep the movement going.

One reason why Louis Farrakhan seems able to inspire many black Americans is that he has "been there" himself. Farrakhan was named Louis Gene Walcott when he was born in 1934 in the Bronx, New York, to Jamaican parents. He grew up in the Roxbury neighborhood of Boston.

He showed signs of early excellence when he learned to play the violin like a professional while still a boy, won honors in track in high school, and became an avid honor student, eager to know more about African-American history. His first black hero was Marcus Garvey. He recalled asking his uncle:

Where is this man, that I might meet him and help him? My uncle answered, 'That man is dead.' I was so hurt that after hoping, all my young years, to meet the right man for our people, that when I

"Tears rolled down my cheeks and I cried and cried because Marcus Garvey was dead."
—Louis Farrakhahn

293

found him, he was already dead. Tears rolled down my cheeks and I cried and cried because Marcus Garvey was dead.

More disillusionment came when he went to North Carolina to Winston-Salem Teachers College, where he experienced racial discrimination firsthand. He abandoned teaching as a profession and became an actor and professional singer, specializing in Calypso songs. In fact, he was working in a Boston nightclub when he first heard about the Black Muslims.

In 1955 Farrakhan went to Chicago to the Muslim Saviour's Day Convention and wasted no time in joining up. He became Louis X and rose rapidly through the ranks.

In recent years, Farrakhan's speeches have attracted more and more non-Muslims, who now flock by the thousands to hear him. At a speech in the Los Angeles Coliseum in 1990, Farrakhan drew a crowd of nearly 40,000 listeners. He remarked that in 1972 he had spoken right across the street, at the University of Southern California, to just 100 people.

In his speech he encouraged Native Americans, Hispanic Americans, and African-Americans to learn to love one another and unite so that they can get what is rightfully theirs in the world. He touched on the many problems facing people of color today:

> We are the original people of the Earth, the family of Almighty God. But there is an assault on our families. You can't have a strong family if you can't have a strong male. In this racist society, the white male is threatened if black, brown, and red come into prominence, so the society is geared to crush them. This brings constant tension between the males and females. We're at each others' throats as if *we* were the enemy.

The Black Muslims' Appeal

Although it is relatively small at this time, the Nation of Islam's official membership is growing. This is due, in part, to the religion's efforts to encourage more African-Americans to join, despite the somewhat challenging Black Muslim living code.

Black Muslims pray five times a day, eat just once a day, and abstain from smoking, alcohol, gambling, drugs, dancing and profanity. Followers are encouraged to dress neatly. The men usually opt for conservative white shirts and dark suits. The women choose to keep their legs and heads covered in public.

The Nation of Islam is also working to overcome its former reputation for racial controversy. During the last few years, Minister Farrakhan has appeared in public and on television to clarify certain of his statements that he says were misinterpreted as being anti-white or anti-Jewish. In his most recent speeches, rather than criticizing other racial groups, Minister Farrakhan has emphasized the potential benefits of "people of color" separating from whites and building their own political and economic structures.

Finally, Black Muslims are playing a somewhat more active role in American politics. Until recently, although being nonviolent and law-abiding, they were very selective politically, rarely voting in regular elections. In the last two years, however, they have voted more regularly for candidates who support their views, and, in fact, several Black Muslims themselves have run for political office on the local level.

SECTION TWO REVIEW

1. **VOCABULARY** Write a sentence for each of the following terms: Black Muslim, Muhammed, Quran.

2. **RELIGION** What is the key part of Black Muslim belief?

3. **BIOGRAPHY** What role did Elijah Muhammad play in the rise of the Black Muslims?

4. **RELIGION** What practices of the Black Muslims differ from those of people outside the religion?

5. **CRITICAL THINKING** Do you think that the establishment of a separate black nation in America would be a practical idea? Explain your answer.

SECTION THREE

CONTEMPORARY AFRICAN-AMERICANS—THE ARTISTIC SIDE

MAIN IDEA African-American authors and artists have made a deep impression on American cultural life.

OBJECTIVES As you read, look for answers to the following questions:
1. Who are some of today's outstanding African-American authors?
2. What African-American painters have gained fame in recent years?

In the realm of literature, many admirable black authors have come to the fore in the 1970s and 1980s. Because there are so many, we have included just a few who have received acclaim. From a cultural standpoint, their awards, whether from white or black society, are not the most important thing. What is especially important is whether they have helped their readers to understand themselves better.

African-American Authors

In 1982 Philadelphia playwright Charles Fuller won the Pulitzer Prize for his drama, "A Soldier's Play." The story takes place in an army camp in Louisiana. The year is 1944, when black soldiers were kept segregated from the whites. Someone has just killed a black sergeant. Who did it? As the play progresses, the audience wonders if white soldiers did him in, or, because of his treatment of the black men under him, whether one of them pulled the trigger.

Ishmael Reed, publisher, poet, and professor at the University of California at Berkeley, has been nominated twice for the National Book Award for both his poetry and his fiction. His *Shrovetide in Old New Orleans* (1976) is a collection of essays describing "much HooDoo about everything." Here he describes Madi Gras in New Orleans:

> I headed . . . to Canal Street, when the carnival suddenly came in upon me. . . . Blacks. Not the . . . glossy "Superfly" . . . types but people who put on overalls and walk down the street holding their children's hands. This is the "field" division of Negro society. . . . They drink corn whiskey and dance at clubs with names like The Honey Hush and do their wash in the Splish Splash Washateria.

Alice Walker's account of a young black woman trying to find love, as well as herself, is called *The Color Purple* (1982). For this book, Walker won both the Pulitzer Prize and the National Book Award for Fiction in 1983.

Gloria Naylor's *The Women of Brewster Place* (1980) also won the National Book Award. In the novel Naylor, a writer-in-residence at George Washington University in Washington, D.C., tells how the black women of an urban ghetto street, Brewster Place, manage to cope amid the harsh reality around them:

> Mattie looked around at the cramped boarding-house room with its cheap furniture and dingy walls. . . . She found an assembly-line job in a book bindery, and she paid Mrs. Press, an old woman on the first floor, to keep [her baby] during the day. . . . Mattie would walk the thirty blocks back to the boardinghouse to see the baby during her lunch break. . . .
>
> She thought about taking night courses at school . . . but what with working six days a week, she hardly ever saw the baby as it was. It was heartbreaking when she missed his first step, and she had cried for two hours when she first heard him call Mrs. Prell "Mama."

Toni Morrison, an editor and the mother of two sons, also has written a series of highly acclaimed novels. Her first was *The Bluest Eye* in 1968. In 1978 she received the National Book Critics Award for *Song of Solomon*. Ten years later, she won the Pulitzer Prize for Fiction for her novel, *Beloved*. "I never played it safe in a book," she has written. "I never tried to play to the gallery. For me, it was extraordinary exploration. You have to be willing to think the unthinkable."

In 1990 Charles Johnson won the National Book Award for Fiction for *The Middle Passage*, his novel about the life of a newly freed slave. Johnson is a professor at the University of Washington.

African-American Painters

Black painters too have gained recognition. Jacob Lawrence is an outstanding example.

Jacob Lawrence's mother enrolled him in an after-school arts and crafts program in Harlem in 1929 when he was twelve years old. She feared that if he didn't have something productive to do, he would end up in a gang. As it happened, young Lawrence fell in with several of the top black artists of the day. One of them was Augusta Savage, who encouraged him over the years and helped him get into a federally subsidized artists' program.

Lawrence was able to paint the images of black history he loved so much in his colorful, distinctive, angular style. After his first show at the Harlem YMCA, he received other grants to paint, as well as an offer to be represented by Edith Halpert, a top art dealer of the day.

By 1965 the National Institute of Arts and Letters had asked him to become a member. In 1969 he and other artists founded the Black Academy of Arts and Letters. And in 1970 he was awarded the prestigious Spingarn Medal, the highest award bestowed by the NAACP. Lawrence has stated his view of the role of black artists today:

> I think the thing for us to pursue is not only to get massive aid and help within the black community, but also not to tear us away from the main community, not allowing people downtown to say, 'Well, let's give them a little something and we can forget about them.'

SECTION THREE REVIEW

1. **LITERATURE** For what drama is Charles Fuller known?

2. **LITERATURE** Who is a leading black poet today?

3. **LITERATURE** What are the titles of some of Toni Morrison's novels?

4. **ART** Why is Jacob Lawrence well-known today?

5. **CRITICAL THINKING** Reread Jacob Lawrence's statement about the black community. From his words, do you think he would have favored the politics of Jesse Jackson or Louis Farrakham? Explain your answer.

THE AFRICAN CONNECTION

VOCABULARY apartheid African National Congress ban Sharpeville Massacre sanctions

MAIN IDEA In South Africa, the struggle for equal rights and justice continues.

OBJECTIVES As you read, look for answers to the following questions:
1. What did the government of South Africa do to exert its control over the nonwhite majority?
2. What was the response of young Africans like Nelson Mandela?
3. Why did the South African government imprison Nelson Mandela?
4. When, and under what circumstances, was Nelson Mandela released from prison?

SECTION FOUR

At the same time that African-Americans were organizing and protesting for freedom in the 1950s, their counterparts in Africa were gaining their independence from European colonizers like Great Britain and France.

Ghana was first. Under Kwame Nkrumah, it gained its independence from Great Britain in 1957. This was just one year after Martin Luther King, Jr.'s celebrated bus boycott struck a blow for civil rights in this country. Within three years, countries across the continent had gained their independence. In southern Africa, however, the minority white governments remained tightly in control. In one part of the region, the struggle to eliminate discrimination is still going on.

299

The Establishment of Apartheid

As you read in Chapter 8, Europeans arrived in southern Africa in the 1600s, forcing the inhabitants off their lands. There they set up the country of South Africa, and it remained a nation ruled by people of European descent, even though whites formed no more than 20 percent of the population.

As the 20th century rolled around, South Africa was the most developed country in Africa, leading the world in gold and diamond production. The whites were determined to remain in charge. In 1948 they gave control of the country to the National Party, which was dominated by Afrikaners. The new government wasted no time in passing a policy called **apartheid** (ah-PART-hide).

Strict apartheid laws were passed to restrict the rights of nonwhites. Neither Africans nor persons of mixed race were allowed to live in white areas.

To keep track of the movement of nonwhites, the government established a system of "pass laws." Nonwhites had to carry passes, or identification cards, that showed where they lived and worked. If they were caught in the "wrong" area or if they were out after curfew, they could then be arrested. In addition, rural Africans were forced either to live on "homelands," which were little more than rural slums, or in crowded "townships" on the outskirts of the white-only cities.

apartheid:
official policy of racial segregation of the South African government to keep the white minority in power.

Nelson Mandela and the Struggle for Freedom

During the 1950s African, Asian, and mixed-race groups spoke out for nonracial democracy. An emerging leader in the movement for freedom was Nelson Mandela.

Nelson Mandela was born in 1918, a noble young prince of the Tembu ruling clan in the Transkei region of southern Africa. Young Nelson could have had it easy. He could have stayed at home and married the young woman his family had deemed "suitable" for him. He could have made a comfortable living from farming and raising sheep.

But that was not his calling. Instead, the inquisitive, aggressive young Mandela wanted to do something more for his people. He later recalled why:

Our people lived peacefully under the democratic rule of their kings and counsellors and moved freely all over their country. Then the country was ours. . . .

The elders would tell us about the liberation and how it was fought by our ancestors in defence of our country, as well as the acts of valour performed by generals and soldiers during those epic days. I hoped, and vowed then [to] make my own humble contribution to their struggle for freedom.

So, Mandela went to the local Methodist school, and after that, studied at University College at Fort Hare, which would produce many of black South Africa's radical leaders. By Mandela's third year, he was already showing signs of leadership. He helped organize a boycott after the white government took away the student council's decision-making power. Mandela was expelled from school for his actions, but still he would not go home, marry the "right" girl, and tend his flock.

In Johannesburg, Mandela met two young men who would become his closest comrades, Walter Sisulu and Oliver Tambo. Sisulu helped him get into law school. Mandela and Tambo, who was also an expelled student from Fort Hare, later became partners and established their own law practice in Johannesburg.

Sisulu, Mandela, and other young black men and women helped form the Youth League of the **African National Congress** (ANC) in 1944. (The ANC had been set up by two American-educated black South Africans in 1912 to work for equal rights.) Mandela and his valiant young comrades vowed to be a "body of gentlemen with clean hands." They would take "direct action," but it would be nonviolent.

African National Congress: organization founded in 1912 to work for equal rights in South Africa.

Mayibuye Afrika—Let Africa Return!

By 1952 Mandela had become President of the Transvaal Branch of the ANC, and, later that year, the Deputy National President. The ANC joined with other anti-government groups to plan a massive "Defiance Campaign." Much like the sit-in's in the American South, the protestors planned to sit in waiting rooms or other places reserved for whites. In particular, the ANC hoped to do away with South Africa's hated "pass laws."

The campaign began on June 26, 1952. Their battle cry was "Mayibuye Afrika"—"Let Africa Return!"

Police immediatley began raiding the homes of the movement leaders, following them and planting informants in their midst. In 1953 the government stripped the ANC President, Natal Chief Albert Luthuli, of his traditional tribal status. Meanwhile, thousands of protestors were thrown into jail.

But even as the government brought more and more pressure to bear, the ANC would not be moved. In 1955 its leaders began organizing a "Congress of the People," that would "speak together of freedom" for all oppressed South Africans. Again, the ANC joined with other resistance groups like the South African Indian Congress, the Coloured People's Organization, and the Congress of Democrats (a liberal white group). The "Freedom Charter" approved at the meeting declared, "South Africa belongs to all who live in it, black and white."

Mandela wrote about the "Freedom Charter" in *Liberation* Magazine in June 1956:

> The democratic struggle in South Africa is conducted by an alliance of various classes and political groupings amongst the non-European people supported by white democrats, African, Coloured, and Indian workers. . . . All participate in the struggle against racial inequality and for full democratic rights.

The South African Government Responds

As far as Mandela was concerned, the fight had just begun. Lashing out, officials arrested him for the worst "crime" they could think of—"high treason." His trial and that of his fellow leaders lasted five exhausting years, from 1956 to 1961. Even then, with all the government machinery arrayed against them, the courts finally had to admit that they did not have much of a case. The charges against the ANC leaders were dropped.

Despite the victory, the cost to the protest movement

had been high. Many leaders had lost their jobs and homes. And the government had formally **banned** the ANC.

ban:
to prohibit by official decree.

Another big problem stemmed from a major ideological split among South African activists. Like their African-American counterparts, they were divided into two camps. The first camp included the ANC. Its position was that blacks and whites should be allowed to live together, enjoying equal rights. This was similar to the principle of integration in America.

The second camp included the Pan-Africanist Congress, formed in 1958, which called for the separation of the races. Led by Robert Sobukwe, the PAC went so far as to call for the expulsion of all whites from Africa.

Winnie Mandela

One of the reasons for Nelson Mandela's success as a freedom fighter was his marriage to the strong-willed Winnie Nomzamo.

By the time Nelson met Winnie, he was already a 38-year old lawyer, famous for his revolutionary practices. Winnie was "captivated both by the man and his dream." For years, she had seen her own father, a school headmaster, struggle for the rights of black schoolchildren. Because of the African extended family structure, her father had up to 30 mouths to feed. In spite of this, he and one of Winnie's sisters sacrificed even more, sending her to Johannesburg to become the first black medical social worker in South Africa.

Through friends, Winnie first met Nelson in 1955, while he was awaiting the outcome of his treason trial. Nelson, in the midst of the most serious crisis of his life, did not talk to the attractive young woman about her budding sideline job as a fashion model in the local black magazines. Instead, they discussed ways of augmenting the ANC's staggering expenses for its courtroom defenses.

In the next two years, they did get around to other topics. Nelson proposed in 1957. Even then, he was frank with her about the hard life he was facing. He told her the struggle was a "commitment for life, like a call to the ministry."

Nelson had to get permission from his parole authorities to marry Winnie. Their wedding was a blend of the old

303

and the new. Winnie wore a Western satin and lace wedding gown in white, but Nelson still had to pay the traditional "lobola" or bride-price of a number of head of cattle in order to marry her.

From the time the couple moved into their little cottage in Soweto (soh-WAY-toh), a huge township outside Johannesburg, they would never have an ordinary life. Soon after they were married, Winnie, pregnant with their first child, was arrested during a protest march. In jail for two weeks, wrapped only in a filthy blanket, she nearly lost the child.

During this time, Nelson was banned from all public appearances, as well as his regular law practice. As a result, he went underground to direct the movement. Even though this meant leaving his wife and small children and any semblance of a "normal" life, Winnie supported him all the way. It was up to her to keep food on the table.

The year 1960 brought the **Sharpeville Massacre**. In Sharpeville, near Johannesburg, police fired on an unarmed crowd of Africans protesting the pass laws, killing 69 and wounding 86. Many demonstrators were reportedly shot in the back as they ran from the police.

This atrocity served to bring the plight of black South Africans to international attention. As recognition of the ANC's efforts to bring change to South Africa, in 1961 ANC President Chief Luthuli was awarded the Nobel Peace Prize. (This was three years before Martin Luther King, Jr., would receive the same award.)

Sharpeville Massacre: massacre of unarmed protestors in 1960 that served to focus world attention on the apartheid system.

Nelson Mandela—South Africa's "Most Wanted" Man

The Sharpeville Massacre had another important effect. It apparently convinced Nelson Mandela that the days of nonviolent resistance were over. Mandela became head of *Umkonto we Sizwe* (Spear of the Nation), an underground branch of the ANC that was founded to commit acts of sabotage and attack targets symbolizing apartheid. Terrorist acts against individuals were ruled out, however.

Over an eighteen-month period, *Umkonto we Sizwe* claimed credit for more than 70 acts of sabotage. Frightened whites would find leaflets announcing, "The time comes in the life of any nation when there remains only two choices: submit or fight." During this period, Mandela also managed to slip out of South Africa to visit countries across Africa, raising funds, and even taking part in military training in Algeria.

Tragically, in 1962 the South African police managed to learn of Mandela's whereabouts and arrest him. The courts sentenced him to five years' solitary confinement and hard labor. In 1964, after another black revolt, the government extended Mandela's five-year sentence to life imprisonment.

Imposing Sanctions

Even though Mandela was not on the scene, the fight went on. At the time, the United States and Western European nations were buying more than 60 percent of South Africa's exports. And, with rare exceptions, these countries refused to vote for economic and military boycotts, called **sanctions**. In 1963, however, the United Nations did vote to ban the sales of arms to South Africa. The World Health Organization, along with other technical organizations, ousted South Africa from their ranks. And South Africa was excluded from the Olympic Games. But it would take nearly 25 more years of pressure and persuasion before the international community could force any true sanctions on South Africa.

Steven Biko—Black Man, You Are on Your Own

In the late 1960s and early 1970s, with Mandela in prison, a brilliant young black medical student named Steven Biko (BEE-koh) helped lead South Africa's protest movement. Biko promoted a "black consciousness" movement, not unlike the black power movement in the United States. He wrote:

> The type of black man we have today has lost his manhood. The first step therefore is to make the black man come to himself; to pump back life into his empty shell; to infuse him with pride and dignity.

Biko's slogan was "Black man, you are on your own!" In 1972 he abandoned his medical career to become a full-

"The time comes in the life of any nation when there remains only two choices: submit or fight."
—ANC leaflet

sanctions:
formal measures usually agreed upon by several nations to stop doing something that is against international law.

305

Archbishop Desmond Tutu

time activist. The government, fearful of having another young Mandela on their hands, soon took drastic action. First, it banned Biko from all public speaking. Then, to try to exert control over his youthful followers, it ordered that all students to attend classes conducted in the Afrikaans' language.

Massive student protests and school boycotts followed. By 1977, an astounding 250,000 students were on strike. And 600 teachers resigned in sympathy.

Once again, the South African police did their evil deeds. In September 1977 they captured Biko and beat him to death.

Bishop Desmond Tutu

Nelson Mandela was in prison. Steven Biko was dead. But opposition to the government countinued to mount.

Religious leaders of all faiths spoke out fearlessly against apartheid. The head of the Anglican Church of South Africa, Archbishop Desmond Tutu was awarded the Nobel Peace Prize in 1984 for his efforts to bring about nonviolent change. Clearly articulating the need for international sanctions against South Africa, Tutu watched with great joy as the United States Congress condemned the South African government in 1986 by imposing economic sactions. United States businesses found themselves facing public censure if they continued to operate as usual in that country.

Mandela Must Be Free!

In 1984 student rebellions to free Mandela erupted again. The South African government offered to release Mandela on the condition that he would agree to settle in the black tribal "homeland" of Transkei. But the black leader refused the offer until the government did away with apartheid. He wrote:

What freedom am I being offered when I may be arrested on a pass offense? When I must ask permission to live in an urban area? When my very

South African citizenship is not respected? Only free men can negotiate. Prisoners cannot enter into contracts.

In the meantime, Winnie Mandela carried on the struggle. She endured months of imprisonment in solitary confinement. Her house was bombed. And her younger daughter, Zeni, had to wait 16 years before being allowed to see her father in prison. Her older daughter, Zinzi, was hounded when she tried to finish her schooling. But in spite of it all, the Mandela family persisted and, finally, prevailed.

Nelson Mandela Freed

In 1990 the South African government was forced by continuing international sanctions to make concessions to its black citizens. It lifted its state of emergency and restored the legal status of the ANC. In addition, after 27 years of imprisonment Nelson Mandela agreed to be released. Triumphantly, he and his wife toured the world, urging that sanctions stay in place until "the total elimination of apartheid and the extension of the vote to all people." In the United States, Nelson and Winnie Mandela met with President and Mrs. Bush and were given a ticker-tape parade in New York City.

Given the rare invitation to speak before both houses of Congress, Mandela recalled the inspiration that freedom fighters in South Africa had gained from their study of American history:

> We would not have made an acquaintance through literature with human giants such as George Washington, Abraham Lincoln, and Thomas Jefferson and not been moved to act as they were moved to act. We could not have heard of and admired John Brown, Sojourner Truth, Frederick Douglass, W.E.B. Du Bois, Marcus Garvey, and Martin Luther King, Jr., and not been moved to act as they were moved to act. We could not have known of your Declaration of Independence and not elected to join in the struggle to guarantee . . . life, liberty, and the pursuit of happiness.

307

Meanwhile, the pressure continued, resulting in 1991 with the government of South Africa calling for the end of all apartheid laws. White voters approved the government's plans in a referendum in 1992, and many nations responded by lifting economic sanctions. But will the changes lead to full voting rights for all the people of South Africa? Only time will tell. Of course, like the United States government, South Africa has never undertaken positive change for its black citizens without pressure. So, still on parallel courses, concerned people of color on both continents continue to fight with determination for their freedom.

SECTION FOUR REVIEW

1. VOCABULARY Write a sentence using each of the following terms: apartheid, African National Congress, ban, Sharpeville Massacre.

2. HISTORY What part did "pass laws" play in the apartheid system?

3. BIOGRAPHY Describe the changes in tactics that Nelson Mandela played over time as a revolutionary.

4. ECONOMICS What part did the imposition of economic sanctions play in the release of Nelson Mandela?

5. CRITICAL THINKING To what degree do you think American history has served as an inspiration to freedom fighters in Africa? To what degree has the struggle for freedom in Africa inspired African-Americans?

CHAPTER TEN REVIEW

VOCABULARY

Write the numbered sentences on a separate sheets of paper. In each sentence fill in the blank with one of these terms: *apartheid, ban, Black Muslim, Rainbow Coalition, Sharpeville Massacre.*

1. A _____ is someone whose religion calls for separation of the races.

2. The policy of _____ also called for separation of the races.

3. The _____ focused world attention on the apartheid system.

4. To drive it underground, the South African government enforced a _____ on the African National Congress.

5. A political organization founded by Jesse Jackson is the _____ .

REVIEWING THE FACTS

1. Who are some of the leading black politicians today?

2. What important point did Jesse Jackson make in his efforts to win election as President?

3. What are the Black Muslims' three main ideas?

4. Who shaped the Nation of Islam into a modern force?

5. Who were two of the leading Black Muslim ministers of modern times?

6. Who are some of today's outstanding African-American authors?

7. What African-American painters have gained fame in recent years?

8. What did the government of South Africa do to exert its control over the nonwhite majority?

9. What was the response of young Africans like Nelson Mandela?

10. Why did the South African government imprison Nelson Mandela?

11. When, and under what circumstances, was Nelson Mandela released from prison?

CRITICAL THINKING

1. ANALYZING In your own words, describe what you think the term "Rainbow Coalition" stands for?

2. COMPARING During the hundreds of years African-Americans have lived in America, there have been two main approaches to coping with life in this country: separation and integration. Describe those leaders and groups—both black and white—who urged separation. Who are some of the individuals and groups who have favored integration?

309

3. DRAWING A CONCLUSION Why might it be argued that apartheid was doomed to failure?

UNDERSTANDING PREJUDICE

1. The families of many white inhabitants of South Africa have lived on the African continent for hundreds of years. Would it be fair to force them all to leave South Africa? Do you believe that would be a racist move? Explain your answer.

2. At the start of the Persian Gulf War, Arab-Americans suddenly found themselves under suspicion, with many being investigated by government agencies. Why do you think this was done? Do you think it could be justified? What earlier episode in American history does it remind you of?

3. African-Americans continue to play a vibrant role in the national economy. Do research to find out about the life either of oil baron Jake Simmons, Jr., or publisher John H. Johnson. Then write a short essay describing your subject's achievements in business and the obstacles he had to overcome.

4. Throughout this book, you have read the history of the African-American people. That history has been a proud and glorious one, one that has often revolved around the efforts of black people to find their place in the American dream. But some people have been dismayed at the recent emphasis on black history as a separate history. Deborah Wright, a black resident of Oakland, California, wrote in a major newspaper of her dismay at the use of the term "African-American":

> Adopting the label African-American is a major step backward. It places emphasis on differences—differences that foster conflict.
> It is hard to understand that 25 years after the civil rights movement, some black Americans are still searching for an identity. What does one hope to achieve by this exercise? We have been colored, Negro, Afro-American, black—and now African-American. Would it be OK to just be American?

What do you think of this analysis? Does it contradict the purpose of this book?

GLOSSARY

This glossary gives definitions for vocabulary words and terms used in *African-American History: Heroes in Hardship*. The page number following each definition tells you on what page the word is first used in the text. Remember that many words can have more than one meaning. The definitions given here are the ones that will be most helpful to you in reading this book.

A

A.D.: the years since the birth of Christ. (1)

abolition: the movement to abolish (or put an end to) slavery. (94)

African National Congress: organization founded in 1912 to work for equal rights in South Africa. (301)

altruistic: showing a selfless concern for others. (101)

American Revolution: the fight for independence by Great Britain's American colonies (1776–1783) (54)

Amistad Revolt: the famous shipboard revolt led by Cinque in 1839 which resulted in freedom for the African freedom fighters. (84)

amnesty: a general pardon by a government for political offenses. (136)

apartheid: the South African government's policy of racial segregation and white supremacy. (300)

asiento: the Pope's plan to divide the world between Spain and Portugal. (32)

B

B.C.: the years before the birth of Christ. (1)

ban: to prohibit by official decree. (303)

Bantu: language and culture groups of people of central and southern Africa. (25)

black Cabinet: the name given to those African-Americans whom President Franklin Roosevelt placed in significant federal positions during the 1930s. (229)

black codes: laws passed by southern states just after the Civil War to restrict the rights of African-Americans. (140)

Black Muslim: a member of the Nation of Islam, a religious group that calls for the separation of the races. (287)

Black Panther Party: political party which sought to take control of the inner cities for black people during the late 1960s. (267)

border states: slave states occupied by the North at the beginning of the Civil War. (123)

Boston Massacre: an incident in 1770 that started when angry colonists taunted British soldiers who then fired into the crowd, killing several colonists including Crispus Atttucks. (53)

Brown v. Board of Education: the Supreme Court decision of 1954 declaring racial segregation in public schools to be unconstitutional. (254)

C

census: an official count of the population. (3)

civil disobedience: the refusal to obey unjust laws, usually by nonviolent means. (256)

Civil War: the war between the Union and the Confederacy (1861–1865), ending in the defeat of the Confederacy and the end of slavery in the United States. (123)

civilization: an advanced level of culture, characterized by organized government and religion, a system of writing, and a class structure. (vi)

collective bargaining: the process of negotiation between an employer and a labor union to settle disputes. (227)

colonization: policy, during the 1700s and 1800s, of sending people of African descent to another country, preferably in Africa. (103)

Compromise of 1850: an agreement by which (1) California was admitted to the Union as a free state, (2) the territories were allowed to decide whether to permit slavery, (3) the slave trade was ended in Washington, and (4) a strict Fugitive Slave Law was enacted. (111)

Confederacy: the southern states that seceded from the Union starting in 1860, forming a separate nation. (122)

cotton gin: a machine invented by Eli Whitney in 1793 for cleaning cotton quickly. (60)

D

discrimination: an unfair attitude based on prejudice toward a particular group of people. (119)

disenfranchise: to exclude from voting privileges. (144)

Dred Scott case: a Supreme Court decision in 1857 declaring that slaves had no rights of citizens and that Congress could not forbid slavery in the territories. (112)

dynasty: a series of rulers from the same family. (2)

E

emancipation: freedom from slavery. (121)

Emancipation Proclamation: order issued in 1863 by President Lincoln freeing all the slaves in the states still fighting against the Union in the Civil War. (129)

"Exodus of 1877": migration of blacks to Kansas and Nebraska to escape harsh conditions in the South. (187)

extended family: a family that includes parents, children, and other close relatives, such as grandparents. (12)

F

Fifteenth Amendment: amendment to the Constitution, ratified in 1870, declaring that the right to vote should not be denied on the basis of race. (146)

Fourteenth Amendment: amendment to the Constitution, ratified in 1868, declaring all native-born persons to be citizens. (144)

free black: during slavery days, an African-American not held in bondage. (43)

Freedmen's Bureau: federal agency set up after the Civil War to help poor southerners and to manage abandoned or confiscated southern land. (155)

freedom ride: a bus trip by protesters in the South during the early 1960s to call attention to discrimination in transportation. (258)

Fugitive Slave Act: a law passed in 1850 requiring people in free states to help capture escaped slaves. (91)

G

Ghana: the first great West African trading empire, located at the southern edge of the Sahara. (15)

ghetto: an inner-city neighborhood from which, for reasons of economics and prejudice, members of a particular group are unable to leave. (265)

Great Depression: the period of severe economic hardship lasting from 1929 to World War II. (225)

Great Migration: the movement of large numbers of African-Americans out of the South, between 1900 and 1920. (218)

griot: an African oral historian. (19)

H

Haiti: the Caribbean island on which a successful slave revolt in 1791 shocked slaveholders throughout the Americas. (86)

Harlem Renaissance: a black literary and artistic movement of the 1920s. (231)

heathen: to a European Christian, anyone who practices another religion. (31)

hieroglyphics: ancient Egyptian writing that used pictures to symbolize words and sounds. (3)

I

imperialism: establishing political or economic control over other countries. (206)

indentured servant: a European who exchanged usually four to seven years of labor for passage to colonial America. (37)

indigo: a plant used to make a black-blue dye. (51)

Industrial Revolution: a shift from hand tools to machines and large-scale factory production, beginning in England in the late 1700s and then spreading to the rest of Western Europe and America. (60)

integration: the mixing of the races. (171)

Islam: the religion founded on the Arabian peninsula by the prophet Muhammad during the 7th century A.D. (12)

J

Jim Crow: referring to laws introduced in the South following Reconstruction that segregated schools, railway cars, and all public facilities. (171)

K

Kansas-Nebraska Act: a law passed in 1854 that allowed the residents of Kansas and Nebraska to decide whether to permit slavery. (111)

Korean War: conflict (1950–1953) in which American troops helped prevent the take-over of South Korea by North Korea. (251)

Ku Klux Klan: a secret organization that grew in the South after the end of the Civil War to promote "white supremacy," often by terrorizing blacks. (162)

Kush: a kingdom established by the Nubians in about 2,600 B.C. in the part of Africa now occupied by Egypt, Sudan, and Ethiopia. (6)

L

Liberia: country in West Africa settled by black Americans starting in 1821. (104)

M

Mali: West African empire that at its height stretched from the Atlantic to the cities of Timbuktu and Gao. (18)

manifest destiny: a doctrine of the 1800s stating that the United States was meant to expand across the continent to the Pacific Ocean. (206)

March on Washington: massive civil rights rally in Washington, D.C., in August 1963, during which Martin Luther King, Jr., issued his famous "I Have a Dream" speech. (259)

Meroë: the capital of Kush. (8)

Middle Passage: the brutal voyage taken by slave ships across the Atlantic from Africa to the New World. (32)

Montgomery bus boycott: the 1955–1956 boycott of the bus system of Montgomery, Alabama, by black citizens protesting segregated seating. (255)

Moor: term once used in Europe referring to any dark-skinned person; from the North African conquerors of Spain. (40)

Muhammad: prophet and founder of Islam. (288)

mulatto: a word from the Spanish, meaning a person of mixed white and black ancestry. (40)

mutiny: a rebellion against superior force. (84)

N

NAACP: organization formed in 1909 to work for the legal rights of African-Americans. (183)

Nat Turner's Rebellion: a 1831 slave revolt in Virginia that frightened white southerners. (89)

Niagara Movement: group organized by W.E.B. Du Bois in 1905 to demand equal rights for African-Americans. (183)

nomadic: referring to people who have no fixed home and wander from place to place in search of food and water. (11)

northern colonies: the English colonies of Connecticut, Rhode Island, Massachusetts, New Hampshire, New York, New Jersey, Pennsylvania, and Delaware. (50)

Nubia: the land south of ancient Egypt, along the great bend of the middle Nile River. (6)

P

Palmares: the republic set up by Africans in northeastern Brazil in the 1600s. (85)

Parliament: the law-making body of England. (52)

pharaoh: a ruler of ancient Egypt (2)

pilgrimage: a journey with a special religious purpose. (19)

Plessy v. Ferguson: landmark Supreme Court case in 1896 that legalized segregation. (172)

poll tax: a fee paid by a person in order to vote. (170)

popular sovereignty: the principle that the voters living in a territory should decide for themselves whether to admit slavery. (111)

Q

Quran: the sacred text of Islam, containing the revelations made by Allah to Muhammad. (288)

R

Rainbow Coalition: Jesse Jackson's coalition of political supporters of all races. (285)

Reconstruction: the period (1865–1877) during which the federal government sought to rebuild the states of the former Confederacy. (136)

Republican Party: a political party formed in 1854 in opposition to slavery; along with the Democratic Party, one of the two dominant political parties today. (111)

S

savanna: a flat, open grass land with scattered clumps of trees and shrubs. (15)

sanctions: formal measures usually agreed upon by several nations to stop doing something that is against international law. (304)

secede: to withdraw formally from membership. (110)

segregation: the separation of the races. (171)

sharecropper: a farmer who works a plot of land in return for part of the crop. (157)

Sharpeville Massacre: massacre in 1960 of unarmed protestors in South Africa that served to focus world attention on the apartheid system. (304)

silent trade: a method of trade in Africa by which goods were left at an agreed-upon place, without actual contact between individuals. (16)

sit-in: a method of nonviolent protest whereby people sit down in a public place and refuse to move. (258)

slave codes: laws passed in the South to restrict the conduct and activities of slaves. (66)

Songhay: largest of the great West African empires, it reached its peak in the early 1500s. (20)

southern colonies: the English colonies of Georgia, North and South Carolina, Virginia, and Maryland. (50)

Spanish-American War: the 1898 war between Spain and the United States, won by the United States. (211)

sub-Saharan Africa: that part of Africa lying south of the Sahara. (14)

Swahili: people living along the coast of East Africa who interacted with Arab traders and merchants. (12)

T

Thirteenth Amendment: amendment to the Constitution, ratified in 1865, that put an end to slavery. (139)

U

Underground Railroad: a secret network of people who helped runaway slaves escape, often to Canada. (94)

UNIA: organization, founded by Marcus Garvey, the goal of which was the return of all black people to Africa. (221)

Urban League: organization founded in 1911 to improve the health, housing, job opportunities, and recreation facilities of urban blacks. (191)

V

Vietnam War: a war from the 1950s until 1973 in which the United States unsuccessfully tried to prevent a Communist take-over of South Vietnam. (259)

W

War of 1812: the war fought in 1812 to preserve American independence from Great Britain. (58)

World War I: a global conflict, fought between 1914 and 1918, in which the Allied Powers defeated the Central Powers. (213)

World War II: a global conflict, fought between 1939 and 1945, in which the United States and its allies defeated Germany, Italy, and Japan. (248)

Z

Zimbabwe: empire of south-central Africa which reached its peak in the early 1400s. (25)

African Images, Harold Scheub (New York: McGraw-Hill, 1972).

The American Negro—Old World Background and New World Experience, Rayford W. Logan and Irving S. Cohen (Boston: Houghton Mifflin Co., 1970).

The American Negro Reference Book, John P. Davis, ed. (Englewood Cliffs, N.J.: Prentice-Hall, 1966).

America's Black Past—A Reader in Afro-American History, Eric Foner, ed. (New York: Harper and Row, 1970).

Amistad 2—Writings on Black History and Culture, Charles Harris, ed. (New York: Random House, 1971).

Before the Mayflower—A History of the Negro in America, Lerone Bennett, Jr. (Baltimore: Penguin Books, 1964).

Black Abolitionists, Benjamin Quarles (New York: Oxford University Press, 1969).

Black American Politics—From the Washington Marches to Jesse Jackson, Manning Marable (London: Verson/New Left Books, 1985).

Black Americans in Defense of Our Nation (Washington, D.C.: Department of Defense, 1985).

The Black Book, Middleton Harris, Morris Levitt, Roger Furman, Ernest Smith (New York: Random House, 1974).

The Black Book—The True Political Philosophy of Malcolm X (El Hajj Malik El Shabazz), Y. N. Kly, ed. (Atlanta: Clarity Press, 1988).

Black Bourgeoisie—The Rise of the New Middle Class, E. Franklin Frazier (New York: Macmillan, 1957).

Black Cowboys, Paul W. Stewart and Wallace Y. Ponce (Broomfield, Colorado: Phillips Publishing, Inc., 1986).

Black Images of America, 1784–1870, Leonard I. Sweet (New York: W.W. Norton, 1976).

Black Protest in the Sixties, August Meier and Elliott Rudwick, eds. (New York: New York Times Press, 1970).

Black Reconstruction in America—1860–1880, W.E.B. Du Bois (New York: Atheneum, 1935).

Blacks in America—1492–1970, Irving J. Sloan, ed. (New York: Oceana Publications, 1971).

Blackthink—My Life as a Black Man and White Man, Jesse Owens (New York: William Morrow, 1970).

Bronzeville Boys and Girls, Gwendolyn Brooks (New York: Harper and Row, 1956).

Brown Sugar—Eighty Years of America's Black Female Superstars, Donald Bogle (New York: Crown Publishers, 1980).

California's Black Pioneers, Kenneth B. Goode (Santa Barbara: McNally & Loftin, 1974).

The Choice: The Issue of Black Survival in America, Samuel F. Yetter (New York: G.P. Putnam's Sons).

The Chronological History of the Negro in America, Peter M. Bergman (New York: Harper and Row, 1969).

Coretta King—A Woman of Peace, Paula Taylor (Mankato, Minn.: Creative Education, 1974).

The Crisis of the Negro Intellectual, Harold Cruse (New York: William Morrow, 1967).

A Documentary History of the Negro People in the United States, Herbert Aptheker, ed. (Secaucus, N.J.: Citadel Press, 1974).

Eyes on the Prize: America's Civil Rights Years, 1954–1965, Juan Williams (New York: Penguin, 1986).

Eyewitness: The Negro in American History, William Lorenz Katz (New York: Pitman Publishing Co., 1967).

Flight to Freedom—The Story of the Underground Railroad, Henrietta Buckmaster (New York: Thomas Y. Crowell, 1958).

From Freedom to Freedom, African Roots in American Soil, Mildred Bain and Ervin Lewis, eds. (New York: Random House, 1977).

From Slavery to Freedom, John Hope Franklin (New York: Alfred A. Knopf, 1967).

The Golden Age of Black Nationalism—1850–1925, William J. Moses (Connecticut: Archor Books, 1978).

Harlem Renaissance, Nathan Huggins (London: Oxford University Press, 1971).

History of Black Americans, Phillip S. Foner (Westport, Connecticut: Greenwood Press,1983).

I Dream a World—Portraits of Black Women Who Changed America, Brian Lanker, Barbara Summers, eds. (New York: Stewart, Tabori & Chang, 1989).

In the Name of Apartheid—South Africa in the Postwar Era, Martin Meredith (New York: Harper & Row, 1988).

319

The Jackson Phenomenon, Elizabeth O. Colton (New York: Doubleday, 1989).

Lay Bare the Heart: An Autobiography of the Civil Rights Movement, James Farmer (New York: Arbor House, 1985).

Living Black in White America, Jay David and Elaine Crane, eds. (New York: William Morrow, 1971).

The Lonesome Road—The Story of the Negro's Part in America, Saunders Redding (New York: Doubleday, 1958).

Makeba: My Story, Miriam Makeba and James Hall (New York: NAL Penguin Books, 1987).

Malcolm X—The Last Speeches, Bruce Perry, ed. (New York: Pathfinder Press, 1989).

Many Thousand Gone: The Ex-Slaves' Account of Their Bondage and Freedom, Charles H. Nichols (Bloomington, Indiana: Indiana University Press, 1963).

The Negro Almanac—A Reference Work on the Afro-American, Harry A. Ploski and Warren Marr, eds. (New York: The Bellwether Company, 1976).

Negro Americans in the Civil War, Charles H. Wesley and Patricia W. Romero (New York: International Library of Negro Life and History Publishers Company Inc., 1967).

No Name in the Street, James Baldwin (New York: Dell Publishing Co., 1972).

One Hundred Years of Negro Freedom, Arna W. Bontemps (New York: Dodd, Mead & Company, 1961).

A Pictorial History of the Negro in America, Langston Hughes and Milton Meltzer (New York, Crown, 1968).

Selected Poems of Claude MacKay, Max Eastman, ed. (New York: Harcourt, Brace, Jovanovich, 1953).

The Shaping of Black America, Lerone Bennett, Jr. (Chicago: Johnson Publishing Company, 1975).

Six Black Masters of American Art, Romare Bearden and Harry Henderson (New York: Doubleday, 1972).

The Struggle Is My Life, Nelson Mandela (New York: Pathfinder Press, 1986).

To Die for the People—The Writings of Huey P. Newton, Huey P. Newton (New York: Random House, 1972).

The Unfinished March—The History of the Negro in the United States, Reconstruction to World War, Carol F. Drisko and Edgar A. Toppin (New York: Doubleday, 1967).

The Voices of Negro Protest in America, W. Haywood Burns (London: Oxford University Press).

We Are Your Sisters—Black Women in the Nineteenth Century, Dorothy Sterling, ed. (New York: Norton & Co., 1984).

What the Negro Wants, Rayford W. Logan, ed. (Chapel Hill, N.C.: University of North Carolina Press, 1944).

Winnie Mandela, Nancy Harrison (London: George Braziller, Inc., 1985).

The Women and the Men—Poems, Nikki Giovanni (New York: William Morrow, 1975).

World's Great Men of Color, J. A. Rogers (New York: Macmillan, 1972).

A SELECTION OF BLACK BOOKSTORES

ATLANTA, GEORGIA

First World Bookstore
805 Cascade Avenue, S.W.
Atlanta, Georgia 30310
(404) 758-7124

Hakim's Bookstore
842 Martin Luther King, Jr. Drive,
S.W.
Atlanta, Georgia 30314
(404) 221-0740

Shrine of the Black Madonna
Bookstore
946 Gordon Street, S.W.
Atlanta, Georgia 30310
(404) 752-6125

Soul Source Bookstore
118 James P. Bawley Drive, S.W.
Atlanta, Georgia
(404) 477-1346

BOSTON, MASSACHUSETTS

A Nubian Notion Bookstore
41 Warren Street
Boston, Massachusetts 02119
(617) 442-2622

CAMBRIDGE, MASSACHUSETTS

Savanna Books
858 Massachusetts Avenue
Cambridge, Massachusetts 02139
(617) 868-3423

CHICAGO, ILLINOIS

Freedom Found Books and the
Underground
5206 South Harper Avenue
Chicago, Illinois 60615
(312) 2888-2837

Third World Press
7524 South Cottage Grove
Chicago, Illinois 60619
(312) 651-0700

DALLAS, TEXAS

Black Images Book Bazaar
142 Wynnewood Village
Dallas, Texas 75224
(214) 943-0142

DENVER, COLORADO

Hue-Man Experience Bookstore
911 Park Avenue West
Denver, Colorado 80205
(800) 346-4036

DETROIT, MICHIGAN

Shrine of the Black Madonna
13535 Livernois Street
Detroit, Michigan 48238
(313) 491-0777

LOS ANGELES, CALIFORNIA

Aquarian Bookstore
3995 South Western Avenue
Los Angeles, California 90062
(213) 296-1633

Esowan Books
900 North LaBrea Avenue
Inglewood, California
(213) 674-6566

NEW YORK, NEW YORK

Liberation Bookstore
131st St. and Lenox Avenue
New York, New York 10027
(212) 281-4615

Amen Ra & Isis Associates
Mart 125
260 West 125th Street
Harlem, New York 10027
(212) 316-3680

PASSAIC, NEW JERSEY

Shabazz Books and Things
393 Monroe Street
Passaic, New Jersey 07055
(201) 478-4124

PHILADELPHIA, PENNSYLVANIA

Hakim's Bookstore
210 South 52nd Street
Philadelphia, Pennsylvania 19139
(215) 474-9495

SAN FRANCISCO, CALIFORNIA

Marcus Bookstore
1712 Fillmore Street
San Francisco, California 94115
(415) 346-4222

WASHINGTON, D.C.

Common Concerns Bookstore
1347 Connecticut Avenue, N.W.
Washington, D.C. 20036
(202) 463-6500

Pyramid Bookstore
2849 Georgia Avenue, N.W.
Washington, D.C. 20001
(202) 328-0190

A SELECTION OF BLACK MUSEUMS

ATLANTA, GEORGIA

Martin Luther King Center for
Nonviolent Change
449 Auburn St., N.E.
Atlanta, Georgia 30312
(404) 524-1956

AUSTIN, TEXAS

George Washington Carver
Museum
165 Angelina Street
Austin, Texas 78702
(512) 472-4809

BALTIMORE, MARYLAND

Morgan State University
Gallery of Art
Hillen and Goldspring Lane
Baltimore, Maryland 21239
(301) 444-3030

BOSTON, MASSACHUSETTS

Museum of the National Center of
Afro-American Artists
300 Walnut Avenue
Boston, Massachusetts 02119
(617) 442-8014

CHICAGO, ILLINOIS

DuSable Museum
740 East 56th Place
Chicago, Illinois 60637
(312) 947-0600

DALLAS, TEXAS

Museum of African-American Life
and Culture
P.O. Box 41511
Dallas, Texas 75241
(214) 565-9026

DETROIT, MICHIGAN

Museum of African-American
History
301 Frederick Douglass St.
Detroit, Michigan 48202
(313) 833-9800

DURHAM, NORTH CAROLINA

North Carolina Central University
Museum of Art
1805 Fayetteville Street
Durham, North Carolina 27707
(919) 683-6211

HAMPTON, VIRGINIA

Hampton University
University Museum
Hampton, Virginia 23668
(804) 727-5308

LOS ANGELES, CALIFORNIA

California Afro-American Museum
600 State Drive
Los Angeles, California 90043
(213) 744-7432

Museum of African-American Art
May Company Crenshaw, Third
Floor
4005 Crenshaw Boulevard
Los Angeles, California 90008
(213) 294-7071

NASHVILLE, TENNESSEE

Fisk University
Carl Van Vechten Gallery
Stieglitz Collection of Modern Art
P.O. Box 2
Nashville, Tennessee 37203
(615) 329-8543

NEW YORK, NEW YORK

Caribbean Cultural Center
408 West 58th Street
New York, New York 10019
(212) 307-7420

Studio Museum in Harlem
144 West 125th Street
New York, New York 10027
(212) 864-4500

ORANGEBURG, SOUTH CAROLINA

South Carolina State College
I.P. Stanback Museum/
   Planetarium
Orangeburg, South Carolina 29117
(803) 536-7174

PHILADELPHIA, PENNSYLVANIA

Afro-American Historical and
   Cultural Museum
7th and Arch Streets
Philadelphia, Pennsylvania 19106
(215) 574-0380

SAN FRANCISCO, CALIFORNIA

San Francisco African-American
   Historial and Cultural Society
Fort Mason Center, Building C,
   Room 165
San Francisco, California 94123
(415) 441-0640

INDEX

This index will help you locate quickly information on any topic in this book. The index includes references not only to the text but to pictures as well. A page number with p before it refers to a picture.